The Buddhist Psychology of Awakening

The Buddhist Psychology *of* Awakening

An In-Depth Guide to Abhidharma

Steven D. Goodman

Shambhala   Boulder   2020

Shambhala Publications, Inc.
4720 Walnut Street
Boulder, Colorado 80301
www.shambhala.com

9 8 7 6 5 4 3 2 1

First Edition
Printed in the United States of America

♾ This edition is printed on acid-free paper that meets the
American National Standards Institute z39.48 Standard.
♻ This book is printed on 30% postconsumer recycled paper.
For more information please visit www.shambhala.com.
Shambhala Publications is distributed worldwide by
Penguin Random House, Inc., and its subsidiaries.

Designed by Greta D. Sibley

Library of Congress Cataloging-in-Publication Data
Names: Goodman, Steven D., 1945– author.
Title: The Buddhist psychology of awakening: an in-depth guide
to Abhidharma / Steven D. Goodman.
Description: First edition. | Boulder: Shambhala, 2020. |
Includes bibliographical references and index.
Identifiers: LCCN 2019014671 | ISBN 9781559394222 (pbk.: alk. paper)
Subjects: LCSH: Abhidharma.
Classification: LCC BQ4195 .G66 2020 | DDC 294.3/42—dc23
LC record available at https://lccn.loc.gov/2019014671

Contents

Preface

A few words about the focus and origin of this book may help to orient the reader. First, the focus: For whom was this written? It was written primarily for those who have or might develop an interest in the very basic Buddhist teachings associated with what Tibetan traditions call the "first turning of the wheel of the Dharma." Here, there are grouped teachings on proper conduct (vinaya), discourses (sutras), and commentaries (shastras), and the basic teachings that came to be gathered together under the rubric of Higher Dharma (Abhidharma). The teachings on Higher Dharma are, for the most part, rather technical, consisting of main points and enumerated lists of basic factors (*dharmas*) of phenomena mentioned in the sutras.

There is a rich codification of such teachings preserved in the early Pali Buddhist traditions and thereafter in the Theravadin Abhidharma literature. In addition, there is a different set of texts used by the living traditions associated with Indo-Tibetan Buddhist lineages, which is the focus of this book. These have been largely preserved in Sanskrit as well as in translation in Tibetan, Chinese, and Mongolian languages. Primary among these texts is the *Treasury of Higher Dharma* (*Abhidharmakosha*) by the fifth-century Indian Buddhist savant Vasubandhu.

My love of the Abhidharma was catalyzed by Emeritus Professor Jaini (University of California at Berkeley), who stressed that a thorough knowledge of the Abhidharma tradition should be the bedrock and starting point for all Buddhist studies. I hope that some glimmers of insight and humor, in spite of flaws in my understanding, may dawn in the minds of readers. Perhaps more importantly, I have also been inspired by the living tradition of Buddhist study and practice, and it is to that tradition and those lineages that I pay homage and gratitude. Scholars and those who are well versed in the original source materials may find this approach too cavalier. This book, therefore, is not aimed at the specialist who can read the original texts themselves. Rather, it is aimed at inviting a fresh look at this noble tradition; it is for those who might seek to refresh their view on Buddhist basics and then, perhaps, to actually apply that view in their practice.

The challenge is to find a way to present the main points of this rather encyclopedic compendium that might inspire and guide the curious modern reader into the profundity and nuances of an "Abhidharma" approach to the view and practice of the Buddhadharma. I have chosen to give an account, based on the compendium itself and the Tibetan commentaries and summaries based upon it, that strives to bring out a lively, relevant, and what might be considered a somewhat novel way to actually apply some of the key approaches of the Higher Dharma for a contemporary nonspecialist readership.

One might ask how the technical language of a fifth-century tradition on the Buddhadharma can provide something relevant for modern times? I have tested and refined the material in this book and have placed a primary emphasis on using conversational, casual, and nontechnical language in order to show, using everyday examples, how some of the central insights of Abhidharma might still be accessible and useful to those who approach the study and practice of the Buddhadharma in contemporary times.

Of course, there will be errors of fact, but hopefully the spirit of inquiry is faithful to Vasubandhu and his heirs. The reader will note that I refer, here and there, to Tibetan Buddhist teachers to make certain points. I do this, in part, because these teachings are vibrant and thriving in the living lineages that they transmit, and I myself continue to be inspired by such examples.

The Origins of This Book

Many years ago, at the newly established Nyingma Institute in Berkeley, California, the head Tibetan Buddhist teacher Tarthang Tulku urged me to begin an intensive study of what was then available of the Abhidharma literature in European languages. To that end, I prepared a rough translation from the French of the "Abdhidharma" section of Etienne Lamotte's *L'Histoire du Buddhisme Indien*, which is now available in English translation. Then I delved into a study of Louis de la Vallée-Poussin's French translation of Vasubandhu's *Kosha*, entitled *L'Abhidharmakosha*, now also available in English translation by Pruden (1991). This background work was soon supplemented by a study of the Tibetan translations of Vasubandhu's work, works written in Tibetan as commentaries on the *Kosha*, and works written by Indian commentators. Finally, I was led to study and translate key portions of Ju Mipham Rinpoche's *Gateway to Knowledge* and the commentary on it by Kathog Khenpo Nuden. This text by Mipham is now also available in English in full, translated by Erik Pema Kunsang.

What I culled from these studies was a desire to present "key points of view" to eager graduate students at the Graduate Theological Union in Berkeley, via its affiliation with the newly established Nyingma Institute. These students were bright and engaged and asked many questions about the diverse categories of dharmas and their arrangement into "conditioned" and "unconditioned." They also asked what any of this had to do with the foundational teachings of the Buddhadharma, such as the four noble truths (suffering, the causes of suffering, the cessation of suffering, and the path leading to the cessation of suffering). From the very beginnings of teaching this material, we explored the possible implications for what emerged as what we might call a special kind of "Buddhist psychology" and how such study might inspire and provoke a new way forward into foundational and transformational practices.

Sometime after those initial presentations, I was invited to explore these approaches at the Naropa Institute (now Naropa University) in Boulder, Colorado, to a lively and engaged group of Buddhist students. In subsequent years, and through many refinements, this material was taught in courses at the California Institute of Integral Studies in San Francisco and at a summer study program at the Rigpa Shedra in Southern France.

Thus, what you have before you is a reworked and edited presentation of these lectures and teaching materials that are based on the Indo-Tibetan textual traditions of Abhidharma. I hope some of these novel approaches may prove to be beneficial in presenting a coherent introduction to the depth and precision of Abhidharma methods to the study of Buddhadharma. Finally, I hope that the light and conversational tone of this book will be inviting to all.

Acknowledgments

I must acknowledge those teachers who first encouraged me to undergo the study and exploration of the Abhidharma: Tarthang Tulku Rinpoche (Nyingma Institute), Chögyam Trungpa Rinpoche (Naropa Institute), Professor Jaini (University of California, Berkeley), and Professor Herbert Guenther (University of Saskatchewan). Without their encouragement and goading, I would not have ventured into these wild forests of study. Secondly, I must thank both Tulku Thondup and Daniel Goleman for reviewing this work when it was still in manuscript form. Their encouragement and kind words are greatly appreciated. Finally, I must thank both Snow Lion and now Shambhala Publications for accepting this book for publication. And thank you to my first editor Dave O'Neal and my final editor Casey Kemp for their attention to form and content. Finally, thanks are due to the editorial skills of Lea Samphel for her work on the notes and many other details. To all the students, colleagues, and recorders and transcribers of various versions of this material over the years, I give thanks and trust that your efforts to bring this study to light will be met with approval. May those in the future who chance upon this study at least be inspired to inquire more deeply into the rich traditions of the Buddhadharma.

The Buddhist Psychology of Awakening

Introduction

In a phrase, all of the teachings of the Buddha might be seen as
concrete methods to go from *duhkha* to *sukha*.

This book presents an approach to Buddhist psychology that tries to make
practical sense of some of the core teachings and approaches of the Higher
Dharma (Abhidharma) according to the Indo-Tibetan Buddhist traditions.
It primarily focuses on the fifth-century Sanskrit classic entitled *Treasury of
Higher Dharma* (*Abhidharmakosha*) by the famed Indian Buddhist scholar
Vasubandhu and on subsequent works written by masters in the Indo-Tibetan
tradition. The importance of the *Treasury of Higher Dharma* continues even
in these present times, as witnessed by Ian James Coghlan's recent translation
of the commentary by Chim Jampaiyang, who is credited with composing the
first commentary written by a native Tibetan scholar (see full listing in references under Chim Jampaiyang, 2019).

The *Treasury of Higher Dharma* is based on the tradition of reflection on
the legacy of the Buddha's discourses (sutras) that were orally transmitted and
studied in and around what was historically known as Gandhara in North-
west India. Based on the encyclopedic text known as the *Great Compendium*

(*Mahavibhasha*)—which today only survives in Chinese translation—Vasubandhu, according to tradition, would lecture on one topic for a day, and, at the conclusion, compose a four-line verse summarizing that lecture in a very concise form; this was done mostly to serve as a mnemonic device for later study. He composed almost five hundred such verses and wrote a commentary on them known as the *Commentary to the Treasury of Higher Dharma* (*Abhidharmakoshabhashya*), which consists of eight chapters (though a ninth chapter, on the nature of the self, *pudgala*, was later added). Those eight primary chapters embody a vast range of erudition, with detailed discussions about the nature of the person and their world, karma, emotional impediments, and meditative states. The technical terms and definitions embodied in Vasubandhu's autocommentary have served as the primary material for almost all subsequent musings on the "higher" meaning of the Buddha's discourses and ethical guidance. There were subsequent commentaries on Vasubandhu's *Treasury* written in Sanskrit and translated into Tibetan as well as original Tibetan commentaries, which are studied to this day in the context of Buddhist colleges of higher learning.

From a doctrinal point of view, for those so interested, the *Treasury* lays out the primary tenets of the Sarvastivadin school (considered one of the eighteen schools that developed in India several hundred years after the death of Shakyamuni Buddha). This school was foundational for the Tibetan traditions understanding of both rules of conduct (vinaya) and the higher meaning of the sutras. The Sarvastivadin views embodied in the *Abhidharmakosha* are not to be confused or conflated with the Staviravadin or Theravadin (Way of the Elders) traditions, which are textually based on the Pali Buddhist Canon and have their own approach to Higher Dharma study; an outstanding example of which is *The Path of Purification* (*Visuddhimagga*) by Buddhaghosa.[1]

Why Study?

The View

Some traditional Buddhist teachers have said that they observe Western Buddhists to have a sincere heart and a sense of practice and its importance, but lack a stable view, which comes from study. Perhaps one way to address this lack of a stable view is to encourage Westerners to use their habitual tendencies to make discriminating distinctions in a new way. The Buddhist term often used to talk about this "new way" of thinking is sometimes translated as the *view* or *right view*. This starts an eightfold list (the eightfold path) that represents the traditional way of explaining how to find oneself on the path to cessation of suffering. The eightfold path (*marga*) was first elaborated by the Buddha at Sarnath when he turned the wheel of the Dharma for the first time. The eight are (1) right view (*samyak drishti*), (2) right thought (*samyak samkalpa*), (3) right speech (*samyak vak*), (4) right conduct (*samyak karmanta*), (5) right livelihood (*samyak ajiva*), (6) right effort (*samyak vyayama*), (7) right mindfulness (*samyak smriti*), and (8) right concentration (*samyak samadhi*). Subsequent writings categorize these eight into three categories: (1) wisdom (comprising 1 and 2), (2) conduct (comprising 3, 4, and 5), and (3) meditation (comprising 6, 7, and 8).

The path indicates both a destination—that is, a place to go—and also the road or way that leads to that destination. If one finds this path and learns how not to deviate from it—or knows how to become aware of the deviation and then find one's way back—this path will lead us to our destination, which Buddhists call "liberation," the cessation of all suffering (*nirodha*, or *nirvana*). *Nirvana* is a term that has worked its way into the English lexicon (most recently as the name for a popular rock group). In the eightfold listing of the path, *view* is given the first place in the traditional explanation of how to distinguish between what is a path to nirvana and what is not—between what encourages and sustains us on the path and what blocks or mystifies us so that we can't make the distinction.

The Path

Many people think that *path* means something like an already-existent road, as if someone already did the hard work and all one has to do is get his or her legs onto it, and as soon as they're on it, everything will go splendidly. But perhaps a more accurate translation would be *journey*. In fact, in the Indian Buddhist context, the Sanskrit word for path, *marga*, is often used with an instrumental grammatical ending (*margena*)—it is "by means of the path" that one goes.

This has been interpreted to mean it is a journey, an inner process of finding our way—by means of intellect and heart—out of the thick forest of confusion and pain and into a clearing from which we can first glimpse, and then perceive more stably, a way of proceeding with a sense of confidence.

Dharma Is Difficult to Precisely Communicate

Now, you might ask, "What does this path have to do with study?" For many people, this question might never arise. For most people, it seems, might never think of a path or journey out of suffering; they are too absorbed with the stresses of everyday life, right? For most people, then, this talk about a path might seem rather strange. Talk about the Dharma is not, in many cases, easy to square with our everyday concerns of "this life." That is not to say it is difficult, but to use the words of the Buddha himself, the Dharma is "profound, easily misinterpreted, and very difficult to precisely communicate so that a particular individual might understand."

This is why the Buddha said that those who are inspired by the sublime Dharma (*saddharma*)—this sublime way of upholding what is most important—would be well advised to learn the habits of precisely communicating in a language and style that is specifically appropriate to the temperaments, cultural backgrounds, and motivations of those who have shown an interest.

These basic Dharma teachings were never meant for the crowd or the pub, at least not the basic teachings. (In time, however, it seems the Buddhadharma was transmitted in many unusual contexts.) These basic teachings are a true and reliable way of learning how to identify and then eliminate sources of pain and suffering.

The Benefits of Study and Practice

At the end of the day, what do we imagine we might get through the study and practice of the Dharma? What do the Dharma treatises promise us, and what are their guarantees? What are the contraindications? What are the side effects? Will we see rainbow colors everywhere if we just sit long enough, are calm enough, are spacious enough, and learn well enough how not to grasp? Well, perhaps not.

Chögyam Trungpa Rinpoche once said that the sign of an advanced

Dharma practitioner is that he or she discovers that life becomes somewhat more workable. And on another occasion, he said that the sign of a good Dharma practitioner is that they no longer feel the need to apologize for the varieties of their neurotic tendencies.

For those of us of who are not advanced practitioners but are of average or lesser capacity and realization, it's important to realize that it is natural—even as a Dharma practitioner, or maybe especially as a Dharma practitioner—that quite often things are not going well at all. Also, if we actually feel we are of average or lesser capacity, we may experience embarrassment and try to prevent others from discovering how truly neurotic we are. The point here is that it is to be expected, and in that sense it is "natural" and even predictable that we defend and deny the range of our rather crazed internal musings. The Buddhadharma reminds us that this defense and denial is to a very great extent just who we are; therefore, there is no point in fighting it or hiding it, especially from ourselves. The Buddhadharma suggests that the cultivation of an attitude of acceptance toward how we are, a mindful acceptance that we will experience many varieties of pleasant and unpleasant mental and emotional states, is "natural."

It is precisely the varieties of everyday "neurotic" experiences that we will explore in this book. The focus will be on the very basic teachings of the Dharma, and we will come to see how these teachings classified as the Higher Dharma (Abhidharma) lay out the variety and dynamics of these ever-changing states.

Finding the Right Medicine

When we consider the first step of the so-called eightfold noble path, right view, it is not at all obvious what the right view actually is. Therefore, it is said that study and practice are necessary, not only to find the right view but also to establish that view in a concrete way, in all the different situations of our lives. Right view is not operating only when we're calm and being "good" Buddhist practitioners but also when we are distracted and when we completely forget all the heart advice of our teachers. The goal is to be free from distraction, both when we're calm and when we're agitated. The way to do this is the heart of "practice"—it is a deep, vital, and not obvious thing.

Sometimes the Dharma is likened to medicine for those who are dying.

There are other ways teachers have characterized the import of the Dharma. A contemporary teacher once said that the purpose of the teachings is to encourage us to become totally free, to be autonomous and flexible, and not to be conditioned or caged—not even caged or conditioned by the teachings themselves. It is said that the role of a good teacher is to skillfully encourage us to come out of all limited perspectives, to reveal to us our secret, hidden faults. Patrul Rinpoche (1808–1887), author of the acclaimed classic on Buddhist practice entitled *The Words of My Perfect Teacher*, puts it starkly. He quotes the Bengali master Atisha (982–1054), writing:

> The best spiritual friend is one who attacks your hidden faults. The best instructions are the ones that aim squarely at those faults.[2]

In the context of the eightfold noble path, those hidden and habitual faults are the ones which block right view from emerging and guiding us on a genuine spiritual journey toward awakening, one suffused with what the Dalai Lama characterizes as clarity, kindness, and insight.

How to Study

Many teachers have stressed the importance of taking delight and enjoyment from study. But, unfortunately—like a little child who doesn't know the actual taste of many foods—we might be falsely encouraged to put everything we see into our mouth, only to find out that it doesn't correspond to our nature, and so we reject or spit out those foods. Some like to approach their studies as if they were invited to an elaborate buffet, or smorgasbord; they are not obliged to eat everything they see but instead choose what they like according to taste, perspective, or temperament. The point is to discover, through experimental "tasting," what brings us to depth and clarity. All that does not bring us to such depth or clarity can be set aside.

One of the ways in which an aversion to certain topics of study may manifest is with a sense of agitation or drowsiness, terms we may generally associate with calm abiding[3] (*shamatha*) or insight (*vipashyana*) meditation practice. But all of us, in our everyday lives, are sometimes agitated or sometimes depressed. We might say that the Buddha encouraged us to understand that being human is more or less to cycle through ups and downs, so there is really no need to apologize for that. We might, in time, come to recognize and accept that these ups and downs are in fact our nature. And, more to the point, we might come to discover that these ups and downs are not at all permanent, or invariant; they are based on the coming together and cooperation of many factors of experience.

So, then, we might say that the study and practice of the Dharma can be understood as a way to explore those many factors of experience and then gradually find ways to diminish and eliminate the painful aspects of their occurrences. Such study and practice can be a way to explore how we are caged in by our unexamined habits of attention, by our viewpoints, so as to come out of such habits.

Many Buddhists practice the Dharma with a sense of guilt, a sense of not wanting to disappoint their teachers. They practice with a sense of anxiety regarding their promises and pledges (*samaya*); they do their prostrations and so on with a tight mind. As mentioned before, whether we are practicing the Dharma or not, we often proceed through this life with this same tight mindset. It seems that our basic attitude doesn't change, whether acting in daily life or in our "Dharma life." It is in that sense that Dzongsar Khyentse Rinpoche once remarked that if we practice Dharma with that sense of fear and uptightness, this is not really Dharma practice; it is mental torture.

So, in short, regarding the material presented in this book, I would like to encourage the reader to find what is useful. If it is useful, use it, taste it, celebrate and enjoy it! If it doesn't go down well, maybe find some other ways to explore this expansive material. The suggestion is that "study" might be a way to deepen and clarify our perspectives on what we ourselves regard as important.

The Buddha's Decision to Teach

I would like to present a brief summary of the very first teachings that the one born as Siddhartha Gautama, who later came to be known as the Buddha, imparted in Sarnath, India, teachings that he gave for the first time publicly after his awakening. The Sanskrit word *buddha* means "having awakened." Tradition reports that something rather astounding occurred after his awakening.

The Buddha is alleged to have not wanted to teach others about the insights that had arisen for him upon that occasion. He said that the Dharma was so deep and its importance so difficult to communicate that he preferred not to do so.

Traditional accounts such as the *Request Sutta* (*Ayacana Sutta*) report that an apparitional being—what we might call a sprite—by the name Brahma Sahampati said to the Buddha, "You have to teach." And Buddha said, "No." Sahampati asked, "Why?" And Buddha replied, "Because the Dharma is deep and difficult to understand." The Buddha then stated, "If I were to teach the Dhamma and if others would not understand me, that would be tiresome for me, troublesome for me."[4]

This sprite goes on to say that he must teach anyway, because he has always taught in the past. And, furthermore, now again, upon his realization, it is the time to share and to teach the appropriate ways to use this precious medicine of the Dharma to cure the painful conditions of living beings.

To this, the Buddha, after a moment of reflection, replied that Brahma Sahampati was right. The Buddha realized that in the past he came to the same point, and therefore he must teach. Thereupon the Buddha walked to modern-day Sarnath, and there he delivered a discourse wherein he is said to have talked about the path for the very first time. This discourse came to be called "Turning the Wheel of the Dharma."[5]

So, why recount this story? Because if the Buddha himself was not in such a hurry, and if the Buddha reflected on the profundity, the nonobvious nature, and the difficulty and the importance of the Dharma, then perhaps we also might be encouraged not to become too anxious about our ability to quickly understand the totality and the depth of his teachings in a short period of time.

The Noble Insights

Within the context of that first discourse, the Buddha—the One Who Had Awakened—spoke of four insights. I would now like to contextualize the traditional account of how talk of path and view arose in the experience of the Buddha. Only after a difficult and long period of study and reflection did the

Buddha come to an awakening. It was in the context of the very first recorded teachings he gave that he said there were four certainties about reality, four noble truths:

1. The truth of suffering (*duhkha*)
2. The truth of the causes of suffering (*samudaya*)
3. The truth of the cessation of suffering (*nirodha*)
4. The truth of the way or path (*marga*) to the cessation of suffering

The term he used for "certainty" was the Sanskrit word *satya*, which is sometimes translated as "truth." However, this word *satya* comes from the Sanskrit root *as*, which means "that which is, that which exists, that which is actually the case." Hence, it is what is "true" in the sense of what is in accord with reality. It is "what is real." Truth is what is in accord with what is real. To translate the full meaning of the word *satya*, most languages would need to use two words with two slightly different flavors: "reality" and "truth." Which one of the two is best to translate the Sanskrit word *satya*? Most English-language books on Buddhism translate it as "truth"; so we commonly see the phrase "Buddha's four noble *truths*." But the flavor of the word *reality* is a little bit different. The Sanskrit word *satya* can mean "what is real," "truly real," or "actually real." In Western philosophy, one sometimes finds a "correspondence theory" of truth; so truth is what corresponds to what is taken as the "real" state of things. It is a friend of reality. It is not fighting it; it works with it.

In the Indian context, there is a strong sense that when the Buddha spoke about these four *satyas*, he was talking about two senses of the term: what is actual and real, and what corresponds with that. In addition to these two senses, the Buddha noted that these "truths" and the reality they corresponded to were not easily understood or even commonly accepted "truths." He had discovered, or awoken to, "noble truths" (*arya satya*). The point here is that this very first teaching of his was not a talk about ordinary reality, nor was this an ordinary talk about reality, nor was this an ordinary talk about what corresponds to reality. The term he chose to signify what was not ordinary was the term *noble* (*arya*). It modifies the term *reality*: these "truths" or "realities" (*satyas*) were noble and nonordinary.

In many accounts of Buddhism, one finds the word *arya* often translated as "noble." But when you hear this word, what does it mean? It carries the sense of that which is above the ordinary; it has a sense of dignity and nobility, something valuable, something most worthy of note.

Here, then, the Buddha is discoursing on "truth" or "realities" that are not common. They are valuable, precious, and not corruptible; their nature won't change. There could be so many ways to translate the adjective *arya* into Tibetan because the Tibetans have many words for honorable, dignified, incorruptible, and valuable.[6] But they chose the word *pakpa*, which means "to be above," "to rise above," or "to go beyond the ordinary." The Buddha was not talking about what common people take to be real—the so-called "truth" of the marketplace, that of a "samsaric perspective"—but, rather, something *arya*, something elevated beyond that, and hence noble.

First Insight: Crowded Space

Precisely what were these noble truths, or insights—these unusual and profound realities—which the Buddha hesitated to speak of in the first place? What the Buddha said is that there are many things that might characterize the life of a living being. He wanted to isolate one predominant tendency and give it first place. He did not say that this is the only experience that living beings have, but he wanted to give first place to an observation that totally transformed him, that awakened him. And the word he chose, of all the words he could have chosen to talk about the wide variety of experiences that human beings undergo, was a very strange word with extremely strange translations. He chose the word *duhkha*, a word that is usually translated into English as "suffering" or sometimes "pain."

Let's examine this Sanskrit word *duhkha*. The first part, "*duh*" is related to the Greek prefix "*dys*" and the English prefix "*dis*," as in, for instance, the word *dys-functional*. *Dys* means something is not working well. It modifies the next part of the word, which is "*kha*," meaning "space." Together, "*duhkha*," just going by the formation of the word itself, might convey a sense of a space that is a bit off, out of joint, crowded, or cramped. In that crowded space, things don't work well. Hence, they are unsatisfactory, and by association, they are "painful." One of the earliest occurrences of the word *duhkha* seems to be a description of a bull cart on which the axles are "*duhkha*," meaning "out of the groove," so that the cart cannot roll on; it is dysfunctional. Now, the opposite of this is the Sanskrit word *sukha*. *Su* is related to the Greek prefix "*eu*," as in the word *euphonious*. Sukha is space that is harmonious. Usually, however, the word *sukha* is translated as "bliss" or "well-being."

We might say that for most people many experiences arise as being crowded; they are potentially or actually suffused with suffering or the cause of suffering. The Sanskrit expression for this is *sarvam dukham* (everything is painful) But it is not obvious what this actually means, and it seems to not correspond to our experiences of happiness and well-being, right? It takes a great deal of study and practice to come to a deep, certain, and settled understanding of what *sarvam duhkham* means according to the Buddhadharma, and why, in spite of it, life is still worth living.

Going from Crowded Space to Open Space

The very first valuable, superior, and uncommon truth that truly is said to be in accord with our nature is duhkha; it corresponds to the fact that we lead our lives duhkha-like, with a lack of spaciousness. We might say, then, that the entire teaching of the Buddha is an instruction on how to find oneself in sukha, "an expanded space," "a space of well-being." Thus, the Buddha taught how to move from "duh-kha" to "su-kha."

In this condensed presentation of the teachings of the Buddha, the concrete methods that show one how to go from duhkha to sukha, known as the path, what remains the same throughout this whole process, is "kha," or "space" (in later teachings, this is referred to as "the expanse," "our basic nature," "our buddha nature," and "our basic goodness"). The crucial point here is that our basic goodness, our buddha nature, the great expanse of what is, has never changed; it is our experience that changes. And it is those changes which, for the most part, we regard as unwanted experiences and therefore as a source of pain and suffering.

The Buddha said that this duhkha, this "crowdedness," is the disease for which the medicine of the Dharma was intended—not to make us new or different, but to concretely reestablish our basic spaciousness and our basic well-being. Many of the teachings of the Dharma encourage us to discover and

12

then to confidently trust in our inborn, natural capacity for spaciousness, our buddha nature, our naturally arising primordial wisdom, our stainless wisdom mind.

Second Insight: The Causes for Suffering

The second insight is that this crowdedness and all the suffering that follows from it is due to multiple and different conditions coming together (*samudaya*). Samudaya is sometimes translated as "cause." What it means more precisely is "the coming together or arising of the conditions" for suffering, and this is how the Tibetans translated the Sanskrit term *samudaya* (Tib. *kunjung*), the occurrence or arising of all (the conditions) pertaining to the presence of duhkha.

This second noble truth or insight, which seems to aptly correspond with our nature, might be rendered as "the pattern or causes of this crowded way of living." It is said that this crowdedness is due entirely to temporary conditions obscuring our basic nature. That is very easy to say, isn't it? What we take to be "ourselves" is precisely this sense of crowdedness, this sense of dis-ease.

In this sense, then, study and practice present ways of recognizing the dynamics of our everyday conditions. Those conditions tend to obscure our possibility of spaciousness as our basic nature. It is as simple and as complicated as that. We forget that our habits of reflection are a concrete, total presentation of our distractedness and forgetfulness of such spaciousness. What we habitually take to be "clarity" or "understanding" can, upon further reflection, often be revealed to be entirely conditioned by temporary and crowded modes of reflection. When we discover this, it is not a matter for despair anymore than we should be despondent when we see clouds in the sky. Only a child or a fool or an idiot would feel that the presence of clouds meant that life was not worth living.

In summary, the first noble truth is that we have a crowded experience of life. And the second noble truth involves discovering the variety of factors that constitute this sense of crowdedness. Such a discovery, moreover, is not bad news; such discovering is the Dharma because Dharma is "that which is in accord with what truly is." We are, here, merely reminding the reader that these traditions of Higher Dharma encourage us to concretely, honestly, and spaciously begin to discover and acknowledge the variety and modes of upset and crowdedness we all experience.

Third Insight: Cessation

The Buddha furthermore said that this coming together of conditions that cause this crowdedness can be completely destroyed—not merely lessened, but "destroyed," or "annihilated." The word he used for his third noble truth or insight about reality was *nirodha*, a word which means "to annihilate." This is a very strong word. *Nirodha* means to annihilate the conditions of this crowded, painful situation.

So far, we've presented the first three of the four noble truths. They are:

1. The fact of crowdedness
2. The fact that this crowdedness is due to concrete, discoverable conditions
3. The fact that these conditions, which are temporary and concrete, can completely cease, they will be annihilated, they will be blown out, better known as *nirvana*

Buddha said that nirvana/nirodha, "the cessation (of all upset)," results in a peaceful (*shanti*) way of being, one which is also relaxing, harmonious, and spacious. But he cautions that this state is not just the opposite of duhkha. When speaking of nirvana, this spaciousness is a radiant mode of being that is beyond all distinction between that which is pleasant (sukha) or painful (duhkha). Therefore, it is called the great or absolute sukha (*maha sukha*). Nirvana is *maha sukha*. It is beyond the distinction of "sunny" or "cloudy." It refers to the radiant, continuous expanse of the sky, which accommodates all weather patterns.

Fourth Insight: The Path to the Cessation of Suffering

The fourth insight or truth the Buddha discovered is that each person has the innate capacity for discovering precisely how to annihilate the conditions that cause suffering. The term he used for this capacity was *marga*—"path" or "journey." This is the capacity to learn how to annihilate the conditions which cause duhkha, this crowded situation, and thereby be moved away from one's former pain and suffering. Traversing the path elaborated by the Buddha-dharma—through study and practice—provides concrete methods for showing us how to live in a more calm and stable way and for showing how one can journey out of the thick darkness and into the light, into the spacious expanse of full and complete being. In a more psychological sense of the teachings on the four noble truths, "path" names the progressive discovery and stabilization of precisely how to go about dissolving, annihilating, and no longer being conditioned by the conditions which cause suffering.

Now, of course, annihilating these conditions will take a bit of work. It doesn't just happen in the same way that Newton, who was hit on his head by an apple falling from a tree, is said to have "discovered" the law of gravity. It is not the case (for most people) that we just see how things are and are then liberated. We don't typically say, "Oh, now I see: all conditioned things are impermanent! Voila! I'm liberated!" That might be so for some individuals,[7] but normally it takes a bit of work. It's not that this entails some type of mental torture, but it does require some sense of spacious, good-hearted inquiry and also some discrimination about which food nourishes us and what is appropriate to how we are at the moment. To extend the metaphor, a good practitioner is one who becomes a bit of a food connoisseur, a *gourmand*. Finding the food that corresponds to our nature is the way, the path—that is, the "path leading to cessation." In that sense, then, all sincere study and practice can be part of the path.

Old-Dog Practitioners

In the Tibetan Buddhist traditions, there is talk about "old-dog practitioners." An old-dog practitioner is likened by many great masters to a rock that sits in a riverbed. For hundreds of years, fresh water has been running over it, and one could imagine: "Oh, that rock is so wet and shiny." But at some point, someone might make an inquiry into the actual nature of that rock. They might lift it out of the river, crack it open, and discover that the inside is completely dry. That is a metaphor for old-dog practitioners—they've been submerged in the river of the Dharma for a long time, but that sublime water of the Dharma has not yet penetrated into their core.

For years, the shiny projection to others of being a "good Dharma practitioner" may have fooled many—both ourselves and others. (Maybe we truly thought we were good practitioners.) In this state of delusion, and yet with a good conscience, we might spend years straying from the path of awakening. One possible way in which we might stray is by developing a lifestyle that we call "being a Buddhist." It becomes habitual. The teachings contain many examples of this. It is important to acquire the tools necessary to recognize whether we are truly on the path or not to ensure we are not deluding ourselves.

What Concretely Is the Path?

This brings us to an important question: What concretely is the path, and how would we know? Remembering the example of the rock in the river, we might reflect, "I'm wet on the outside, therefore I must be a good Dharma practitioner. I have the costume, I have my meditation beads and my altar, and I have my good feelings of devotion, so that should be enough." Well, apparently it's not enough. The Buddha said there were eight aspects to this path, the so-called eightfold path. Each of these aspects of the path might be seen as indicating a cautionary tale, an indication, a possible repertoire for mindful monitoring, so that at any point we can check whether or not, "Dharmically" speaking, we are drifting away from the path.

How do we know whether we are on the path? We may have expectations that one day we will find the path. That means we may have a view that's based on hope and fear. We may think, "I hope to be on the path, I fear not being on the path, therefore I am on the path." Well, that doesn't really seem to correspond to the reality of the path.

The main point here is this: although all study and practice of the Buddhadharma is to stabilize us on the path, the path itself is not the main point of the Dharma. So what, then, is the point? The main point is arriving at the destination that the path leads to. That goal or destination is the cessation of suffering, and once one arrives, one no longer obsesses about "the path." The journey is complete.

The Eightfold Path

The point of studying the Dharma is to discern and stabilize right view, to cut through the conditioned patterns and causes of crowdedness and discomfort. One might note that, in practice, one applies the four noble truths in reverse: We learn how to be on the path (fourth noble truth) so as to cut through and cease (third noble truth) the conditioned patterning (second noble truth) of discomfort and pain (first noble truth).

But how do we walk the path and discern whether we are on it or not? There are eight aspects to the path, and though we will be concentrating on the first, possessing the right view, it's important to remember the other seven. In addition to right view, there is right thought. We might think right thought and right view must mean the same thing, but the Buddha made a distinction and he put right view first.[8]

Completely Pure View

The very first item mentioned by the Buddha in his elaboration of the eightfold path was *samyak drishti*. *Samyak* is translated as "right," "correct," or "genuine;" and *drishti* can be understood to mean "view," "understanding," or "perspective." The Sanskrit root of *drishti—drish*—means "to see" in the sense of "to understand" or "to comprehend." It is a very deep metaphor, using the eye metaphorically as the organ of insight. This "seeing" as a metaphor for understanding or discerning is well attested in much of Indian philosophy. It is also present in European philosophy and is a notion that has been around since the time of the Greeks. "To see," here, means to discern or to understand.

What we think we understand is a way of being, a way of seeing how to proceed. But the Buddhadharma cautions that our "normal" way of seeing is suffused with habits of understanding that are best characterized as being pervasively unsatisfactory. This "seeing," this "drishti," undergirds and perpetuates the causes of suffering. By contrast, "right" seeing (*samyak drishti*) is the way of understanding which is correct or genuine. It is defined as a way of being and understanding that leads one to the precise knowledge of how to annihilate or overcome every cause, source, and condition of suffering. This is the view, the "right view," in the Buddhist sense. It is the reason for studying and practicing the Dharma.

Just as the term *suffering* sometimes causes a problem in our understanding because it's a very profound, deep, and nuanced realization of the Buddha, we are not talking about "right" in any ordinary way. It does sound like right versus wrong, doesn't it? It sounds like there is a right view and wrong view, a good view and a bad view. We've even heard the term "wrong view" or "perverse view" mentioned in Buddhist texts. If we hear this, we might become anxious. No one wants to have a wrong view. I must, therefore, be quite cautious. The Sanskrit term *samyak,* "right," is translated rather interestingly into Tibetan as *yang dakpa. Dakpa* means pure, and *yang* can have the sense of over and over again (*yang yang*), like a process of refining, so as to get to the quintessence. It's like a view that is completely pure or has been completely purified.

A completely pure view will help us discern and stabilize being on the path. Therefore, study and practice are ways of purifying our view. So rather than "wrong view," we might say instead "view that is still in need of purification." It is good to remember that right view is listed first in the list of the eightfold noble path. Given their profound nature and importance in the foundational insights of the Buddha, each one of these eight aspects of the path could be studied separately for a long time; one could, perhaps, even spend a year in retreat reflecting on each one of them.

Completely Pure Thought

Pure thought is what is in accord with right view regarding that which impedes and that which promotes engaging in the path whose destination is the cessation of all suffering.

Completely Pure Effort

We don't simply have views and thoughts; we have intentions and we engage in effortful activities. Even if we're a really lazy person, we have to make some effort in our laziness, in our diversions, right? In fact, it is very difficult to be completely lazy. Luyipa, one of the eighty-four *mahasiddhas* celebrated in the Indian Tantric Buddhist tradition, is said to have made his spiritual attainments (*siddhis*) great (*maha*) by maintaining his laziness with tremendous effort and no distraction. It's not so easy. The point here is that study and practice take a great deal of confident effort. We are encouraged to develop a habit of such pure effort.

Completely Pure Mindful Reflection

Pure mindfulness is a broad subject. The main point, which subsequent Buddhist writings have greatly expanded upon, is the cultivation of "mindfulness" (*smriti*), meaning "not drifting away from the chosen object of concentration (*alambana*)," and "alertness" (*samprajanya*), meaning becoming alert to when one has drifted away from concentrated focus and then returning to the object of contemplation. These days, there are numerous mindfulness-based practices that have been adapted for use in secular contexts and whose main aim, it seems, is to reduce stress and anxiety. These modern practices are rather effective at stress reduction, but they have been criticized by more traditional Buddhist teachers (and their followers) for not being in full accord with the Buddhist eightfold path. That is, they seem to be ends in themselves, and they are not geared toward the Buddhist goal of the complete cessation of suffering. What can one say about this? Such is the current state of things.

Completely Pure Speech

When we talk about wholesomeness and unwholesomeness, right and wrong action, there's this famous list of the ten unwholesome factors: three for body and three for mind, and, interestingly, four for speech.[9] Maybe with respect to our habits of expressing ourselves, a little bit of extra purification is necessary? What are those four wholesome speech actions? They are (1) to renounce lying, (2) to give up sowing discord, (3) to abandon harsh speech, and (4) to renounce worthless chatter.

Completely Pure Conduct

Pure conduct is how we are with others. Are we promoting a sense of well-being or not?

Completely Pure Livelihood

Pure livelihood refers to how we make our living. The Buddha cautions his followers to refrain from accepting pay for particular occupations that may bring harm to others or for producing objects that result in increasing the pain and suffering of others.

Completely Pure Meditation

Pure meditation, the last in the list of the eightfold path, refers to practices which deepen the inquiry into the nature of reality (*samadhi*). They are meant not as an end in themselves but rather to aid one along the path to the cessation of suffering.

This eightfold path has been likened to a wheel with four spokes. The first four of these eight aspects of the path—completely pure view, thought, effort, and mindful reflection—are likened to four spokes of a wheel. Three of these aspects of the path—completely pure speech, conduct, and livelihood—are the hub of a wheel. The circumference, the rim of the wheel, is the aspect of completely pure meditation. All eight factors, then, need to be in place or the wheel will not properly turn.

The Abhidharma
and How It Relates
to Our World

What Is the Abhidharma?

In Sanskrit, *Abhi* means "making manifest." *Dharma*, in this case, means "what can be known or cognized," "the plurality of factors of reality," or simply "what there is."

Somebody could say, "Why bother? Why should I care about knowing how to directly perceive reality?" That is an excellent question. The point of the Buddhist teachings is that the direct perception of reality is necessary in order to be truly free. Our capacity to learn how to directly perceive reality is the *sine qua non* for traversing the path, without which one cannot be truly free. In fact, how free we are depends on how directly we perceive reality.

Of course, these days in the West any talk of a true reality is regarded by many as rather suspect. There are those who would say, "It's a matter of opinion," "One man's meat is another man's poison," or "Life is just as you like"—anything goes. This is what the Buddha calls nihilistic. So this notion of "the direct perception of reality" is, perhaps, the most important definition of Abhidharma.

There are three aspects to this definition: the first aspect is making manifest. You could do a whole study of Buddhism in terms of what is manifest and what is not yet manifest. The second aspect is direct perception. The third is this famous reality. In Tibetan it is called *de kho na nyi*, "just what is."

The Seventy-Five Dharmas

Now, to further elaborate on dharmas as "factors of reality" or "what there is," there is a list of seventy-five dharmas (see page 209). We could look at it like we would a periodic table of elements with all the different atoms, from hydrogen through einsteinium. There are lightweight atoms and heavyweight atoms, each with their own characteristics, their own quantum spin (at the level of quarks), and their own capacity to engage in conditional relations with other atoms to make molecules. These molecules combine with other molecules to make bigger molecules. And sometimes, as with carbon, an atom continues making long strings called polymers, such as plastics, which we may later use as a plastic bottle.

We can see polymers in their functional aspect, as, for instance, a plastic bottle, but we don't see the molecular structure of the polymer itself. This distinction between the way things really are and the way they appear is crucial and is a distinction that is elaborated upon in the Abhidharma (and in subsequent) literature. It is said that the listing and understanding of the various factors of existence and their interactions is, in fact, the way things are. It is, however, difficult to be aware at the level of the flowing interactions of the dharmas themselves. We shall see that Vasubandhu, following the traditions he studied in Gandhara, found it more amenable to classify the seventy-five basic factors of existence into a grouping of eighteen elements (*dhatus*) or, in another grouping, as twelve sense bases (*ayatanas*). At the level of the way things actually are, not only in Western science but also in Abhidharma, there is an understanding that there is a fundamental plurality of different energy patterns, which in Western science, until recently, we called an "atom," meaning "not divisible." *Atom* is simply a word for a fundamental pattern of energy. Of course, nowadays, we say that not even the atom is so fundamental. What are the current and most fundamental building blocks that make up atoms? They are called quarks, which have rather wonderful names: *beauty*, *strangeness*, and *charm*.

In a similar way, the Abhidharma tradition has a very subtle and precise way of presenting what makes up our entire world, both physically and nonphysically, perceptually, cognitively, somatically, physiologically, and so on.

The equivalent to this atom (or quark) in the Abhidharma world is called a dharma. The study of the Abhidharma can be understood as consisting of becoming learned about both the essential features of these dharmas and also how these dharmas work together.

Why should that be of importance to us? It is important because, just as in the study of physics, the study of the Abhidharma also shows the basic factors of existence and the basic laws that regulate their coming together. This makes up the entirety of what we call so casually and imprecisely "my world," "my life," "my emotions," "my thoughts," and so on. It is not as we would like it to be, or think it ought to be, or hope that someday it will be, but is precisely as it is and has always been.

Abhidharma study, then, moves us from the imprecise language of thoughts, emotions, feelings, intuitions, and desires into the precise language of the coming together and uncoming together of dharmas, in this case, seventy-five dharmas, which are discussed and categorized rather like an atomic chart of basic factors of existence.

The Importance of Precision

These days, of course, most people who call themselves Buddhists don't know the names of these various aspects of reality. We might be inspired by the teachings, recite the sutras for inspiration, or even do some practices of the Vajrayana traditions, or maybe we simply pray for blessings from the teachers. But if someone asks us questions about the precise meaning of the words we use to characterize our understanding and our experiences, our confidence may become rather shaky.

There are many styles for engaging the Buddhadharma. For instance, there is the style of studying and learning—in addition to practice—how to be more precise, in a spacious way, with our capacity to make distinctions. His Holiness the Dalai Lama and many other great Buddhist teachers have stressed the precise, almost "scientific" mode of the Buddhist teachings. It does not contradict the other mode that involves faith-based practice with an open heart. In fact, many teachers have stressed the benefit of bringing both modes together.

Some people love the feeling of the Dharma but don't like to study precise words used in the authoritative texts. Others love the precise words, but if they are invited to open their heart in a ritual context, they feel they are following some cult. Perhaps it is good to find the right balance.

The *Treasury of Higher Dharma*

The first turning of the wheel of the Dharma consisted of the teaching on the four noble truths, the teaching on proper conduct, and the teaching on the four mindfulnesses as found in the Pali *Satipatthana Sutta*[10] and in the Sanskrit *Sutra on Establishing Mindfulness (Smrityupasthana Sutra)*.[11] *Smriti* is a Sanskrit word for mindfulness.

On the basis of that first turning, those who came after the Buddha made commentaries. It is in this context that the great scholar Vasubandhu—the half-brother of Asanga and one of the great jewels of India—wrote a magnificent work called the *Treasury of Higher Dharma* or the *Abhidharmakosha*.[12]

As mentioned before, Vasubandhu himself merely summarized all the different streams of Abhidharma teachings that existed at the time that he lived (in the fourth to fifth centuries of the Common Era) in the area of Gandhara (present-day Kashmir). Tradition recounts that Vasubandhu gathered all the different views extant at that time, and on the basis of those views he would lecture all day. After his lecture, he would go home and summarize that lecture by composing one *karika*, a four-lined summary verse. We have these lines of text in Sanskrit, Chinese, Tibetan, French, and English.[13] On the basis of those summary verses, he then compiled them into almost five hundred verses, called the *Verses That Contain the Treasury of the Abhidharma (Abhidharmakosha-karikas)*.

Verses and Commentary

After Vasubandhu wrote these verses, he then wrote a commentary (*bhasya*) on them. The verses and commentary together are called the *Abhidharmakosha-bhashya*.[14] *Kosha*[15] means "treasury," and treasure means something of great value. Remember that these verses together with their extensive commentary composed by Vasubandhu is considered an encyclopedic "treasure" of information on how to make manifest the direct perception of reality. It contains an account of all the possible interactions between the basic factors of existence, the dharmas.

According to tradition, one would memorize the verses (*karikas*).[16] When I first heard "verses," I thought, "It's poetry." But actually they are very terse and condensed verses, with almost no grammar, and you can barely make sense of it. In the living traditions of Tibetan Buddhism, monastics memorize these verses simply as a mnemonic device. They aren't meant to make sense of the verses by themselves.

In his commentary Vasubandhu explains what each particular dharma, or factor of reality, means. Then he tells us that some thinkers in the tradition have different views on the meanings of some key points. Often Vasubandhu cites the names of the people who posed certain questions or objections. And then we have Vasubandhu's response to the effect of, "Ah, so you say. But in truth this is based on the following error of your thinking . . ." He does this not to shame the person asking the question but rather to sharpen the sword of their capacity to note distinctions relevant to the wide variety of specific points.

Discernment

In fact, what is being exercised and what is working here is one out of the seventy-five factors, or dharmas, the one we call "discernment" (*prajna*).[17] The discussion of prajna that comes from the *Abhidharmakosha* states that it is itself a "dharma," a factor of reality, which is present as the capacity to make fine, precise distinctions with respect to the nature and functions of all other factors. It is that special dharma that makes it possible to have knowledge of all the other dharmas—to have precise knowledge of the other dharmas. The Sanskrit phrase that defines this discernment is *dharmanam pravichaya*.[18] In this book, following along with Vasubandhu, we will be exploring our own capacity for discernment in order to clarify the meanings of the variety of distinctions that account for the multiplicity of our experiences.

Other Traditions of Abhidharma: No Conflict

The basis for our discussions of Higher Dharma are teachings based on what in the Tibetan Buddhist traditions are classified within the so-called first turning of the wheel of the Dharma; it is the so-called Way of the Listeners

(Shravakayana), or sometimes classified as the "Hinayana" (the Lesser Way), which does not delve into Greater Way (Mahayana) formulations of similar topics.

The main text that was studied by Tibetan Buddhists for so-called Mahayana Abhidharma is the *Compendium of the Higher Teaching* (*Mahayana Abhidharmasamuccaya*),[19] a text attributed to Vasubandhu's half-brother Asanga. The approach of Vasubandhu, which we follow here in this book, contains seventy-five dharmas, whereas the Mahayana approach contains one hundred dharmas. There is, however, no real contradiction in approach.

Although we follow the listing of seventy-five dharmas in this book, it is not the only way. The nineteenth to twentieth-century Tibetan master Ju Mipham Rinpoche, in his *Gateway to Knowledge*, discusses ten expert knowledges mentioned in Maitreya's *Discriminating between the Extremes and the Middle* (*Madhyantavibhaga*). And then, in accord with this schema, he engages in a presentation of these dharmas, combining both Shravakayana and Mahayana definitions of them.

The point here is that whether one studies the *Abhidharmakosha* of Vasubandhu or the *Abhidharmasamuccaya* of Asanga, or both, there are no major contradictions. The lists are somewhat different, but the basic dynamic principles are the same: everything is dharmas, and they can be divided into conditioned and unconditioned dharmas. Both the Shravakayana and the Mahayana Abhidharma accept that. And both the Shravakayana and the Mahayana Abhidharma agree that conditioned means arising due to causes and conditions and being subject to dissipation; both approaches accept that reality is an unconditioned state, not subject to causes and conditions.

The Mind Is Sharpened by Clear and Distinct Definitions

In the great Indian traditions of study, one makes concrete lists and then goes very carefully by the list. This is not to say that Indians were interested in collecting lists, but it was felt—as a matter of pedagogy—that the mind is sharpened by having very clear and distinct definitions that precisely orient the mind and attention. These definitions were thought to be necessary in order to truly hit the target referred to.

For example, in *The Words of My Perfect Teacher*, Patrul Rinpoche speaks of three defects, six stains, and five wrong ways of remembering when you study. The five wrong ways of remembering are:

1. Remembering the words but forgetting the meaning
2. Remembering the meaning but forgetting the words
3. Remembering both but with no understanding
4. Remembering them out of order
5. Remembering them incorrectly[20]

He says it's not enough to come out of a teaching and say, "It was such a great teaching, it was so profound. The teacher was so inspiring." But then when asked what was said, you reply, "Oh, it doesn't matter, it was just so inspiring." According to Patrul Rinpoche, this is a defect. Having a defect doesn't mean we're going to hell or we're going into a deep precipice and never returning. It just means it will delay us a bit on our way to directly perceiving reality. This way of going through lists is meant to help sharpen the intellect.

The Four Categories of Butön

Those who knew the Dharma very well thought that perhaps this word *dharma* was the deepest and most important word of all. The great Tibetan Buddhist scholar Butön (1290–1364) wrote a magnificent work called *A History of Buddhism*[21] and was instrumental in compiling the first widely available Tripitaka, the collection of the Buddha's teachings. In doing this, he closely studied the variety of available texts. In his *History of Buddhism*, he divides the discussion of the meaning of this key word *dharma* into four sections:

1. Different referents for the term *dharma*
2. The etymology of the word *dharma*
3. The definitions of dharma
4. The variety of types of dharma in the sense of Buddhist teachings

1. Dharma as Referents: Ten Referents by Vasubandhu

Butön's first section is called "Different Referents for the Word *Dharma*." Here, Butön quotes Vasubandhu. In addition to the *Abhidharmakosha*, Vasubandhu also wrote a text called the *Proper Mode of Exposition*,[22] in which he laid out a number of distinctions about the Dharma. The Tibetans in particular fastened on to one section of this work, wherein he lists ten different senses in which the word *dharma* is used. For each referent, Vasubandhu gives the definition and then quotes how the word *dharma* is used in the Buddhist context. It's very concrete. Just to hear this makes us appreciate the nuances of the multiple ways in which this word *dharma* is used. According to Vasubandhu, *dharma* can mean a number of things:

1. What can be known or cognized:[23] Dharma is the plurality of factors of reality, as in the expression, "dharmas are conditioned or unconditioned."

2. The path to liberation itself:[24] This meaning is represented in the expression, "Dharma is completely pure view."

3. Nirvana:[25] We observe this meaning in the expression, "I seek refuge in the Dharma."

   Interestingly, Vasubandhu says, in its true sense, this expression means full and complete enlightenment, nirvana.

4. Mental object:[26] There are certain things which are a "dharma basis."[27] This is a technical term that refers to whatever is exclusively an object for the mind itself and does not depend on sense fields; that is, it is not an object for visual, auditory, olfactory, gustatory, or tactile perception.

5. Merit:[28] This is exemplified in the expression, "They behaved in accord with the Dharma."

6. This life:[29] This meaning is conveyed in the sentence, "Worldly beings are attached to this present life, to worldly dharma." Dharma in the sense of worldly dharma means precisely, from the Buddhist viewpoint, to only have regard for this life as it is, with no thought for lives to come, no thought for the karmic implications, and so on.

7. Teachings of the Buddha:[30] This is expressed in the quote, "The

Dharma consists of Sutra, Vinaya, Abhidharma, and so on." There are twelve divisions of that.

8. What is subject to change or aging:[31] This is observed in the sentence, "This body is endowed with the dharma of aging."

9. Religious vow:[32] This is dharma in the sense of an intention to lead one's life in accord with ethical norms, in the sense of "the four dharmas of a monk or a nun."

10. Worldly custom:[33] This is dharma in the sense of cultural conditioning, as in the expression, "The dharma of that country, the dharma of those people."

In this book we will focus primarily on "dharma as what we can know" (definition 1) as well as "Dharma as teachings of the Buddha" (definition 7). To distinguish these two, we will capitalize the word *Dharma* when it refers to the Buddha's teachings.

2. Etymology of "Dharma"

How is the Sanskrit word *dharma* formed? There's a general sense and a special sense. The general sense comes from the root *dhir*,[34] which means to uphold, to maintain, to support, or to sustain.

The special sense is *saddharma*[35]—highest, supreme, or sublime Dharma; that is, Dharma as the highest teachings, Dharma as applied to Buddhism. Because saddharma—the sublime Dharma, the Buddhadharma, the teachings of the Buddha and his heirs—is so important, there is a list of three different senses of saddharma:

1. The Dharma of the Buddha,[36] the one whose teaching is supreme

2. The Dharma that is the supreme[37] Dharma applied to Buddhism (In this sense, *sad*, supreme, and *dharma* are appositional, the same)

3. The Dharma for the supreme ones,[38] those who are blessed and temporarily flexible enough in their hearts and minds to take the teachings seriously into their lives (This is the most important sense of saddharma for us here)

3. Dharma as a Buddhist Teaching

In the *Abhidharmakosha*, Vasubandhu says that saddharma as a Buddhist teaching is twofold:

1. Dharma as a means of conveying, called "Dharma of scriptures"[39]
2. Dharma as understanding itself, called "Dharma of realization"[40]

There's the means of conveying through text (and text here means whatever medium is used to convey the teachings)—the Dharma as means. And there is also Dharma as end result, as realization, as full and complete understanding; it is that which this "means" is aiming at.

4. Variety of Dharma Teachings

The fourth category of Butön is the variety of types of dharma in terms of teachings. They are:

1. The three turnings of the wheel of Dharma
2. The teachings in all their multiplicity and variety; if they are Buddhadharma, they are of unique taste[41]

What's special and precious about the Buddhadharma is that it is wholesome, good, and in accord with reality. It is said a superior practitioner, upon merely hearing the name of a Buddhist text, can completely realize the essence of that teaching. The less capable have to descend to studying the contents. That's why titles are given such wonderful names: because there's a *tendrel*[42] here, an auspiciousness in the name. Buddhadharma is considered to have the special quality or flavor of being good in the very beginning, in the middle, and even at the end. This is the case because it is said to accord with reality. That's one sense of what's unique about such teachings.

To return to the term unique or one taste," what is this taste? It's said to be unique, wonderful, and good. It is said to have the taste of liberation (*vimoksha*) itself.[43] Every word of the Dharma, if it is truly Dharma, and every combination of the words has the true, invariant taste of leading to liberation. This is the traditional view that motivates Buddhists to study the works of the

Buddha and the commentaries, and to put them into practice so as to achieve the goal of complete liberation from suffering. Thus, when one studies and practices, one should never disparage or become impatient with respect to the sublime Dharma.

Needless to say, the above perspectives represent what anthropologists call an "emic" perspective—that is, an "insider" perspective that accords with those attitudes held by practitioners within the Buddhist traditions. There are, of course, "outsider" perspectives, "etic" approaches, which are, for the most part, the approach of so-called academic, historical accounts of Buddhism.

In the Shravakayana traditions, they say that although the Buddha is no more, one yearns to see the living presence of the Buddha. The Buddha, anticipating this concern, was said to have declared, "Whoever sees the Dharma sees me." The Buddha, as the one who shows the way, is fully present and complete in and as the Dharma.

Discernment (Prajna):
The Dharma That Makes It Possible to Know Dharmas

How can these teachings be good in this way? They are good because we ourselves are fundamentally good. We are fundamentally wholesome; therefore, we are entirely capable of accessing that free, open, and boundless ground of goodness. And we do so by learning what to accept and what to reject in accord with our natural capacity to nurture the roots of goodness, what Chögyam Trungpa Rinpoche called our basic sanity.[44]

What is the name for the capacity to do this? In Sanskrit the term that is used is *prajna*. We've already discussed the importance of this factor of existence, this dharma. You might be familiar with prajna from the prajnaparamita[45] ("wisdom that has gone beyond") literature such as the *Heart Sutra*, which is well known in Zen Buddhism. In this context, prajna means "wisdom," but here in these Abhidharma contexts, it means "discernment," our capacity to note distinctions that are important for our quality of life, our capacity to nurture the roots of our own basic goodness. Remember, this is a definition that comes from the *Abhidharmakosha*. Remember that prajna is one of the factors of experience and is defined as the capacity to precisely discern the nature of the factors of existence.[46] To re-emphasize this crucial point, here "prajna" is one dharma that has as its definition the capacity to know dharmas. We might think of it as the gossamer thread connecting us to our buddha nature.

The application of discerning factors of reality is part of the path—combining both view and practice together. What, then, is involved in applying or bringing out this prajna?

1. There is prajna in terms of how to listen.[47]
2. There is prajna in terms how to reflect on what was heard.[48]
3. There is prajna in terms of meditation—how to go deeply with what one has reflected on.[49]

There is a famous list about how to properly listen, reflect, and deepen—the so-called four reliances—that is enumerated in the *Explanation of the Profound Secrets Sutra* (*Samdhinirmochana Sutra*).[50] The list reads:

1. Rely on the Dharma that is being spoken and not the person speaking.
2. Rely on the true sense and not the mere words.
3. Rely on the definitive, stable meaning and not the provisional, contextual meaning.
4. Rely on the primordial wisdom aspect and not the intellectual, perceptual aspect.

At this point, one might ask, "What is so special or higher about the Abhidharma?" Traditionally there are four different meanings for "higher" (*abhi*) in the word *abhidharma*:

1. Making manifest:[51] Abhidharma is a way of study and practice that manifests the direct experience of reality. This is the main characteristic of "*abhi*."
2. Doing something over and over again repeatedly:[52] This is Abhidharma repeatedly and in various ways showing the different groupings of the factors of experience (the five aggregates, twelve sources, eighteen elements, etc.).

3. Surpassing or dominating:[53] Here, *abhi* means that by knowing the particular and generic aspects of these dharmas, these factors of existence—by knowing the specific, concrete characteristics as well as the multiplicity and general patterns of reality—one will be able to surpass the views of one's philosophical adversaries. Here, the primary philosophical adversary that we may want to surpass is not outside us; it is our temporary tendencies toward "wrong view." This is not like waging war outside. This is a way of surpassing our wrong views and limited patterns and conclusively dominating, settling, and stabilizing all doubts and controversy regarding spiritual practice.

4. Complete comprehension or realization:[54] This is *abhi* in the sense of having full comprehension of everything whatsoever, which we are told consists of those things that are actual and those things that are only mental constructs.

2

Everything Is Dharmas

Which Way Will the Frogs Jump?

My task in this book is to convince you that Abhidharma study and practice, which is often considered boring and just lists of lists, can actually be enlivening and loads of fun. Here is the analogy: There is a barrel of frogs here, and, at the moment, the barrel is closed. If we feel there is some movement there, maybe we are afraid or maybe we are interested in those frogs inside. My task in this book might be likened to opening the barrel and gently spilling out the frogs and then encouraging you to feel confident that, judging by the type of frog, you know which way it is going to jump. And then, of course, the big surprise is to remind you that these frogs and the way they jump are us.

We have a habit of saying, "There is a problem" or "I have a problem." But the first problem is "I." "I am a problem." "I think, therefore there is a problem" or, as some would put it, "I think, therefore I think I am." In the Buddhist tradition they call this an unwarranted inference.

Just because we think, we should not imagine that this corresponds to an "I." Our understanding of reality gets us through the day, but in reality, what is it made of? Why should we take any interest in that? Just as in the example of carbon atoms that can be arranged in long chains called polymers to take the shape of a plastic bottle, we might think, "It's enough to have the plastic bottle, isn't it? Why bother learning about polymers?" But maybe, if we know what that bottle is made of, we can change its form and discover how to mold plastics for other uses.

In fact, just to think of dharmas as many different things already brings an increase of mental space. One sign of mental spaciousness and being relaxed is the capacity to laugh. It is difficult to maintain a narrow mental view and laugh at the same time. You might try it; it's very difficult, right? One of the epithets of the Buddha is He Who Can Laugh. He was also called the Great Analyzer.[55]

My task here is to show you that learning how to analyze the seemingly chaotic and jumping-around nature of our thoughts might be likened to opening the lid of a box containing lots of frogs. Maybe we can learn to laugh while we investigate the nature those unruly "frogs."

Sarvam Dharmam: Everything Is Dharmas

We shall now finally delve into the list of the seventy-five different mental and emotional factors (chart 1) according to the Abhidharma. These are the categories of all different kinds of dharmas and how, like wild frogs, they jump about. According to the Abhidharma, these dharmas and their patterns of interactive behavior make up all of life: both "me" and "my world."

These basic factors of existence, these dharmas, constitute what truly exists in all of its particularity and variety. This list of seventy-five dharmas is regarded by the Higher Dharma tradition as comprehensive; it accounts for the entirety of our actual and possible existence. This is a total picture of everything that one needs to know in order to accomplish full and complete enlightenment. As mentioned before, everything is constituted by dharmas (in Sanskrit, this is expressed as *sarvam dharmam*).[56] This word *sarvam*, "everything," is used over and over again in the teachings of the Buddha. "Everything," here, means all-inclusive, nothing missing, a full and complete teaching.

Remember my previous question, "Why bother? Why don't we just open our hearts and rest? Isn't that what the teachings are all about?" Well, that's great if you can do it. These teachings seem to suggest, however, that opening to what is and resting in that is not so easy. There are many impediments, blockages, and doubts. There are so many contradictory thoughts and feelings.

THE SEVENTY-FIVE DHARMAS

CONDITIONED				UNCONDITIONED

I	II	III	IV	
Forms	Mind	Concomitant Mental Factors	Elements Neither Substantial Forms Nor Mental Functions	
1. Eye	12. Mind (*chitta*)	13.–22. General	59. Acquisition	73. Space
2. Ear		Factors	60. Nonacquisition	74. Cessation
3. Nose		23.–32. Primary	61. Similar Class	Due to
4. Tongue		Wholesome Factors	62. Perceptionless	Discrimination
5. Body		33.–38. Primary	Serenity	75. Cessation
6. Form		Factors of Upset	63. State of	Not Due to
7. Sound		39.–40. Primary	Nonperception	Discrimination
8. Smell		Factors of Nega-	64. Serenity of	
9. Taste		tivity	Cessation	
10. Touch/Textures		41.–50. Minor	65. Life	
11. Imperceptible		Factors of Upset	66. Birth	
Forms ("other")		51.–58. Variable	67. Fleeting	
		Factors	Stability	
			68. Decay	
			69. Impermanence	
			70. Name	
			71. Word	
			72. Letter	

The Seventy-Five Dharmas according to the *Abhidharmakosha* (see appendix 1, column III, for a complete list of the factors and for the Sanskrit and Tibetan names)

In fact, the Higher Dharma names and catalogs those energies that block the heart from being open. One might say, then, that the study of what opens and what blocks the opening of the heart is the very core of the Abhidharma.

The Discernment of All Dharmas

Let's look at prajna, discernment, which is factor 18 from the list of seventy-five on the chart. We've already defined it as the dharma that allows us to *know* dharmas. In the *Abhidharmakosha* (chapter 1, verse 2a), Vasubhandu responds to the question, "What is Abhidharma?" by stating:

Abhidharma is pure prajna with its following. Prajna . . . is the discernment of the dharmas.[57]

Even if you were to stop reading now, you would already have something wonderful. You would know that the Abhidharma, the highest teachings of the Dharma, consists precisely, and in an absolute way, of undefiled wisdom, as the capacity to know what arises *as it arises*. This knowledge is a treasure because it is this knowledge that leads us out of the mire of transmigration.[58] This is the absolute meaning of Abhidharma. Vasubhandu (*Abhidharmakosha*, chapter 1, verse 2b) also states:

> It is also prajna, and the treatise that brings about the obtaining of pure prajna.
>
> In common usage, the word Abhidharma also designates all prajna that brings about the obtaining of Abhidharma in the absolute sense of the word; . . .[59]

To paraphrase this, the word *Abhidharma* designates all discernment of dharmas, bringing about the Abhidharma. Remember, this word *abhi* means making manifest direct perception of reality as it is. *Prajna* is the name given to that which makes that manifest—the direct perception of reality as it is. Now we know something about Abhidharma in the absolute sense and something about Abhidharma as a treatise. In this sentence, Vasubandhu is using the term "Abhidharma" in both senses. Vasubandhu continues:

> . . . defiled prajna whether it is innate or natural, or whether the result of an effort, the result of hearing, reflection, absorption, receives, along with its following, by convention, also the name Abhidharma.[60]

We also give the name Abhidharma to the way in which prajna works when it is not pure. That means Abhidharma and this treatise also talk about the way in which our capacity to note distinctions is defiled.

We have two senses of the word *prajna*, two ways in which we can discern the way things are: (1) purely, which allows us to directly perceive reality as it is, and (2) impurely (prajna in a defiled sense), which is the result of being caught up in effort due to hearing, thinking, absorbing, and so on, in an unclear way.

Dharma Bears Its Own Unique Characteristics

Vasubandhu continues: "Dharma is that which bears (dhārana) its own spe-cific or unique characteristic."[61] This is one of the senses of the list of ten ref-erents for the word *dharma*. What Vasubandhu indicates here is that each of these seventy-five dharmas has a specific, unique characteristic. Previously, we used the analogy of atoms and quarks. We don't say, "I think it was probably hydrogen, but maybe it was helium. I'm not sure. Anyway, there was a little bit of energy, and what does it matter?" We learn, instead, to know the precise characteristics of the atoms (or quarks and so on). It is rather the same with the dharmas. Precision is key.

There are concrete effects due to the specific workings of these various dharmas. Every love affair and every war can—at the level of analysis—be to-tally accounted for by these seventy-five dharmas. However, the Abhidharma is not studied in order to make a full account of every war and every love affair. However, it does help us to not be surprised when love affairs sometimes turn into a war. This is the nature of defiled dharmas, of defiled prajna.

Otherwise it's as if someone who is not a skilled doctor went into a room and engaged in a display of being shocked and disgusted by the full mani-festations of the symptoms of an illness. Why are we shocked? Why are we surprised when someone gets upset? From the point of view and practice of the Abhidharma (and indeed the Buddhadharma), when conditions are ripe, upset occurs, and when conditions are right, upset dissipates, and these con-ditions we can know—dharma is that which bears its own specific or unique characteristic.

To conclude this section, Vasubandhu writes:

The Abhidharma is called *abhi-dharma* because it envisions[62] the dharma which is the direct object of supreme knowledge, or the su-preme dharma, [which is] nirvana [itself].[63]

Conditioned and Unconditioned Dharmas

Let us examine the chart of the seventy-five dharmas. There are two great divisions in the chart:

1. Conditioned dharmas (1–72)
2. Unconditioned dharmas (73–75)

Conditioned Dharmas

The section on "Conditioned Dharmas" is divided into four major categories:

I. Forms, which consist of eleven specific dharmas
II. Mind, which consists of one dharma
III. Concomitant (or working together) mental factors, which are further divided into subgroups (see appendix 1, column III, for more details)
IV. Elements neither substantial forms (column I), nor involved in mental functioning (columns II and III), which consists of true factors that do not depend on a truth or reality in a present moment of experience (in other lists, these are presented like what we might call in physics "laws that regulate the coming together of dharmas")

We will spend most of our time exploring those dharmas listed in column III. We will address such questions as: What are the general factors of being alive? What are the factors that help open our heart? What are the factors that prevent us from opening our heart? What factors can be either opening or closing, depending on the situation? And we will explore those dharmas listed in column IV and address such questions as: What are the general laws that regulate this coming together and also their dissipation?

Unconditioned Dharmas

However, all of these seventy-two conditioned dharmas are rather beside the point if it wasn't for the very last column, those of the unconditioned dharmas, those factors which name the possibility of freedom and liberation from suffering. Without that, probably no one would be interested. In order to give

a full picture of all the dharmas, in addition to the dharmas that come together and go apart, there are three dharmas that are not created and not conditioned. These include dharma 73, space itself.

In addition to space there are two ways to understand cessation of suffering
(*nirodha*), dharmas 74 and 75. One sense of cessation, that of cessation with
remainder, refers to the awakening of the Buddha under the bodhi tree. The
term *with remainder* is used to indicate that, although his defilements had
ceased, the Buddha continued to teach and be seen and heard by many beings
for over forty years. That is what is meant by "cessation with remainder." The
other sense, dharma 75, "cessation without remainder," refers to the final nirvana (*parinirvana*), or "death," of the Buddha, which leaves no remainder.

The Coming Together of Dharmas

Remember, everything that occurs is due to the working of dharmas, so we
might ask the questions, "How come all of these factors aren't always working
together all the time? What has to happen in order for some factors to lock
into place, and what has to happen for those factors to be unlocked and no
longer be working? How does impermanence work, and how does language
work?" The answer to these questions is listed in this fourth column.

To play the Abhidharma "game," this special mode of analysis, the answer
has to be given in terms of dharmas. Then, to formulate the same question
as an Abhidharma question, we might ask: "Which dharmas are responsible
for the coming together of dharmas?" Just by hearing this, we move into the
technical way in which an *Abhidharmika*—one who practices Abhidharma—
thinks about these things.

Acquisition and Nonacquisition

The dharma responsible for the coming together of dharmas is 59: *acquisition*.[64] The dharma that is responsible for disengaging groupings of dharmas
is 60: *nonacquisition*.[65]

Birth

The dharma that is responsible for the coming into existence of a situation is 66: *birth.*[66] Birth here does not mean birth from a mother but the coming about of a new situation. If you think about it, it is strange that something new can occur. We have this habit of saying, "I have a new boyfriend, a new girlfriend, a new job, a new teacher, a new understanding, a new kind of goat cheese, a new whatever." But that does not mean we understand its characteristics. From the viewpoint of dharmas, what is responsible for this experience of *newness*? It is 66: birth.

Fleeting Stability

The other strange thing about experiences is that they don't immediately dissipate. They seem to be stable for a while. If we have a new boyfriend or girlfriend, this is good news. If we are newly unemployed, this is bad news. But to give a full presentation of a situation or experience, to say that it is new is not enough; it also sticks around for a while. In order to underline the impermanence of it, I call it *fleeting stability* (67).

For a while we are here, and the general characteristics of this "here" situation is the sole ground that makes scientific investigation possible. Think about it: if it were the nature of all reality to instantaneously arise and dissipate, it would be impossible to engage in that famous repetition of the experiment. There has to be a relatively similar situation, a stability, in order to communicate or investigate anything at all. In fact, it is one of the hallmarks of mental health.

When the stabilities of ourselves and another individual are not harmonious, when the rate of decay of remembering or reflecting is different among individuals, we say we're not compatible. It starts with something small like "The timing is a bit off here; it's incompatible." That is the "seed syllable" before we say, "There is a problem." And the full visualization of that samsaric practice is, "We must banish something." All of this comes from differences of stability.

That which is extremely unstable is often regarded as negative, as if there is some force that wants or desires things to be stable. We categorize things and situations as good or bad depending on their *stability*. If something is painful, it is good if it is extremely unstable. If something is pleasurable, it is bad if it is extremely unstable. However, no matter how stable it is, sooner or later it will completely dissipate in terms of its current pattern. It won't disappear, it *decays* (68); it undergoes a transformation to the point where its general characteristics are no longer appropriate as a full explanation.

And both in India and in the West, great and lesser philosophers have wondered about whether or not what has changed is the nature and essence, or only an accident, of its qualities. The fact that there seems to be a movement from dharmas called *birth* (66) to dharmas called *stability* (67) to dharmas called *decay* (68) is given the name *impermanence* as a separate dharma (69).

Impermanence

Impermanence is the name given to the fact that all conditioned elements (all elements from 1 to 72) arise, stay for a while, and then decay. This is that famous "impermanence." It is one of the marks of conditioned existence. In the Abhidharma, conditioned existence consists of seventy-two separate, analyzable factors. However, how do we usually understand "impermanence" in these contexts? Dzongsar Khyentse Rinpoche once asked why so many people think that impermanence is bad. He then suggested another way to think: Imagine that my current situation of not having a Mercedes-Benz is impermanent. Expanding this sense, we can think that our current situation of not being a full and complete buddha is actually impermanent!

3

*Exploring the Nature
of Self and Reality*

Ourselves as a Stream

There is a great deal to study, and if we think this is boring and we don't have time, I can hear Vasubandhu's laughter because, from the viewpoint of the Abhidharma, these factors are what we see whenever we look into the mirror, this swirl of jumping frog potential.

If we feel embarrassed or if we laugh, all those passing moments of embarrassment, laughter, and boredom are completely accounted for as simply the coming together and the dissipation of dharmas. One moment we are embarrassed, the next we laugh, then we stop. This is what we are: a movement or a stream of unending "coming togethers" and "going aparts."

What is amazing, according to the Abhidharma and according to the Buddha, is that we as that stream can know the stream. That's fantastic news. There are only two ways the stream goes—knowing itself or not. Whether we study the Abhidharma or not, the stream will still flow.

In what follows, I'd like to say something about what it is to ignore the concrete subtlety of the various movements, why it is given such importance in the

Buddhist teachings, what this has to do with self or ego, and why self or ego is considered the "bad guy" in Buddhism.

The Conditioned and the Unconditioned

But before addressing these very important questions, I'd like to revisit the distinction between the seventy-two conditioned dharmas and the three unconditioned dharmas. What do the terms *conditioned* and *unconditioned* mean? What do all of these seventy-two conditioned factors have in common, and how are they different from the three unconditioned dharmas? What does the "un" in unconditioned—the *a* in the Sanskrit *asamskrita*[67]—mean? And again, why should we care about these "not" conditioned factors? Without knowing what unconditioned means, we do not know what cessation (of suffering) itself means. How do we know whether we have reached the end of the road? To ask the question about what is unconditioned is to ask the question about enlightenment itself.

Vasubandhu spends quite some time on this point, and he tells us that when he was studying, there were at least four separate schools and controversies on this one point about the meaning of conditioned in contrast to unconditioned.

Although Vasubandhu discusses four different ways of understanding the meaning of conditioned (*samskrita*) and not conditioned or unconditioned (*asamskrita*), he finally settled on what henceforth became the classical definition: "not" is taken to mean "not caused" (*ahetuka*).[68] Not conditioned or unconditioned means there was never anything that caused it to come about. Conditioned means, then, it does come about due to specific causes (*hetu*) and conditions (*pratyaya*).

Now we might think that the study of "causality," the dynamics of cause and effect in Buddhism, is the full and complete teaching. But we now learn that causality itself has absolutely nothing to do with those three not conditioned dharmas since they weren't caused. Think a bit: this might mean that we can't "produce" cessation, right? How can we produce a state that cannot be produced? How can we cause something that has no cause? Many thousands of pages have been written by Buddhists on this point, on this famous riddle of awakening—the cessation of conditioned factors.

Expressing Reality: Two Traditions

Now I would like to talk about a certain type of tightness. In the West, and according to some psychologists, *ego* is believed to be healthy and necessary, but in Buddhism ego seems to be not only unnecessary but "bad."

I Am That

In some of the noble traditions of India before Buddhism arose, there were treatises that spoke of a self (*atman*).[69] In Brahmanism, and later, in the so-called Hindu traditions, this self, or soul (there are various ways it has been rendered into English), is considered a "good guy"—that is, it is viewed as a very positive, spiritually important thing. Yet in most instances, we find that same term *atman* in Buddhist texts as a negative thing, a "bad guy," something to be seen through and abandoned. What I mean by "good guy" and "bad guy" here is that the word *atman* in Brahmanical/Hindu contexts refers to—in a very dynamic and subtle way—a spiritual insight into an invariant and dynamic way of being. In these traditions, *atman* signifies the most essential sense of what we are and *brahman*[70] refers to the invariant nature of the universe; it is the natural state of what is. These esoteric spiritual traditions of Hinduism consist of the investigation of how to discover and live in the light of seeing the identity between *atman* and *brahman*, but in Buddhist traditions, *atman* is regarded as a fixation that, when clung to (*atmagraha*), actually serves as the primary cause of suffering. So, in short, "self" (*atman*) is "good" in Hindu traditions, but "bad" in Buddhist traditions.

This identification is encoded in the famous expression *tat tvam asi* from the Upanishads, which in archaic English is translated as "that thou art." That is to say, it means something akin to "I am that," "you are that." The "that" is brahman and the "I" or "Thou" is atman—and they are the same. This very famous expression is considered a quintessential truth of the Upanishads.

The Buddha of course was not born a Buddhist. He was a member of the Shakya clan and said to have been of the warrior (*kshatriya*) caste. He lived some five hundred years or so after the Upanishads were said to have developed, so he surely knew the traditions of the famous brahman and atman very well. But he also seems to have known of another famous tradition of the Upanishads, one that is less quoted by Buddhists when they want to show the differences between Buddhist and non-Buddhist traditions: We refer here to the Upanishadic phrase regarding the ultimate that is "not that, not that" (*neti neti*).

Not That, Not That

Many scholars feel that there is an "apophatic" tradition of Upanishadic thinking which was very sympathetic to a line of teachings developed by the Buddha, a tradition in which one would search for what is most basic in the universe and discover that it wasn't "that." This "negative" use of language regarding the ultimate did not mean there did not exist any such thing as "the ultimate," but rather that one could not express what "it" might be in language.

This approach suggests there's an acknowledgment of the limits of naming what is most fundamental, a recognition that what is most fundamental cannot be named. All the names for this so-called fundamental nature can never hit the target of what is most fundamental because it is boundless; that is, it cannot be bound by language. In time, this way of reflecting grew into a tradition in the Upanishads. In time, a slogan developed that is as famous as *tat tvam asi*. It is the statement that whatever we think is "it" is not "it." This came to be expressed as *neti neti*, "not that, not that."

Thus, there were these two traditions of thought prior to Buddha's awakening—the tradition of "that thou art" (*tat tvam asi*) and the tradition of "not that, not that" (*neti neti*). Both were understood to have the same target—reality. Both traditions of characterizing what is absolutely real still exist today, not only in India but also in Buddhist traditions throughout the world. Some say we can positively characterize what is absolutely real; others suggest that we can use language only in a "negative" way to indicate the limits of language in the presence of what is absolutely real.

The Four Extremes

In the tradition of apophatic discourse—using negative language that points to the absolute nature of reality—there came to be Nagarjuna's famous exposition of four extremes.[71] They are:

1. Do things truly exist? Can we assert something truly exists? No.
2. Do things truly not exist? If we can't say that things truly exist, then surely we can assert that they must not exist. Can we say things truly do not exist? No.
3. Do things sometimes both exist and not exist? Perhaps sometimes things truly are and sometimes they truly aren't; perhaps they are both. This famous third option was subject to various interpretations. One way of interpreting "both" here is in a temporal sense: So it is the case that it *sometimes* is and *sometimes* isn't? Again, Nagarjuna says "No."
4. Do things never sometimes exist and not exist? Then, it must be the case that we can assert with certainty that it truly *is the case* that it never sometimes is and sometimes isn't? Again, Nagarjuna says "No."

Note in particular that the "not being able to establish" is not the same as establishing the opposite case.

These are the famous four extremes, and they can be regarded as a robust or turbocharged version of *neti neti*. Because of such talk, many people think that the essence of Buddhism is essentially *apophatic*, and some think that the essence of Christianity is *cataphatic*, as if there was no "not like that" tradition in Christianity, nor anything similar to "God is love" in Buddhism.

Misunderstanding Self, Soul, and Ego in Buddhism

We've spent a bit of time talking about self and ego in the tradition of the Upanishads because this kind of talk is extremely important in the Buddhist tradition. But since most of the early figures who translated the words of the Buddha into Western languages were conditioned by Christian thinking, we find absurd translations and thoughts such as "Buddhists say there's no such thing as a soul, ego, or self."

Perhaps to skirt these confusions, His Holiness the Dalai Lama says over and over again that the essence of all religions is love. I myself have never heard him give a teaching at an ecumenical conference in which he said there are two kinds of spiritual traditions: those who think (deludedly) that there is a soul and those who know (definitively) that there is no soul. But many people seem to take this business of the existence or nonexistence of the soul as a matter of life and death.

In Buddhism, there is the habit of saying that those who think that there is something called a soul or God suffer the wrong view or the extreme known as "eternalism." On the other side, of course, those for whom the word *soul* or *God* is an opening—an ethical, kind, and loving word—think, "Oh, those Buddhists, those nihilists, those God-denying heathens, who pay no attention to the salvation and loving-kindness of our Lord, they are to be pitied; they are to be converted; they are to be shunned." To summarize: this simple word *soul* has caused great confusion.

Obsessive Fixity

The Buddhist meaning of the word *atman* is "obsessive fixity."[72] Now you might ask, "What does this have to do with the famous ego?" Let's explore how this famous self and ego as a "good guy" or a "bad guy" is used in Buddhism.

Let's look again at the four noble truths. The cause of suffering is said to be clinging (*trishna*, literally "thirst").[73] Take the metaphors of Buddhism in all of their concrete splendor. *Trishna* means you are suffering from thirst—you are so dehydrated that you obsessively think only of the one thing that will alleviate your thirst—as if you were dying; all you can fixate on is finding water. In the desert you might even hallucinate its presence; the thirst is so strong that it might produce a hallucination, and the name of that hallucination, according to the Buddha, is that there is a self (atman). According to this metaphor, because this is based on an obsession, which is the cause for the continuation of suffering, this sense of atman is taken as something "bad," as discussed before,

According to Buddhist teachings, we thirst (trishna) in three different ways, and *atman* is the name given to the obsessive quality of our thirsting—to our obsessive fixity. I use the word *atman* here to avoid its translation as ego, soul, and self. *Atman* is just a word that's used to talk about any of the three following kinds of obsessions that are the cause of suffering:

1. We want certain things to be permanent, to not change.
2. We want something to be unique, to have never happened before.
3. We want things to be independent, not depending on anything.

We regard, obsess, or plan about things as if they were permanent (or stable), unique, and independent—hence all the practices on impermanence. Impermanence here refers back to our three friends from column IV (refer to the seventy-five dharmas chart on page 38): birth (66), stability (67), and decay (68).

A perfect example for taking things as unique or singular is thinking of only this life. But if we think of dependent co-arising in terms of carrying over the course of many lives, we can think of things differently, that is, subject to change and dependently arisen. This famous metaphor is used by Nagarjuna in a text known as *Letter to a King*.[74] Here, Nagarjuna tells a king that if he had insight into how many lives he had already undergone, and were to make a heap of the bones from each of those previous lives, that mountain of bones would be higher than Mount Meru.

And finally, we want things to be independent as opposed to dependently arisen. Many types of meditation seem to be specific antidotes for this habit in which, thirsting and hungering for some certainty, we grab on to something as if it were permanent. As an exercise we can imagine that our close companions—perhaps a boyfriend or girlfriend—have a "past" of many previous lives, and if their bones were right now piled in front of us they would make a heap taller than the tallest of mountains. Yes, still, we want things to be stable, to be unique, and independent.

So, to summarize this important point, in Buddhism "self" (atman) is the name given to any or all of these three tendencies toward fixation. That's the technical definition. From this perspective we might see how "ego," "me," and "myself" are simply habitual tendencies of fixation. We cling to these static notions of ourselves and of others. You can see how ego and self are a bit secondary. It is said, in fact, that we grab on to this.[75] We might call it "static cling"!

Cutting Through the Fixity: Anatman

It is said when we begin to have insight into this obsessive clinging as the primary dynamic of suffering, then the quality of that clinging begins to break up a bit. There are two ways in which the breakup of that clinging is indicated. We will primarily focus on only one of these ways: no self, which in Sanskrit is *anatman*.[76]

This famous anatman is an insight that, according to the Tibetan tradition, has been called the basic Shravakayana insight. It defines, in part, what is meant by Shravakayana. There is a certain level of insight into how this atman works, so that it loosens up a bit with respect to being a "person,"[77] which is Sanskrit for "my sense of who I am," "my personality," "me."

When we say, "I have a problem," "I" is already the problem. Who is this "I"? Is this person really permanent? Or is it not so solid or fixed? Many Buddhist practices have as their aim coming to experience this so-called person as not so permanent, unique, or independent.

In fact, personhood and personality is not so fixed. All the categories of the conditioned dharmas (the five aggregates,[78] the twelve sense bases,[79] and the eighteen elements)[80] are the impermanent, multiple, dependently arising factors that give a full account of this so-called me and my so-called world of experience, allowing it to not be so fixed. And the benefit—what we gain—is that the upset, the veil that masks our true openheartedness, is cut through. The veil of upset is ripped asunder. By applying the analysis of these Abhidharma categories, in groupings of five, twelve, and eighteen dharmas, we will see that this so-called "me" is not so fixed. The benefit is that one can rip the obscuring veil of upset when things don't go our way.

Arhat: To Have Conquered the Enemy

To conclude this section, the name given to that stable state in which the veil of upset has been thoroughly cut through (*klesha avarana*)—the goal according to the Shravakayana tradition—is said to be the state of being an arhat, a noble one, one who has conquered the foe of emotional upset. Arhat is glossed as foe destroyer.[81] It is said that through this basic practice of seeing through the fixity of the personality, one cuts through the crippling effects of emotional upset so that you have slain this enemy. The enemy is upset itself.

Stuckness of Habit Patterns

In these Buddhist traditions and also in Western forms of psychotherapy meant to help those whose ego has been damaged, the damage is understood to be an inability based on a kind of *stuckness of patterns*. The point is not to be stuck, and to learn how to become unstuck. What, then, would Buddhists say about the Western notion of the necessity of having a "healthy ego"? A healthy ego from the Abhidharma point of view consists entirely of having stabilized those conditioned factors in that category called *wholesome factors* or *positive mental factors*. These include factors such as confidence, self-respect, decorum, equanimity, and so on.

The Buddhist View of Personality

If you ask a Buddhist what the Buddhist view of personality is, there are possibly two extreme responses. One extreme response would be, "There is no such thing as personality." But if a psychologist asked a Buddhist to elaborate, and pointed out certain recurring features of that Buddhist's behavior (which anyone can see) and also inquired about their habitual ways of thinking, their habits of hopes and fears, that psychologist might awaken the Buddhist from this dogmatic slumber of thinking that there was no personality. In that case, then, that Buddhist might reply differently. They might say: "Oh, now I see what you pointed out. Well, we Buddhists say with respect to that: 'get over it.'"

This exemplifies the two possible views some students of Buddhism have with respect to the existence or nonexistence of a personality. Either response may, in fact, be regarded as unskillful or unhelpful, depending on the situation. As the Buddha reminds us, we should communicate according to the temperament and openness of those we encounter, and Buddhist teachers do tend to teach according to the circumstance and capacity of those present.[82]

Personality Types, Basic Temperaments

What does Buddhist thought say about personality types or basic temperaments? The Buddhist tradition might have the earliest recorded classification of personality. It's called *A Designation of Human Types* [83] and is one of the Abhidharma texts in the Pali Canon. The term for human types in this text is "personality" (*pudgala*). This term is the name for a kind of fixity, a reference point, or habit that we tend to rely on. As we've already discussed, cutting through this fixity and habit is, in part, the goal of Buddhist study and practice, for as long as we are bound to such reference points of self, me, and mine, we keep the wheel of suffering turning in full swing.

What do Buddhis say about the variety of personality types? The ancient text *A Designation of Human Types* states that there are three basic personality types: you are either (1) a greed type, (2) a hate type, or (3) an ignorance type. [84] These are character or personality types, karmic habits deeply rooted in early development. We can imagine them as orientation and survival strategies, like the Western notions of humors as discussed by Paracelsus (melancholic, choleric, bilic, and sanguine). [85] As such, they are not to be conflated with overt displays of anger, greed, or confusion, expressions of upset which might arise in different circumstances. These three possible temperaments are more deep-seated. They are congenital and constitutive (a materialist, one who only believes in the material reality of things, might say they are genetic).

Greed Type

A person who is a greed type or who has a greed temperament is one whose dominant pattern, sense of reality, and sense of normalcy is created and maintained by a style of responsiveness characterized by "greed." Why so? How does this work? Here, greed is the general tendency—from childhood up through adulthood—to feel most affirmed, real, and normal when one is allowed to absorb or merge with what is presented as an experience (or to merge or absorb into an experience) with no blockage or hesitation. For such temperaments, this is the normal, most comfortable way of responding in everyday situations. We might call such types "blenders" or "mergers." When they are allowed to do that, they feel good and normal. For them, it is the most natural way of responding. It corresponds to how they experience the world, themselves, and other people. They tend to choose their careers and friends according to what is most in accord with such responsiveness. For such types, any interruption, any suggestion that something might impede that blending or merging, is often experienced as a disconfirmation of who they are, and so it is unsettling and potentially disturbing.

Hate Type

Such greed types tend to have stylistic conflicts with those of a hate temperament. A hate type doesn't mean one is running around being angry. The hate type is the most spacious, most happy, most real and normal because they have a great capacity to emotionally create distance from a new experience. That allows them the space to analyze, to make distinctions, and to note differences in the sudden onslaught of experiences. The hate type could be called "the separator," "the distancer." They become claustrophobic when asked to just take things as they are, to not ask questions, and to not go into things.

No matter which type we are, we can all learn which situations shut us down and which situations open us up. A hate type is in contradistinction to a greed type. A hate type's sense of reality is *affirmed* through pushing away and resisting the way in which reality is presented at first glance. They are not accepting it just like this. This is energetically the opposite of the greed type.

Let's give a concrete example of an interaction between a hate type and a greed type. One day, a greed type was reading a book and said to their friend (a hate type), "This book is fantastic!" Then, that friend picked up the recommended book and noticed such things as: "When was it written? Oh, that means it's about ten years out of date. What's the bibliography like? Who does the author cite? Oh, the author is citing a person whose work has been superseded." And the hate type continues in that manner.

As a hate type, that's how they explore and engage. They distance themselves, moving the object away from them so that they can actually bring it into focus. This is their way of gaining a foothold into the material of that book. But the greed type, who recommended that book, says, "Why do you always have to criticize everything?"

The hate type responds, "But I *wasn't* criticizing, I was finding my way into the book. That's my way of engaging—not only books but most subjects I am drawn to. I seem to first take a critical stance in order to access it." This is a typical example of how these two personality types might interact.

Ignorance Type

Ignorant or delusional types may be thought of in two ways. First, and most broadly, one can say that *all* beings are ignorant insofar as they do not (yet) comprehend reality. This "not knowing" (*avidya*) [86] is said to bind beings to the wheel of suffering; unbinding from that is often called an "awakening" (*bodhi*) [87] from the sleep of delusion. Secondly, and more narrowly, there are beings called "tortured ones" or "hungry ghosts", [88] who have been so traumatized that they feel neither safe to merge with something, as do greed types or "attractive types," nor safe to distance themselves from things, as do hate types or "distancing types." They're somewhat shut down. We might reflect here on a possible extreme case of ignorance, on what it might be like to be an extremely deluded type, in the sense of not being able to discern what is real or true.

In *The Words of My Perfect Teacher* by Patrul Rinpoche, there is a wonderful discussion where he takes the example of the hungry ghost, a *preta*, which is one of the modes of sentience in samsara. In Patrul Rinpoche's discussion, he talks about how samsara is not spiritually beneficial to engage with, and he goes on to say a preta is dominated by terror and hallucinations. For them there is no basis for distinguishing what is real from what is not, and this causes a pattern of terror in the entire organism. It's said that the dominant upset that characterizes a preta is an avarice that can never be satisfied. We might think that this represents a greed type. But these are only categories; we can be a bit loose and think carefully about them. The idea here, from a psychological point of view, is that there is an underlying terror for those who have been so shut down due to physical, sexual, and/or emotional abuse. It's known very well.

Dissociative identity disorder (formerly called "multiple personality disorder") might be understood as an extreme form of the deluded or ignorance type, where the fixity is closed and split because it is not *safe* to be either a greed or a hate type. For them it is not safe to be a type that merges because to be present and to merge may mean total annihilation. Nor is it safe to make distinctions because this may be monitored and sensed by someone who will come and annihilate them. It is not safe to relax, and also it is not safe to put one's voice forward, so to speak, and so these beings survive by *not being present at all.*

A student once asked me to translate a question to a Tibetan lama. She asked: "How do you give a direct introduction to the nature of mind to someone with multiple personalities?" So, I tried to think how to translate multiple personalities, and I came up with, "somebody who has many minds." Thereupon, the lama laughed and said: "Multiple? But we can't even say there's one mind."

Tathata: Reality

Buddha Nature

Once again, our goal is to repeatedly manifest the direct perception of reality rather than changing our personality. So then, what is reality? The Tibetan term that was sometimes used for reality is *de zhin nyi*; in Sanskrit it is *tathata*,[89] meaning thusness. One of the names of the Buddha is the Tathagata,[90] the one who has "thus gone" or "went like this." And we are encouraged to reflect that this understanding of tathagata is our true nature. We have the nature and capacity to go like "this"; in Sanskrit this is called *tathagatagarbha*.[91] *Garbha* means we have the potential or the capacity to move, to change, to develop like "this." "This" means as the Buddha did. In the technical sense, "buddha" was not a person; it instead names the open, luminous state that never undergoes suffering; that is sometimes called "awakened." The Buddhist teachings clearly say that enlightenment cannot be different from reality. So to directly encounter or perceive reality and to have full and complete realization is the same thing. Of course, I simplify!

The analogy that is often given for enlightenment is the sky: The sky does not change. Whether or not one is a Shravakayana follower, the sky is still the same. Reality itself does not have the label Buddhist, Hindu, or Jewish.

In a text called the *Uttaratantra* (*Sublime Continuum*),[92] it is said that this buddha nature, this reality, which is our innermost essence, is the great self (*maha atman*), beyond both the "self" of non-Buddhists and also beyond the "not-self" of Buddhists.

Buddhists asked themselves the same question: What is the true invariant nature of this reality, this buddha nature? They knew they weren't alone in the world; they lived among those with different views, and they wondered, "Do those who are not Buddhists have buddha nature?" And they indeed understood that non-Buddhists and Buddhists have the same essential abiding capacity to overcome all suffering.

We should not be surprised that even Shravakayanists have buddha nature from the perspective of Mahayana. Even eternalists have buddha nature. Even nihilists, all bodhisattvas, all mahasiddhas, all serial killers, and all suicide bombers have buddha nature. If you think this isn't fair or not right, go argue with Maitreya, who authored the *Uttaratantra*.

When we judge others as good or bad—and to be human is to judge—our judgment never touches their buddha nature. It is now accepted, especially in the Mahayana traditions, that all living beings (not only humans) have this buddha nature. It is a precious thing. That is why, in part, it is considered a grave karmic error to kill or hurt other living beings.

In the Mahayana tradition, it is a vow, and a form of mental training, to honor the buddha nature of all living beings. From an Abhidharma point of view, the way to do that is to find a way to directly perceive reality because what blocks us from being able to directly perceive the reality of our own buddha nature is a wrong view of the way things are.

Coming back now to our discussion of conditioned versus unconditioned dharmas, this "reality," which we are encouraged to directly perceive, is an unconditioned dharma. It is said that the Abhidharma is high because it leads to a complete spiritual transformation, one that will not change: it leads to the direct perception or realization of reality. This reality is not only a problem for us here, it has been an intellectual problem for countless Buddhist practitioners. To put it in a nutshell: How do we know whether this "reality" is the reality that is being talked about? Upon what basis do we decide what enlightenment is? I don't say this to discourage us but to suggest that it is very deep and profound.

So reality, full and complete enlightenment, our buddha nature, a state that is unconditioned by causes—all of these terms more or less speak of the same thing.

4

Six Channels of Perception

Now, according to the Abhidharma, the whole apparatus of our experiences works through six channels of perception, that is, through our five sense-based faculties and one non-sense-based faculty.

1. Seeing

Seeing is one of the ways in which we obsess. Let's be very precise: we have a habit of seeing something, and we hope it will last or we fear it will last. We hope something we see is unique or independent, or we fear that what we see is unique or independent.

Seeing means, very concretely, anything that we experience, remember, or contact that has shape and hue. We're not talking about movement at this point. It's more like a freeze frame. Movement is a bit of a fiction, and we invest a lot in this fiction. Even a film is just one frame after the other—the trick is to move them at the rate of twenty-four frames a second, and then there is this fiction that is corresponding to the way things are. But in a scientific mode of analysis, it's just frames or pictures. Don't obsess about what you're seeing; mind the gap.

2. Hearing

According to the basic classification of hearing in the Abhidharma, there are four divisions: hearing nice sounds, hearing not nice sounds, hearing sounds that are produced with intention, and hearing sounds that arise due to no intention (like earthquakes or rain). But for all this wide variety of things heard, we obsess; we hope and fear in the way of thinking of it as fixed, unique, or autonomous.

3. Smelling

Another channel for our obsessional activity is that of smelling. Again, the basic classification is smells that we like and smells that we don't like.

4. Tasting

We have sweet, sour, bitter, salty, pungent, and astringent tastes. More or less, all human beings have these ways of making distinctions about tasting. Between smelling and tasting, there develops the career of a gourmand, someone who obsesses about minute differences of taste and smell. We again hope and fear with respect to the fixity, uniqueness, and autonomy of various tastes and smells.

5. Touching

There is interior and exterior touch. Interior touch is what we call hunger pangs, the grumbling of the stomach, and certain kinds of movement with respect to orifices. If you had stomach problems, it would be this channel of touch. Here, we don't talk about the mental component but just the physical component of being sick. You can do an entire analysis of being sick according to the working along these channels.

6. Cognitive and Affective Aspects

This channel six includes all possible experiences which are not "sense based" (mental, as distinguished from the five senses). It includes both what we call mental factors and also affective (emotional) factors. We might say there are affective and cognitive aspects that have a *common channel* that is separate from seeing, hearing, smelling, tasting, or touching including joy, anger, hatred, fear, shame, sadness, guilt, and so on. Cognitive aspects are thought, insight, doubt, remembering, and so on.

In sum, then, there are six channels through which our obsessional habits run. According to the traditions of the *Abhidharmakosha*, our cravings and thirsts don't run anywhere else; they only are activated along six channels. We might call this a hexamodel of experience. Obsessional modes of experience—which are the cause of suffering—in terms of "channels" are everything in terms of fixity, singularity, or independence. Part of getting into recovery and becoming sober from the drunken, casual habits of nonscientific inquiry is to learn precisely how everything we experience is experienced only as moments of seeing, hearing, smelling, tasting, touching, and this famous number six, which I like to call "other," defined as neither seeing, nor hearing, nor smelling, nor tasting, nor touching.

Memory

Something we can experience that is not seeing, hearing, smelling, tasting, touching, is *memory*. This is how the Abhidharmikas would analyze memory: "Is memory something we see or something we hear? No." We say, "this memory" or "I remember," but memory itself is a label. We never have something that could be called a memory. Memory is a word we use to label a concrete experience. If we're asked to talk about that experience, we may say, "I remember . . ." But it has a concrete arising because we're not continually remembering. It sticks around for a while and then it goes away.

We might ask, "But in my memory, I'm seeing, aren't I?" The answer is "no." There is all the difference in the world. In calming meditation (shamatha) practices, often referred to these days as "mindfulness" practices particularly when focusing on an external object, the moment we are looking at something is a moment of seeing. When we space out and start remembering things we saw, in the context of shamatha, this is called a distraction; it is the operation of channel 6. We then bring ourselves back to seeing, back to channel 1.

Three Places of Concentration during Calming Meditation

For shamatha with an object, three (of the six) modes of channel processing are primarily used.

Seeing (Channel 1)

The first mode is seeing. Channel 1 shamatha such as focusing on a flame. A flame doesn't mean your idea of a flame or some flame you may remember but concretely seeing, looking at something like the shape and color of an actual flame. Or, as is common in Tibetan Buddhist practices of shamatha with an object, this may involve focusing on a syllable or letter drawn on paper, perhaps several yards away from the practitioner.

Touching (Channel 5)

You may practice meditation with awareness on the in-and-out breath. This is channel 5 shamatha, or the calming meditation on touch. In many of the practices on mindfulness of breath, there are primarily two channel 5 methods. There is focusing on the point of where this breath touches in the place of the nostrils during the out breath and the in breath. Another channel 5 shamatha with breath is to feel the point of the rising and falling of the abdomen and to count the breaths there. The reason we sometimes do this is to help avoid spacing out. One is instructed to be aware of the direct sensory perception of breathing. If you then start thinking about other things, this is called a distraction, and one has "switched channels." One has gone from channel 5 to channel 6.

Mental (Channel 6)

The third method is channel 6 shamatha, as, for instance, if you have an image of the Buddha in your mind. All focused internal visualizations are channel 6 shamatha. Additionally, we can say that all panoramic awareness (vipashyana) meditations are also channel 6 since they do not involve paying attention to things that are externally seen, heard, smelled, tasted, or touched.

Cutting through the Fixity

To summarize, so far, all this talk about channels and calming practices is meant to bring the flavor of the Dharma to us in an Abhidharma way—remembering the fourfold meaning of *abhi*: (1) to make manifest in a concrete way; (2) to do so repeatedly; (3) to overcome all our wrong and narrow views; (4) so that we will have a full realization. This is a good test to apply to determine whether or not any of these various aspects of the Abhidharma are hitting their target.

It is said that if we learn how to pay attention, which means developing the habit of knowing which channel is "broadcasting," that is a way of cutting through this obsessional fixity of our experiences. The Buddha said that this obsessional quality can end. We can discover the liberating experience of seeing through the habitual frustrating fixity of our experiences. That's the goal of Buddhism.

Unsticking Personality

A basic Shravakayana approach to cutting through this fixity is to recognize that this so-called personality is not always fixed. This is exemplified in the phrase "the personality is not fixed" (*pudgala nairatmya*).[93] Remember *pudgala* means personality, another word for all those habitual patterns of channel firings; *nair* means "not"; and *atmya* is short for atman, which we've discussed at length, meaning here "fixity," "static," or "stuck." The hope (and promise?) of Buddhism is that this so-called personality, this six-channeled or "hexamodel" processing, is not static. How is that fixity destroyed? It is destroyed by the application of the medicine of the application of the categories of wisdom and insight of the Abhidharma.

Aggregates, Sense Bases, and Elements

I will give you the list of the three wonderful wisdom categories. We have the five aggregates (*skandhas*), the twelve sense bases (*ayatanas*), and the eighteen elements (*dhatus*).

It is said that the eighteen dhatus were taught to counteract a specific wrong view with respect to the way things are. And the twelve ayatanas and the five skandhas were also each taught to counteract specific wrong views. Vasubandhu and all the great commentators down to the present, including Jamgon Mipham and others, tell us precisely that the categories of the aggregates, elements, and sense bases were taught for specific and different reasons. What were these specific reasons? Vasubandhu uses three categories:[94]

1. The category with respect to how we are wrong or how we do not understand
2. The category with respect to the intellectual capacity
3. The category with respect to the way in which we like to learn

Eighteen Elements (Dhatus)

According to Vasubhandu, the dhatus are divided into six channels, which are again divided in terms of "capacities," "fields" or "objects," and their "integrational function." In terms of capacity, we have eye (channel 1), ear (channel 2), nose (channel 3), tongue (channel 4), and body (channel 5), and then Vasubandhu uses the term *mind* (channel 6). But, Vasubandhu cautions, "Don't think there is something concrete called 'the mind.'" In the second column, field/object, we have forms, sounds, smells, tastes, touches, and "stuff," which is both affective (emotional) and cognitive.

In terms of integrational function, we have visual, auditory, olfactory, gustatory, tactile perception, and consciousness; it is the capacity to integrate into an experience. Visual perception means the capacity to integrate the information that comes from forms through the eye. For visual perception to occur, it is not sufficient to have an eyeball and some form. There must also be the integrated capacity to become aware, and that is visual perception, which might be likened to our visual cortex in the brain; without it, there will not arise an experience of seeing.

Now we have a list of eighteen dhatus organized in a hexamodal way. We said previously that the elements, sense bases, and aggregates were each taught to counteract a specific wrong view with respect to the way things are. Vasubandhu said, that the dhatus are taught with respect to those who are confused about the relationship between channels 1–5 (non-mental) and channel 6 (mental). These eighteen categories are dynamically taught so that we will know that processing reality through the first five channels is different from processing it through the sixth channel. They provide a concrete experiential point that we can return to in our own practice.

Through so-called dhatu analysis, we can learn to distinguish, at the level of our experience, the precise difference between a moment of concretely seeing a form (channel 1) and a moment in which we remember or fantasize seeing a form (channel 6). In the same way, we can learn to distinguish a moment of concretely hearing (channel 2) from fantasizing or remembering we're hearing (channel 6). We learn to distinguish the difference between processing through the first, second, third, fourth, or fifth channel, and through channel 6. This is the teaching of the dhatus that counteracts the confusion between nonmental and mental, the wrong view that everything we do is the same.

Vasubandhu says that these dhatus are taught for those of the least capacity. They are taught for those who desire or need a very big, elaborate teaching. Atman (fixity), in the case of the dhatus, is to be confused about *forms* (any of the first five modes of processing) and *chitta*, or mind (the sixth channel). The dhatus are taught to counteract thinking that everything is form or thought; we can't make any distinctions. It is as if there was no relation between the application of our wisdom mind and changing the quality of our lives.

Sense Bases (Ayatanas) and Aggregates (Skandhas)

The teachings of the ayatanas, which reflect a completely different scheme, are said to be taught to counteract the wrong view that everything we experience is tangible form, as if there were no sixth channel. According to Buddhists, this is the error in the view of a modern scientific materialist analysis, in which mind is just considered to be biochemistry. It is a view that all thoughts are just macro-molecular dances, so to speak, and that everything we think, feel, or hope for is seen to be replaceable molecules. This teaching is for those whose capacity is average and for those who respond to a pedagogy that is less elaborate.

Finally, it is said that skandhas are taught to counteract the wrong view that everything that happens is just mind. They counteract the wrong view of atman just being chitta, just being mind. The skandhas are taught to those who say, "The mind, that's me, it's God; I am that." There's no differentiation. Everything is mind; it's all the same. Skandhas are taught to counteract atman, or the fixity that dwells on permanence, uniqueness, and independence. We see that there's a plurality of factors. Four of the categories of the skandhas have to do with mental "stuff." That means we need a lot of differentiation. This is for the superior practitioner who only needs a short teaching.

Everything Is Streaming

How does this tight pattern called atman, this fixity or tightness (my working definition), work as it flows out along the six channels of seeing, hearing, smelling, tasting, touching, and "other"? How does this sense of a self or this tightness work as we experience things according to our habits of sensory and mental awareness? It works in seventy-two specific energy-pack ways.

If you are interested in a full, complete teaching on this tendency toward permanence, uniqueness, and autonomy (that is, this fixity), and if you want to know how it actually works—not on a surface level, but on the molecular, atomic, and subatomic level—you need the Abhidharma definition of absolute truth. The technical definition of the absolute truth according to the *Abhidharmakosha* is: Anything that remains after there has been a thorough smashing and analysis of everything, physically and mentally. This *smashing* is like using a supercollider to smash an atom; it is applying discernment of the correct view of not-self that smashes all fixity.

The question is: How does this fixity concretely work? How do these conditioned dharmas work? This is the question we are asking in a general and increasingly more specific way. Recall that the Shravakayana approach is to see that the tightness called the person is not fixed; it can loosen a bit. The insight or the practice of breaking through the fixity of the person is a Shravakayana approach. And the prize, the cherry, is that we get rid of the obscuring effects of upset.

Now, what do the Abhidharma traditions say is the actual condition of being human if this fixity is not the true picture? This fixity, this self, is a generalization, an abstraction or distortion, a surface presentation. The term that is used for characterizing living beings from the Abhidharma point of view is that we and our world is a streaming (*samtana*);[95] everything is a stream, a continuous flow of cooperating factors.

You will find lovely translations of Tibetan texts that state, "referring to my mental continuum," which more precisely is "me as continuum," not "my continuum." It's a continuum of dharmas. The flowing of these energy packets in a more or less disordered and anxious way is concretely how permanence, uniqueness, and autonomy as a fixation keeps the muddy stream going. Sometimes this continuum or stream flows in a moment that we call seeing, and sometimes we call it hearing, smelling, tasting, touching, or "other." This "other" (channel 6), which is all that is mental, all that is emotional, also includes all the great insights, such as "I like," "I don't like," and "I remember."

In fact, this continuum does not always consist of the same number of dharmas. According to the Abhidharma, the number of energy packets flowing at any time defines where—that is, in which realm—we are. The existential terms *being* or *existing* are not at all divorced from this deep analysis of flowing. "I flow, therefore I am."

How the Stream Flows: The Three Realms of Samsara

What does this analysis of these energy packets and how we flow have to do with our experience? And what is the relation between these eighteen dhatus and the seventy-five dharmas? For now, simply rest assured that all seventy-five dharmas are fully and completely embedded and accounted for in these eighteen.

This flow, this tightness, does not always occur in the same way. We can say that the tightness flows in three different ways:

1. Sometimes it flows as the desire realm.
2. Sometimes it flows as the form realm.
3. Sometimes it flows as the formless realm.

All of samsara is made up of the desire realm, the form realm, and the formless realm. This is a teaching not only known in the Shravakayana traditions but all the traditions of Buddhism. This teaching of these three aspects of worldliness, the triple world of samsara, is another way of responding to the question of how this tightness, this anxiety, flows. The good news is that since there are different ways in which the stream flows, that means we can change; and in fact we do.

The Desire Realm

In many Buddhist traditions, the desire realm is said to consist of six realms: there are three lower realms[96]—the hell realm, the hungry-ghost realm, and the animal realm; and there are three higher realms—the realms of human beings, demigods, and gods. Generally speaking, we pray never to be reborn in any of these six realms, where certain dominant patterns of the stream get very muddy, such as anger, craving, jealousy, and so forth.

It is said that all of the eighteen factors that we listed are fully and completely flowing and streaming as one's life as being "in" the desire realm. This is how it is for most people—for those who do not practice the path—that is, they just work, maybe have a family, maybe have a pension, and then die. Some Buddhists would call such individuals "common foolish people," as they make no effort to free themselves from the realm of desire dominated by emotional upset, with all six channels blooming, fully flowing in a muddy way.

The Form Realm

In contrast to those in the desire realm, some people do something a bit different with their lives; they create some spaciousness. They meditate, they reflect, they do "spiritual" practice. And these spiritual practices produce experiences that are quite different. They are not so dominated by desire and aggression; they experience altered or transpersonal states. And these states seem to form a coherent pattern, a protective, bounded situation that feels steady or spacious. This is the meaning of "form" of the form realm. There's the form, or *gestalt*, of an unusual set of experiences that are coherent; they are not so dominated by desire. It is said that when the stream flows as this form realm, not all eighteen factors are working. There is a suspension or nonoperation of two channels. That is to say, when one is meditating, one is temporarily different, as if one has gone to a new realm. This is the Abhidharma analysis of meditation.

There is still a stream: it is conditioned; it is samsara; it won't last. But while it lasts, there might be a bit of a relief. Meditation here means something very specific. These realms are beautifully described in terms of which dharmas are working and which ones aren't. Here, two channels are not working, not flowing: smelling and tasting. It is as if to say that the totality of the individual is a bit in suspension when in this meditative realm, the realm of form.

We should know that this form realm consists of a very precise structure, described in terms of different kinds of concentration.[97] It is said that there are four such concentrative states, which are fixed, coherent meditative patterns. When we are in them, or more precisely, when we are that, we are not so dominated by anger, jealousy, and arrogance. We are a bit above it. In depictions of samsara, the form realm and its four concentrative states are represented as higher than the desire realm.

The Formless Realm

The formless realm is, of course, "higher" than the form realm, and it goes all the way up to the so-called peak of worldly existence (samsara). As such, these are temporary states; they are impermanent. Not all samsara is bad as an experience—but it is still samsara. The main idea is to go beyond samsara. That's why altered states of consciousness, whether induced through drugs or through meditation, from the Buddhist point of view, are still samsara; those states will not last and we will all "come down" from them. How long have human beings been having such experiences, how long has samsara been happening? The Buddhist answer is: since beginningless time, forever. People have been having far-out experiences forever. They wrote about them, they set up little groups to induce them, and then, sometimes they said: "This is enlightenment." From a Buddhist point of view, however, this is not the case. In fact, shockingly, one might even say that the practice of Buddhism is not at all about "experience." It is about *awareness*, which is invariant through all experiences.

So, then, what is it like in the formless realms? Experiences are more diffuse; it is a very altered and extremely transpersonal state. It is said that in this sublime (yet still samsaric) state ("sublime samsara" should be an oxymoron) only one channel is working. Only channel 6 is working. The habit of tightness flows in the formless realms only along one channel; "I am" only that one channel firing. There is no seeing, no hearing, no smelling, no tasting, and no touching. What is left? Only channel 6.

How does experience arise when there is no sense or possibility of seeing, hearing, smelling, tasting, or touching? Although still dominated by a kind of fixity, it is an extremely relaxed and spaced-out fixity. Many people seem to think that formless-realm states are enlightenment. But when they go to their spiritual teacher, he or she will say that it's just an "experience." It is conditioned and will go away. The point here is that "enlightenment" does not go away.

What then are the names of these formless-realm states, these very sublime states in which only one channel is working?

1. The field infinite as the sky
2. The field of infinite consciousness
3. The field of nothing at all
4. The field of neither perception nor nonperception

The names of these states describe the very subtle differences of how our fixity flows at the very peak of samsara in which only channel 6 operates.

Exercise in Sixfold Processing

To understand all this, we have to use our capacity to make distinctions. We have to use the dharma known as prajna, or wisdom. See if you can experience this sixfold way of processing; see if you can develop a bit of an Abhidharma "habit." If you're hearing something, notice you are hearing something. See if you can note the difference between concretely looking at something—as the Vietnamese master Thich Nhat Hanh says, really entering into the dimension of the concrete, sensual presence of the color and the shape—or remembering something. We have the habit of blurring the two. We often have one moment of concrete, visual contact that is followed by twenty or thirty moments in which we're spacing out before coming back to what we see. An Abhidharmika becomes adept in noting these distinctions. See if you can actually experience a difference. According to the Abhidharma, this helps to cut through the fixity of our obsessional patterns.

PART TWO

Elemental Analysis

5

Dhatus and Channel Processing

The "Abhi" Way

In the Abhidharma analysis—which is just a systematic, analytical way of presenting the basic teachings of the Buddha that are contained in the sutras—there is a well-known set of three schemata for presenting the teachings: the five aggregates (skandhas), the twelve sense bases (ayatanas), and the eighteen elements (dhatus). In the *Abhidharmakoshabhashya*[98] it says that these schemata are taught in order to counteract particular wrong views regarding the status of the self. These are taught in accord with the individual's capacity to understand and what the individual desires by way of length of a teaching.

To remind ourselves, the Abhidharma is a way of inquiring into the Buddhadharma in an *abhi* way. And *abhi*, here, means "in order to manifest"—so it's ultimately about how to directly manifest and fully make evident, through such study, a direct perception of this famous "reality." It is said that *abhi* in Abhidharma is *abhi mukhya*,[99] "to make manifest the actual state of how things are." And this is done by learning about the skandhas, ayatanas, and dhatus in their particularity.

Counteracting Specific Errors through Dhatu Analysis

The dhatus are taught specifically to counteract the error with respect to a false self, a crippling sense of fixity that we understand to be the root cause of continual suffering. All these categories and schemes are ways of directly cutting through the root causes of suffering, and one of them is this fixity called the *self.* We spent quite some time already on why this is not such a good translation. In the context of the Abhidharma, this fixity is defined very carefully as any habit of perception or reflection which we hope or fear to be permanent, unique, or independent (which cannot be influenced).

The error with respect to the existence of a self or a fixity that the study of the eighteen dhatus counteracts is the error of being confused about the difference (meaning not knowing precisely, at the level of experience, the difference) between moments of seeing, hearing, smelling, tasting, and touching, on the one hand (channels 1–5), and moments that are not seeing, hearing, smelling, tasting, and touching, on the other (mental, channel 6).

This confusion is summarized as being confused about forms and mind (in Sanskrit, this refers to *rupa* and *chitta*, respectively). Forms here means anything that we can contact. Forms refers to things "out there" that we can see, hear, smell, taste, and touch (channels 1–5). And then there is the sixth channel, "mind," better translated as "other," meaning everything else that anyone could ever experience, including moments of inspiration and moments of despair. It is said that this mode of analysis is put forth in order to experientially have a sense of the difference between the sensory modes (channels 1–5) and the nonsensory mode (channel 6).

The Eighteen Elements

The eighteen dhatus are listed in the following table according to how Vasubandhu explains them:

	COLUMN I	COLUMN II	COLUMN III
CHANNEL	CAPACITY	FIELD/OBJECT	INTEGRATIONAL FUNCTION
Channel 1	1. eye	7. form	13. visual perception
Channel 2	2. ear	8. sound	14. auditory perception
Channel 3	3. nose	9. smell	15. olfactory perception
Channel 4	4. tongue	10. taste	16. gustatory perception
Channel 5	5. body	11. touch	17. tactile perception
Channel 6	6. mind	12. "stuff" (dharmas)	18. consciousness (mental awareness)

The eighteen dhatus are divided in three columns: capacity, field/object, and integrational function. (See also the chart on page 94.)

Column I: Capacity

The first column, capacity,[100] consists of dhatus 1–6. The Sanskrit term for capacity is *indriya* (Tib. *wangpo*). This term *indriya* is a favorite word in the Abhidharma and was given its own chapter in the *Abhidharmakosha*. And in that chapter, they tell us there are twenty-two such capacities, such as the capacity and manifestation of being a biological man or woman. Here, in this context of six "capacities," however, indriya refers to the capacity to process information, and the dhatus in this column are as follows:

1. *Eye:* The text makes very clear that "eye" here in the Abhidharma is used as an indriya, as a capacity to process visual information; it does not just mean the physical eye that can be dissected. If there is a defect of the "eye" indriya, even though there may be forms that could be processed, the processing will not occur.
2. *Ear:* When we speak of "ear" as the capacity to process sound, we are not talking about the part that you can pull when somebody is not behaving the way you want them to. We are not even speaking about the part inside, the part that we normally associate with hearing in the West—that is, the physiological aspect. Rather, we are talking about the ear's intact functioning capacity in a living being.

3. *Nose:* This is the capacity to process smells.
4. *Tongue:* This is the capacity to process tastes.
5. *Body:* This is the capacity to process tactile sensations, but also the capacity to experience rumblings in the stomach, movements in a bit more interior way.
6. *"Mind":* Vasubandhu said this is different from the other five. The difference is that we can locate the site of functional processing for the first five. There is no localized site for the functional processing of something called "mind."

Column II: Field

The middle column, dhatus 7–12, takes the name "field." We might say "perceptual field," or more commonly, "objects" of the senses—the objective or perceptual field. But remember, it also includes, as dhatu 12, non-sense-based objects, such as objects of cognition and emotion.

7. *Forms:* Here, this means "shapes and colors." There is a functional linkage between the "capacity" to process visual information, called the eye (1), and a visual "perceptual field," which may be objectified (7). If analyzed, this visual field consists of shape and color. More precisely, it consists of configurations and hues.
8. *Sounds:* This is the perceptual field linked to the ear.
9. *Smell:* This is the perceptual field for the nose.
10. *Taste:* This is the perceptual field for the tongue.
11. *Touch:* This is the perceptual field for touch.
12. *"Stuff":* This refers to dharmas—various nonsensory factors of existence. The field for mind as a capacity to process nonsensory based information is not a perceptual field.

Therefore, dhatu 12 is the field of everything that might be processed that is not perceptual. We came up with a list of examples—memory, fear, and so forth (see part 3). I call it "stuff," lots of stuff. In this tradition there is a list of forty-six separate dharmas, energy packets, that may be the target of processing.

In each case there is a strict horizontal correlation between column I and column II, a specific linkage between the capacity to process and that which is processed. According to the Abhidharma, you cannot see sounds, you cannot hear forms, and so forth. We can only see colors and forms, hear sounds, use the nose for smelling, and so on. How do we account for the experience that sometimes occurs where we have the impression of more than one channel at the same time? The English term for this is *synesthesia*. The Abhidharma answer is very simple: there is a rapid oscillation *between* the channels, which—because we don't have an open heart and a calm mind—we couldn't experience at the level that it was happening. And that applies for everything.

Column III: Awareness as Integrational Function of "Mind"

According to this teaching on the integrational function of mind, in order to have a full moment of an experience called "seeing," it is not sufficient only to have an intact functional capacity to process and a field that is waiting to be processed. We can think of examples where both are present, and yet there will not arise the experience called seeing. Consider someone with an injury of the visual cortex. The visual cortex is located neither in the eye nor in the field that we are going to process. You could even make a test and show that information is coming in at the level of the eye, but there would not arise a true report that the person is seeing something. Seeing has something to do with a *higher integration* that brings seeing into *consciousness*. Modern-day materialists and those who follow neural net theories call this integrative factor "the brain," but there are both philosophical and cognitive-science disputes about the efficacy of this attribution.

According to the Abhidharma and Buddhism, the elements of this third column are not material things. They nevertheless name something that neither column I nor column II account for. It is not sufficient to simply have the field and the capacity that can process it in order to have an experience. We also need an intact functioning third thing, the capacity to *integrate*, so as to bring it to *consciousness*. There are many examples of brain damage or psychological damage that might interrupt the arising of, for instance, a moment of awareness of "seeing"; the interruption of the integrative functioning of (column III). We might call column III the "integrative functioning." The Sanskrit term for this is *vijnana*, which is often translated as "consciousness." It means "a way of knowing" (*jnana*), which is "divided," "specific," or "differentiated." It is differentiated according to the channel or mode that is operative. We could call it "differentiated knowing" or "channel-specific processing."

Visual perception refers to the eye vijnana, meaning the integrative function of knowing along the specific channel that is activated through contact with the capacity to process visual information and the presence of forms to process. In short, we might call this "the integrative capacity for seeing," the channel-specific processing based on the eye. Channel-specific processing, with the eye as its basis, indicates the integrative aspect that is necessary in addition to the presence of the eye and the form. This integrative function could be compared to the visual cortex.

Review of the Three Columns

- *Column I:* The capacity to process sensory information. We have something called eye; without that we could not see. Eye here means the *capacity* to process experiences. Older translations seem to call these column I items "organs," but that is misleading, for Vasubandhu reminds us that they do not refer to the organic, anatomical, physical aspect of the so-called "organ," but rather to its capacity to process specific kinds of sensory information.
- *Column II:* The field or domains of what there is to process (to see, and so on), the stuff to process.
- *Column III:* The integrative function of channel-specific processing, which is dependent on columns I and II working well.

Dhatu Shorthand: The Language of Processing

Remember, the only reason we are doing this analysis is because of the question of how we can concretely experience the difference between a moment of seeing, hearing, smelling, tasting, and touching, on the one hand, and anything else, on the other hand. It is said that, "For one moment of a full experience called 'a moment of seeing,' there have to be three intact factors that are synchronized and working together."

This is the analysis according to the dhatus, and so I have developed a bit of a dhatu shorthand in order to become a bit bilingual, to speak the language of processing reality in this way. For example, we can note a moment of seeing as:

- [*eye–form–visual perception*]/*moment 1*

The number outside the right-hand square bracket, "1," indicates there has been one moment of visual processing, which itself consists of the three dhatus 1, 7, and 13.

Here would then be a dhatus analysis schematic of three moments of experience: moment 1 is the moment of seeing (channel 1), and moments 2 and 3 are thinking about what was seen (channel 6):

- $[1–7–13]/1 \ldots [6–12–18]/2 \ldots [6–12–18]/3$

Dhatus 1, 7, and 13 are connected with dashes to indicate that they are actually functioning together. The name given to these dashes between 1, 7, and 13 is "contact" or "rapport." [101] It is said that in order for there to be any moment of seeing, all coordinated aspects have to have contact. If any of them is damaged, or absent, there will not arise an experience called "seeing." This applies to any of the six channels, which are named based on the numbering of the capacities.

The shorthand actually names the "capacity" (*indriya*) for processing as the first number, the second number names the object field (*alambana*),[102] and the third number in the brackets names the integrative function (*vijnana*).[103] Thus a moment of seeing can be noted as $[1–7–13]$, and a moment of hearing can be noted as $[2–8–14]$. The act of "seeing" is a firing of channel 1, and it means that there is contact among these three functionally working dhatus.

You'll note that this is a very special way of regarding our experiences and is not, at first, easily understood in terms of its analytic power. For now, it's enough to know that in every moment of seeing there are three factors working well together, and these factors are: the *capacity* to process information, the *information* itself, and the ability to *integrate* it into awareness in a specific way. In each case—that is, in the specific processing with respect to the ear, nose, tongue, body, and mental processing—all three factors have to be present.

"We" Are That Streaming

The name given to these various moments that follow one another one by one is a "stream." We *are* that stream. Here we can understand how dhatu analysis cuts through a wrong view about the fixity of what is. That means that we could take the totality of everything that's been described from the viewpoint of a fixed self and rewrite it very flatly and simply in terms of six different kinds of channels working in a functional way to bring about what we call an experience; and then we have another experience and then another experience.

If you wanted to write someone's biography from an Abhidharma point of view, there would be the moment they were born—call that "ground zero." Then, from the moment that consciousness is functioning (call it moment 1, perhaps), the individual is subject to information processing along the six channels—controlled or uncontrolled, precise or imprecise, kind or unkind. We can present this information, but we should be aware that all that this dhatu analysis tells us is *which* channel is operating; it says nothing about the content. That might not be so interesting to read, but this corresponds to what is actually going on according to Abhidharma.

It's not the case that we can't make generalizations from having just this flat list about the quality and flexibility of the individual. To give an example, for most individuals, one moment of sensory experience—that is to say, the firing of any of the five channels—is followed by many more moments of non-sensory-based firings. After just one moment of seeing (channel 1), we're catapulted into many moments of thinking about stuff (channel 6).

Let's graph this according to the schema we developed. We might say there are two moments of channel 1:

- $[1–7–13]/1 \ldots [1–7–13]/2$

This is then followed by a third moment of channel 6 and a fourth moment of channel 6:

- [6–12–18]/3 ... [6–12–18]/4

To simplify even further, we can write this whole sequence of four moments as follows, listing *only* the first element of the channel, but remembering that all three columns must be working for an experience to arise; Thus, 1 = seeing, 2 = hearing, and 6 = "other" (thinking, feeling, and so on), showing first the channel (two moments of channel 1, then two moments of channel 6, followed by a forward slash and the number of the moment, in the temporal sequence of four. It would look like this:

- [1/1, 1/2, 6/3, 6/4 ...]

Here the square brackets indicate a snippet of the experiential stream (*samtana*).

The Difference between Seeing and Thinking About What We Saw

This sixth channel indicates that there is the capacity, called "mind"; it is the capacity to process non-sense-based information; and there is the capacity to integrate this into a full experience. We can think, we can have fantasies, we can feel, and we can reflect that.

We have yet to explore the "context" of channel 6. So far, we are simply talking about which channel is firing. And so the exercise we just performed was simply and precisely to see if, in our own experience, we can note a difference between channels 1–5 on the one hand and channel 6 on the other hand. The Abhidharma analysis of experience suggests that we can know the difference between directly perceiving something sense based—directly seeing, hearing, smelling, tasting, or touching—and thinking about what we saw, heard, smelled, tasted, or touched.

One way to facilitate awareness of our differentiated experiences is by employing the practice of shamatha. For a fast-moving mind that is easily distracted, it is difficult to be aware of the subtle differences between the five sense-based channels and channel 6. Those differences are there, but they not usually accessible to us at the level of experience. An analogy from film is that the practice of shamatha involves slowing down the rate (the number of frames per second) at which the film is projected. It helps us tune in to the specific frame of the streaming "movie." Noting such differences in experience is the goal, and slowing down facilitates that.

Manas and Vijnana

One may wonder about the difference between *manas* ("mind" as a capacity, dhatu 6 in column I) and *vijnana*, ("mind" as the integrative function, dhatus 13–18 in column III). The Abhidharmikas felt it necessary to address these distinctions regarding the working of "mind." In the case of seeing (channel 1), for instance, it is sufficient to note that, besides having a capacity for visual processing (dhatu 1) and a visual field being processed (dhatu 7) there needs to be "mind" as an integrative function (vijnana), in this case dhatu 13 for the experience of seeing to occur. In that sense, then, "mind" refers to the six possible channel-specific integrative functions.

In the case of channel 6, that is, non-sense-based experiences, there needs to be the integrative function called *manovijnana* (mental integrative functioning, dhatu 18). They differentiate two senses of "mind": mind as the *capacity* to process non-sense-based experiences and mind as the *integrative functioning*. In sum, this so-called dhatu analysis classifies all seventy-five factors of experience (dharmas) into eighteen dhatus—a threefold hexamodal model.

The Tuning of Perception

Our mind edits enormous amounts of information that it's getting from channels 1–5. For example, we do not actually have a visual *experience* of everything that our eye is taking in. There is a selective process.

This is true for each of the channels—for each of them, there is a selective attentional processing. Learning how to apply dhatu analysis is a process of education. Even in the West, there are ways to "educate the senses." We might say that someone who is a great connoisseur of tasting wine educates the palate. One who is gifted in bodywork educates tactile capacity. There is potentially a wonderful field of comparative work between such Western educational methods and the approach of the Abhidharma. For instance, according to Gestalt psychology, the primary way in which the perceptual field to be experienced is structured is in terms of foreground and background. Mindful of this, I translated column II (alambana) as "object field" and not simply as "object." This suggests that there is always a selecting, an objectification, a reification, a fixity in the moment; there is some experiential delimitation within the contours of the perceived field. The field itself, however, is more or less unlimited.

We *learn* to objectify our experiences; in fact, "experience" can be understood as an objectification process. The developmental psychologist Jean Piaget has shown that the stages of developing as a child consist, in part, in the child being able to distinguish different aspects of the visual field and then retrieve them. In fact, a healthy functioning sense of "self" seems to have something to do with *educating* our ability to negotiate differences at the level of perceptual fields. From the viewpoint of the Abhidharma, such an educational process can be understood as the exercise of channel 6, the capacity to reflect and remember our previous sense-based experiences. If we willfully want to remember something, we might have an idea of what that something was, and then somehow we try to retrieve it.

The Nature of Contact

It is rather straightforward how the contact between the three columns works with regard to channels 1–5, but the nature of this contact between mental stuff—that is, between dhatus 6, 12, and 18—is more difficult to understand. Contact seems a bit mysterious; a mild way of putting it is that it's terribly subtle and quick and we don't "notice" it.

At the level of experience, according to this schema, we do not have access to this moment of contact. What we do have access to, as an example, is a "moment" of seeing, and for that to occur, there has to have been contact between dhatus 1, 7, and 13. These three factors, however, are not amenable to being *experienced*. Dhatu analysis only accounts for what is *necessary* for an experience to occur. It's not like in a sports event where we can do an instant replay and slow it way down for one moment of seeing to be able to say, "Ah, there's the eye, ah, it hit the visual field, and here comes that integrative ability, into the goal, goal!"

Will: The Capacity to Regulate Channel Firing

Is This Schema Reality?

It may seem like this dhatu analysis schema and how it works is only intellectual; it is imposed on our experiences, but the Abhidharma traditions assert that this is *actually* how we function. This is the way it is. This is what's actually occurring all the time. It's just one darn thing after another. But, you might wonder whether the "contacts" are not accessible through experience. If we can't experience it, then is it not just speculation?

From an analytical point of view this dhatu analysis asserts that "contact" is merely a designation for the proper and coordinated functioning of columns I, II, and III. Lack of contact accounts for why we sometimes do not have an "experience" of seeing, even though, for instance, there is an eye (dhatu 1, column I) and also a visual field (dhatu 7, column II).

Flexibility in Firing

What's the Abhidharma-analysis understanding of a realized being? We might already have a bit of an idea about this. For many ordinary people, all six channels are firing without knowing what's going on (and they call it their life, and they wonder why they have problems). We are just thrown from one situation to another. And this felt sense of thrown-ness, of being out of control, afraid of the silence of infinite space, the existential crisis of being at all, such things have been talked about in the West at great length, right?

Those who meditate and have access to the so-called form realm (*rupa dhatu*) are able to stabilize their awareness. At those levels of awareness not all eighteen dhatus are operating. But those channels haven't been destroyed. Rather, they're just not operating. For instance, a temporary suspension of experiences of smells and tastes (channels 3 and 4) can be understood as an indication that one has stabilized certain meditative states. It doesn't mean that those channels are defective; it's just that they're not working at those moments. They're just not occurring.

In the more subtle realms of meditative stabilization, the so-called formless realms (*arupa dhatu*), there is no arising of sense-based experiences—no firing of channels 1–5. In the formless realms there are only dhatus 6, 12, and 18; only channel 6 is broadcasting. For those moments in the formless realm "we" are channel 6 processors. Our world of experience is entirely constituted by channel 6 operations. In this sense, then, one might say that "who" we are, "what" we are, and "where" we are, are the same thing: The "who" is the "what," the "where" is the "who," and so on. If taken seriously, such an Abhidharma approach powerfully deconstructs those strong dualistic fixations of "self" and "world" and that dissolution of duality dissolves or erodes our habitual fixations, thereby reducing or completely ceasing causes of suffering.

The Capacity to Regulate Channel Firing

A practitioner can learn at will to have a continuing series of channel 6 firings. Or, if one is focusing on a sense-based object of "seeing," then a channel 1 firing. In the latter case, we can stay with that channel 1 with no distraction into channel 6. Here "distraction" is understood as the firing of a channel that is *not* the channel that you want to be focusing on. Fortunately, we, as a streaming of such firings, have some control; we can learn to regulate what channel we want to focus on and also for how long.

We might say that part of a definition of a "realized" being is one who has the capacity to cultivate regulatory control over *which* channels are firing and *for how long*. But there is still a great mystery here. How is it, if we are, for instances simply having a moment of seeing (channel 1 firing), that we might *decide* to switch to another channel? It is said that we don't have control at the level of the channel firing itself. Well, a response to this mystery about what determines our movements from one moment to another moment and the patterns of being somewhat out of control are explored by the Abhidharma under the topic called *karma*. In the Abhidharma schema of seventy-five dharmas, karma relates to 15 (*chetana*), which is variously translated as "will" or "volition." In fact, there is a full and complete teaching on karma in chapter 4 of the *Abhidharma-kosha*. That chapter provides a detailed analysis of how this "will" works.

The Order of the Channels

Vasubandhu says we place the order of the channels not with respect to how they fire—because anything can happen—but with respect to two criteria: (1) their relative strength of operation and (2) the point of functionality on the fully standing body. So, the strongest channel is listed first, and then the less strong is listed, and so forth. Another point of processing is that it applies to an erect standing human individual. Channel 1 is the highest point on the body. So it's listed first, both according to strength and to location on the body.

First, with respect to strength according to Vasubandhu we can see things further away from us than we can hear things. Of course, we might think of instances where this isn't true. For example, sometimes it takes a while for a sound to travel to us, as when we see a man or a woman on a ledge and they shout in our direction, but we don't hear them, or maybe because of an interfering wind. Nevertheless, it's said that seeing (channel 1) is stronger and can operate over a longer distance than hearing (channel 2). Smells (channel 3) have to be a bit closer than sounds for us to "experience" them. And "touch" (channel 5) seems to require a bit more intimacy than either seeing or hearing. The sixth channel, "mind," is, however, off the map. Vasubandhu reminds us that, unlike the sense-based perceptions, "mind" is not physically located anywhere.

Now, according to location, in the erect body, in a normally constructed individual, the point of processing for channel 1 is above the point of processing for channel 2. But wait a minute, isn't the top of my ear higher than my eye? Here, we use the word "eye" and "ear" not in reference to physical structure, but rather as the place through which they process information. In that sense the capacity for visual processing is located higher up than the place for auditory processing.

Exercise: Seeing and Thoughts of Seeing

So, how does this schema help counteract the wrong view of a sense of self and help us experience everything as just perceptual or nonperceptual flowing? Let's return to a question that was previously posed: How at the level of experience can we distinguish any of the five sense-based channels from channel 6? Can we find a way to experientially differentiate these two types of situation—seeing and then having some *thoughts* about seeing; seeing and having a *memory* of seeing; seeing and having a delight or a depression about seeing? These are differences between channel 1 and channel 6.

Training in shamatha with focus (*sa-alambana shamatha*) is learning to focus on channel 1 (if you're looking at something) or channel 5 (if you're attending to your breath). Can you note when you're staying with your breath (channel 5)? Can you note when some thoughts are coming (channel 6)? And can you notice when you bring yourself back from channel 6 to, in these cases, either channel 1 or channel 5? You can notice that there is a difference, right?

To summarize, the Abhidharma makes precise statements about the way in which perception and cognition function. Up to now, we've explored how the six channels work, and now we will begin to explore the experiential content. We will see how all of the seventy-two conditioned dharmas (out of seventy-five) constitute the content of these channels.

In the dhatu analysis, out of eighteen, fifteen have to do with sense-based experience. This is a very good teaching for people who space out, who spend too much time in their head. We might discover, if we calm down, the precise differences between a moment of seeing and a moment of thinking about seeing or remembering that we saw. Can you discover the difference?

6

Tuning In to Experience

The point of Abhidharma in the Buddhist teachings is to find precise ways to tune in to our experience.

Tuning In to a Gray Rectangle

Perhaps you explored my suggested experiment of trying to see concretely, at the level of experience, and to note if it's possible to be aware that there is a difference between channels 1–5 on the one hand and channel 6 on the other. If I say channels 1–5, we should remember that this means the channels of seeing, hearing, smelling, tasting, and touching, respectively. This is the Abhidharma way to use shorthand for experiential analysis.

We are resting our eyes on this gray rectangle. Let us be very precise now. I am using the word *gray* and the word *rectangle* to help you find the target for channel 1 tuning. It's like a TV guide. There is a program coming on called "gray rectangle." It's a hot new program. We're interested, so we're tuning in.

Frame-by-Frame Processing

But "gray" and "rectangle" are just pointers. When we actually do tune in and experience the program in a concrete, direct, and nonintellectual way, we are using our eye (dhatu 1), channel 1, to process the information. The information is coming from the target area ("gray" and "rectangle"), dhatu 7, and with this contact we are able to integrate this into what we might call an experience, dhatu 13, a moment of channel 1 processing.

A better way of referring to a "moment" of experience might be to use the term *frame*. This also allows us to think of the metaphor of film, where the rapid movements from one frame to another (at a speed of more than twenty-four frames a second) allows us to experience the sense of continuity—a verisimilitude—that seems to be true to what we encounter in so-called real life. Until the invention of video cameras, films used to consist entirely of frames which can be edited (cut) and reordered. What we are suggesting is that each experiential moment of channels 1–5 is a frame and it has a direct, nonconceptual structure.

Now let's return to this frame, this moment, for finding the target of our gray rectangle. When we hit the target, when we actually begin to process channel 1, there is a bit of a gap, or a difference, between our habits associated with the word *gray* and the word *rectangle*, which involve hearing those words (channel 2), thinking about what they refer to (channel 6) and then attending to this target with our eyes in terms of this specific hue pattern (channel 1), this specific delimited field of hue, and the shape or contours, the borders or the limitations of this field. This is all one frame, and it comes to us as a bounded pattern.

Using Channel 6 to Precisely Focus Channel 1

Let's now look at the gray rectangle and note that above it there is a black vertical object. But it is not the totality of what there is. Because if we are encouraged to look above the rectangle and to focus only on the vertical black object and we focus on the contours and the hue of that target, that black vertical object, that's another experience, it's another experiential frame.

If we are then encouraged to move our experiential capacity to the point of contact between the upper edge of the gray rectangle and the visually accessible bottom part of the black vertical object (the intersection between the rectangle and the vertical object), then we can do this. But the words are rather vague. The question might arise: Are we focusing on just the very bottom part of the black vertical object or on the very top of the gray rectangular field that is just below the very bottom of the black part?

Can you pay attention to precisely where these two differently tinted and configured "spaces" meet? There may in fact appear a shaping that is different from either one of these separately. We can tune into the totality of the rectangular field called "gray" by pulling back in our focal length, or we can move our attention to the vertical black object, which might be slightly more difficult.

If we are encouraged to move to the *intersection* of these two perceptual fields, we have to change our focal length in which we are not paying attention to what comes above, nor below, neither to the right, nor to the left of the intersection but only to the *intersection* itself. It is important to remember that all of these capacities to tune in to precise presentations of hue and shape are channel 1 processing. This is a concrete example of how, by using channel 6 processing, one can be led to settle into our capacity to have a visual experience in a precise way.

Shamatha: With and Without a Focus

Classically, it is said that shamatha practice is divided into two types: calming the mind using an object or a focus[104] and calming the mind without a specific focus.[105]

Speaking in the fashion of the Abhidharma, we can say that, traditionally, the methods for focus of our attention, in the manner of shamatha with an object, favor the use of three different classes of focus: seeing (channel 1), touching with breath (channel 5), or internal visualizations (channel 6).

Remember: when we say "object" here, we do not mean a physically existing external thing, not some "ontological object," but rather what might be called an "epistemological object," an object in the sense of what is known to us in experience, what we are in experiential contact with. The Abhidharma is more or less agnostic on the externally existent status, the physical existence, of the sensory fields. From a practice point of view, Abhidharma is most interested in accounting for *experience*, and they tend to leave aside the vexed question of externality and existence apart from an observer or experiencer.

Two Ways of Regarding the So-Called Object

There are two ways of regarding the object: either as (1) column II *in contact with* column I, or (2) column II *in contact with* column III. This is the distinction between an object (column II) in the sense of needing to rely on contact with the sensory capacity (column I) and an object (column II) in the sense of being known through contact with the integrative function of awareness (column III).

Vasubandhu does note, however, two different senses for how to understand column II content. He says that the *sensory* domains, or fields in column II (dhatus 7–11), are sometimes called "objects" (*vishaya*)[106] when referring to their dependence on the *capacity* to process them (dhatus 1–5, column I). This is when one wishes to talk about the sensory field emphasizing the contact being made with the so-called capacity for sensory processing (called the "eye" and so on), those "visibles," and the other four senses. This is a way of acknowledging that what we call a sensory thing, a sensory occurrence that has something to do with what we might call the seemingly "physical capacity" to process sensory information. But Vasubandhu then goes on to say that these same "sensory domains" (column II) are called "epistemological objects" (alambana) with respect to their contact with the integrative function (vijnana) of column III (dhatus 13–17). Vasubandhu clarifies that the same "content" (column II) is differently named according to which column of "contact" one wants to focus on, contact with either column I or column III.

COLUMN I	COLUMN II	COLUMN III
CAPACITY	FIELD/OBJECT	INTEGRATIONAL FUNCTION
indriya	← *vishaya / alambana* →	*vijnana*
eye	form (hues and shapes) seen	visual awareness

Concretely in experience, a gray rectangle is a gray rectangle. But a rose, for example, in dependence on our capacity to process our awareness of it, might be visual or olfactory, right? If the nose is involved, that is channel 3 processing.

Alambana

The "object or field" as something known is called the epistemological object (alambana). Generally speaking, Buddhist practice lineages are almost exclusively interested in this sense of the epistemological objects. To use the example of looking at the gray rectangle, they are not so interested in going into an analysis of what physical or material stuff that grayness is made out of. Rather, they are interested in the visual pattern that is present for us in a moment of seeing with respect to how it gets integrated into experience. An epistemological object is an object constituted in a moment of knowing. By "knowing" we can also understand "a moment of experience." And these experiential moments are not at all necessarily confined to occasions of formal meditation.

In fact, when Buddhists talk about shamatha with or without an "object" or a focus, they use the word for epistemological object—*alambana*. Shamatha is classified as either with or without an epistemological object. This is a "meditational object." That's a field of awareness that is constituted, or that comes about, during or through meditation. We might say as a generality that when we do a visualization, we can refer to what arises in our mind as a "meditational object."

How We Experience the "Object"

Now that we've made the distinction between two senses of "object," we can say that, according to Abhidharma analysis, one does not entertain questions concerning the sense in which this gray rectangle may "exist"—apart from my moment of knowing it or when I am not contacting it. It's like the story told by the Buddha of a man who had an arrow in his eye. Before the man would allow the doctor to remove the arrow, he wanted to know who shot the arrow, where were they from, etc. And the reply was: do you want the arrow out or not?

The point here is to overcome our experiential myopia, to get a wider perspective, to use our inherent wisdom mind in a precise way, one that aids us in going beyond suffering. To the frustration of Western philosophers, the living Buddhist traditions, which have a very precise and subtle way of talking about experience, are rather shockingly disinterested in the issues about externality and materiality. Of course, there are texts that explore these topics here and there, but they don't seem to have been popular, especially in texts on meditation and in practice lineages.

The Relationships between the Columns

Let's recap. Column III, the integrative function, has a direct relationship with column II, but it is no more direct than column I. How is there contact between column II and column III and between column I and column III? How can you have an integrative relationship and an experiential relationship with, say, a rose? What is commonly said is that the emitting region called rose, a visual field, is a physical thing. We have something in our eyes called rods and cones. It's a filter, isn't it? We know that butterflies "see" flowers differently. Their capacity for visual experience is different from that of humans, right? They have a different filtering process. This doesn't necessarily correspond to the object; the emitting region is filtered. What gets through the filter, the hue and the shape, which in our previous example is gray and rectangular for us, was filtered by the rods and cones in the eyes, right? If we were flies, the filter would be different. A fly's column II will be different from a human's column II.

The point is this: the same emitting region (column II) is filtered differently (because of column I), which then needs to be further processed and integrated (column III) for a visual experience to arise. Even though we have the filtered gray rectangular field (column II) and the filters of sensory capacity are working (column I), it's still possible not to have an experience of seeing. There could be an interruption or dysfunction in column III—something wrong with the integrative function.

Examining the Nature of Experience: Phenomenology and the Abhidharma

Experience and Remembering That Experience

Using the example of the gray rectangle, we now have an idea of what channel 1 processing might be. Next, you are invited to close your eyes and see if you can bring into presence, with a relaxed and stable focus, your memory of your former experience called gray rectangle. Then open your eyes again and focus precisely at the gray rectangle for about 30 seconds. The mind will wander. Bring it back to the gray rectangle. Again, close your eyes and calmly bring to presence the gray rectangle.

The claim in this exercise concerning the gray rectangle is that there are two different channels working. When our eyes are open and focused on the target, it is channel 1. And when our eyes are closed and we are bringing into presence the gray rectangle as a memory, it is channel 6. And the claim is made that experience of seeing the gray rectangle (channel 1) is different from the experience of remembering the gray rectangle (channel 6).

Here is another exercise: Keeping your eyes open, simply ask yourself the following questions: Do you remember having your eyes open and actually having looked at the gray rectangle? OK, good. Now, with your eyes closed, can you bring into awareness having seen that gray rectangle? Are those two experiences of "gray rectangle" the same or different?

Describing Experience Precisely

There is a wonderful little book by Edmund Husserl called *The Phenomenology of Internal Time Consciousness*. The book describes a concrete study using hearing (what we call here "channel 2") and remembering what has been heard (what we call "mind" or "channel 6") for finding a way to describe, very precisely, subtle distinctions between a present moment of hearing a piece of music (channel 2) and remembering that one heard a piece of music (channel 6).[107]

The Buddha and Vasubandhu knew the variety of ways in which we experience reality are subtle, deep, and profound; they are difficult to understand at the level that they occur. The common language we use and our common nonmeditative, nonquiet ways of getting through the day seem to diminish our capacity to precisely focus on the deep and subtle aspects of experience. And it is this habit of blocked focus that determines what we call reality. Husserl was interested in finding a language to describe our experiences at a deep level. He was interested in "not talk about things, but the things themselves," that is a radical way of attending to how we actually perceive by using language that is, attuned to those phenomena. This approach is referred to as "phenomenology" and there are a number of contemporary Western philosophers, such as Evan Thompson, who are exploring Husserl's approach in the context of Buddhist thought. Husserl was not primarily interested in how objects may exist materially, a question scientists might be interested in. Nor was he interested in problems of externality—that is, in how objects might exist out there, when I am not experiencing them. Husserl used the Greek term *epoche*, a word meaning "to put in abeyance" or "to put in brackets," to put aside all our theories about perception and to enter more directly into a subtle and deep experience of the perceptions themselves. He claimed to have discovered a way to show how one could move from imprecise reflections to a more precise experiential language regarding our experiences, and he developed ways for demonstrating that kind of precision.

Most importantly for our explorations, Husserl was interested in suspending judgment (epoche) in learning how to remove the sedimented habits of theory, of imprecise language, bit by bit, so that we might come to the experiences themselves.

Cartesian Split: Dualism, Not Differentiation

Descartes famously said that there are two separate things (Lat. *res*). One is called extended things (Lat. *res extensa*), which makes up the so-called objective aspects of our experience constituting the world of things that are seemingly "out there." The other is subjective, "thinking stuff" (Lat. *res cogitans*). This duality is known as the Cartesian split, and it has been regarded as a powerful statement on the dual nature that dominates all human knowledge. The Cartesian split has been quite influential in the development of the material sciences in the West. It represents an altogether different way of understanding direct knowing.

If we run this Cartesian split through the same channel model we have been using, we could say that this split removes channel 6 completely from channels 1–5, or, more accurately, we could say that column II and channels 1–5 make up the outer stuff (*res extensa*) that science claims to "objectively" study as something separate from us. Then channel 6 and column III make up this "thinking stuff" that we call the subject. This dualistic approach seems to assert that there are two separate domains that then interact. One should note that there is a difference between a dualism and differentiation. Differentiation, or variety, means that at the level of experience things are not uniformly and continuously the same. Differentiation is what we are trying to develop with the Abhidharma.

How Husserl's Mode of Investigation Heals Dualistic Approaches

Husserl's method of investigation can be thought to have healed this Cartesian split or at least to have put it into suspension. Husserl said that at the level of experience we can never find an actual separate distinction between thinking stuff and extended stuff; what we find in experience as our experiences are *experiences*. As such, experience does not come with a label of internal or external.

On the level of experience, for example, when we are actually in touch with that gray rectangle (channel 1), the question of what it is made out of or what it is going to be after we are not looking at it never arises. Both Husserl and the Abhidharmikas were interested in analyzing the qualities of different kinds of perceptual objects with respect to which channel they were constituted by. Do the Abhidharmikas deny the possibility of anything existing externally? No, they are agnostic. They set it aside. They say it has little to do with learning how to lead a compassionate life.

Husserl's Subject-Object Complex (Resolving the Dualistic Mind)

Husserl attempted to bypass the dualistic Cartesian split by suggesting that "extended stuff" (*res extensa*) is actually just the objective pole in experience. He used the Greek term *noema*, meaning the *known* object or the objective pole, and instead of Decartes's knowing stuff (*res cogitans*), Husserl uses the Greek term *noesis*, meaning the *knowing* act, the subjective pole.

Husserl said that for every moment of experience there is a subject-object complex, what he called a *noetic-noematic* complex. They are co-constituted. It is not the case that there are two separate things that then come together. Of course, for the purposes of analysis (channel 6) we can say that it seems that there is a *noetic* (subjective) aspect and a *noematic* (objective) aspect, but, Husserl asserts, these are never *actually* separate in experience.

According to Husserl, analysis shows that there is a subject aspect and an object aspect in virtually all experiences. This subject-object processing of experience is often expressed in Buddhist texts as a gloss on the meaning of the term "mind" or "mental awareness" (chitta). "Mind" in this sense is an apprehending-apprehended complex, or a subject-object experiential processing (*chitta is grahya grahaka*).

Here, "object" refers to the object pole, the apprehended aspect of a whole experience (Husserl's noema, Buddhism's grahya)[108] and "subject" refers to the subject pole, the apprehending aspect (Husserl's noesis, Buddhism's grahaka).[109] It is important here to remember that Husserl's "subjective pole" (the noetic aspect) is not a separately existing subject. Experiences come to us as a whole and at the same time, and the word for "at the same time," in Buddhist parlance, is contact (*sparsha*), or dependent co-arising. We can also use the terms *interdependence* or *functional correlation*. All these seemingly separate things are not actually given to us in actual experience.

According to dhatu analysis, what we call "experience" is actually hexamodal processing; simply moments of channel 1–6. In summary, it seems that dhatu analysis is quite consistent with Husserl's method of analysis of perception. Think: Where in dhatu analysis do you divide where there is the self, the experiencer, or the stuff experienced? Where do we account for the wrong view that there is a split? From the view of dhatu analysis, all we have are moments of seeing, hearing, smelling, tasting, touching, and "other." Even to think like this is said to help overcome the painful breach. It helps cut through the wrong view that there is a fixity of mind that is separate from stuff to apprehend.

"Time" Is an Abstraction

When Husserl comes to the main point of his work describing the differences between hearing a melody, remembering that one heard a melody, and so on, he discusses the perception of movement. The experience of elapsed time is demonstrated by, for example, the difference between hearing a note and hearing a melody. Husserl shows that time is an abstraction; it's a habit that we have—in order to make sense out of our experiences. Time itself is never given to us as an experience as such.

Prajna: The Dharma That Makes Possible Precise Knowledge

Let's conclude this chapter with a quick point. When we are doing dhatu analysis, not analytically but as a practice, the practice is simply to be present at the level of our experience. That is to say, we can note that there is a difference between looking at a gray rectangle and the experience of remembering having looked at the gray rectangle, which is also different from producing in our mind the gray rectangle. That which allows us to make this distinction is called discernment, wisdom mind (prajna), factor 18 on the list of the seventy-five dharmas. It is the energy packet, the dharma, that makes it possible to have precise knowledge about energy packets. Poetically—to mix a Mahayana notion with a Shravakayana one—I call it the gossamer thread, the

Abhidharma proof, of our buddha nature. We may be dimly aware that there are experiential differences, and in that case it is thought of as defiled wisdom mind. Or we might be anxious and concerned about the differences that we experience. We are not calm and confident; we suffer these differences. Nevertheless, all such occasions of being able to note differences, this capacity to note differences is inherent. Discernment, as a dharma, accounts for the possibility of opening up and discovering how to cease the causes of suffering.

7

Moments for a Meditator

A Fixed Sense of Self

At this point, a bit of a review may be helpful. According to the teachings of Buddhism, the cause of continuing suffering is maintaining a tight holding pattern, being tight in the heart and in the mind. But we don't know we are tight; we experience it as normal. As a result of this normal tightness, things do not work so well for ourselves and others. This tight holding pattern has been variously described and translated as "self" or "ego," which is not such a good translation for *atman* (in Sanskrit), a technical term that describes how this tightness keeps on being tight.

There are three aspects that keep this pattern that causes suffering going. The first is that we proceed as if our experiences are permanent. We hope that the permanence of things that we like will continue, and we fear that the permanence of things that we don't like will come our way. This desire for permanence maintains a structure of tightness, which is a cause for suffering. The second way in which we perpetuate suffering is due to the fact that we regard things as singular, unique, or special. And we hope that things we like, which are singular and unique, will continue, and we fear that singular or unique things that we don't like may come our way. The third way in which we keep this pattern tight, which causes suffering, is that we imagine that they're situations that are independent of causes and conditions; we think they are autonomous, that they are independent, that they can't be touched, that they are in a special realm. And we hope to be connected with this can't-be-touched, independent-of-causes-and-conditions special realm if it's a special, independent realm that we like; and we fear being connected with what we imagine to be a situation that is independent of causes and conditions if we don't like it.

Atman: Stuckness

When a Buddhist, a Buddhist teacher, or the teachings of the Buddha remind us that there is no atman, no permanent, unique, or independent experience, we might be a bit shocked. This lack of permanence is a conclusion that can be reached on the basis, which is both intellectual and experiential; it's not something established at first glance. I think for most of us it seems to contradict our actual experience. We proceed through life with a more or less permanent or fixed sense of self. The point here is that habituation or "thirsting" (*trishna*) for such permanence can be discovered to be the cause of our continuous suffering.

In order to cut through or go beyond those causes of suffering, we're encouraged to inquire into this stuckness, this fixity called the self, both mentally and meditationally. And all the traditions of Buddhism say that when we do make an inquiry into this tight and troublesome way of proceeding, we can discover that this pattern is not so permanent; it's not unique and it is not independent of causes and conditions. This is a discovery born from analysis, even though it's contradicted in our internal fantasies, our hopes and fears, and in the external expression of our speech and in our physical behavior with others. We proceed as if there were something to hold on to. The Buddhist teachings say that there are very precise and powerful techniques for breaking up or making more spacious this tight holding pattern. And as a result of this blasting through, breaking up, or making more spacious, one discovers that there is not such a tight self, or the self is not well founded.

The Collider Beam of Discernment (Prajna)

How is it possible, being so dominated by this pattern involving the self, that it can be blasted apart, either analytically or meditatively? There is a word that's given to indicate how it is possible to discern and then cut through this self; it is *prajna*. Prajna is said to be that factor, that basic aspect of being human, which allows us to discern and discover how those habitual patterns of our life actually work. We might say that when we experience a sense of permanence, when we suffer this fixity of being a self, our prajna is a bit sleepy. It's there, but it's a bit sleepy. And when we begin to wake up, it is this factor of prajna that helps us wake up. Prajna allows us to blast through this sense of self, the cause of our sufferings. We should be clear that this sense of self is not some minor aspect of our life but rather a term for the tight, crowded, confused, and anxious patterns which make up my life.

To put it a different way, to say, "I have a problem" is tautological. The sense of that "I" is a problem already because "I" is the name given to that tight pattern; it fosters painful habitual clingings. It makes it possible for cravings to "have" or to "not have" things arise. If I have something I like, I don't call it a problem. But even if we have something, we are afraid of our separation from it: we don't want to be separated from stuff we like, and we don't want to be connected to stuff we don't like. Prior to that, there is already a tight difference, a holding pattern, and that's called self. The good news is that this can be cut and blasted through. The bad news is that it's not necessarily quick or easy.[110] There are very precise techniques, both meditative and analytical, for breaking through or making more spacious this tight pattern called self.

Let's imagine the self as a ball, a tight pattern, a very tough particle, one that is hard to break apart. Let's say it's like an atom. And let's say that one had a very powerful collider beam, a powerful, coherent energy source that could be focused on that ball. Now let's say we ran that beam back and forth until it was really revved up, and then we opened the gate and allowed it to hit this target, which is an analogy for that tight pattern of self. What would we discover?

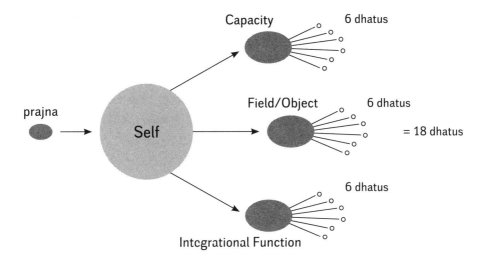

The Abhidharma, according to this analogy, is nothing other than talk about how this beam of discernment smashes this seemingly permanent and unitary self. Then what are the little bits and pieces, or these energy packets, which result from this colliding beam?

Let's put some Abhidharma names on them. The name of the collider beam is prajna. Prajna, in this case, is not being used in the sense of wisdom as a rather spacious expanse. Here, rather, prajna is defined as the focused energy that splits and differentiates the basic energy packets known as dharmas. In fact, prajna itself is an energy packet, one of the seventy-five basic dharmas. What is very special about this energy packet is that it can be in a dormant, nonexcited, nonfocused state, but under certain conditions it becomes a rather coherent, powerful force moving in one direction. It's defined as an energy packet that can coherently and forcefully move forward, smashing apart, distinguishing, and coming to a definitive conclusion about the nature of other energy packets. This is the application of our discriminating mind.

If the tight pattern of self is smashed by the collider beam of prajna, there results the discovery of many factors (dharmas) that make up that which is supposedly fixed. The collider beam smashed the atom of atman into many subatomic particles (dharmas). The Abhidharma is the study of the characteristics of those subatomic particles, those dharmas. One "collision beam experiment" done by the Buddha shows that if you hit the target of the self in a certain way, you get three subdivisions: capacity, field, and integrational function. But if you smash those subdivisions further, each of those three can be further smashed into six. Three multiplied by six gives us eighteen dhatus, eighteen subsmashings or energy packets as particles, which work in a dynamic and spread-out way.

Energy Packets Called Dhatus

We have the names of these energy packets. These six capacities, six fields, and six integrational functions coalesce or work together in a very specific pattern. There is a kind of horizontal grid, ray, or matrix, sorting them into rows. This schema, this way of showing the results from having the collider beam of discerning wisdom smash into this tight, fixed pattern of self, is represented by the analysis at the level of the elements (dhatus): Column I is the capacity (sometimes called "organ") to process information. What all these subatomic particles have in common is their capacity to process information. Column II, the field and object, is the information being processed. There are two senses in which this can be understood: it's either the information to be processed, which indicates its closeness with the capacity, or it's the information that can be integrated or, to use a computer term, compiled into a program known as perception. Column III, perception, indicates those factors, those energy packets, which compile or integrate the information into and as perceptual experiences.

This represents a complete picture and review of what we've done up until now.

Perception

Earlier translations of column III sometimes use the term "consciousness," for example, "visual consciousness" for dhatu 13. But I think that "perception," or "perceptual awareness" is closer to the Abhidharma use of the term in dhatu analysis. Perception here specifically means the minimum conditions that must be present at the level of cooperating energy packets for there to be a moment of seeing, hearing, smelling, tasting, touching, or "other." And remember that "other" (channel 6) includes such things as cognitions (general, analytic), emotions (primary, secondary), and so forth. The level at which we have access to this schema as living, reflecting, feeling human beings is a moment of perception.

But generally, we do not have access to 1–18, to each single dhatu. These interactional dynamics, which are quite specific, are not accessible to us at the level of experience. Most people can't get into what's actually going on there. It's enough to say that there is a moment or a situation of seeing, hearing, smelling, tasting, touching, or "other" things. This is said to be a full and complete way of describing accurately one situation after another; there is nothing missing. Becoming fluent in this type of Abhidharma analysis is like learning how to be bilingual—learning how to translate our normal, alienated, tight ways of proceeding through life into Abhidharma language. We don't experience every single dhatu; this dhatu schema was arrived at through extensive meditative and analytical inquiry, one in which there had to be a very high and coherent energy beam of discernment that smashed apart ordinary ways of experiencing. This dhatu analysis is somewhat like processing at the pixel level of a digital photograph; at that level the ordinary "whole" picture is not experienced.

In what follows, I will refer to each row simply as channel 1–6. If we're broadcasting on channel 1, we're having a moment of seeing, or, using the language of film and cinema, a frame.

Becoming Bilingual

I'm trying to help us become bilingual. That means being able to go from our ordinary experience to an Abhidharma analysis, both intellectually and meditatively, and then from an Abhidharma analysis back to our ordinary experience. Now, what's the advantage in that? According to the Buddha, being able to have experiences at this level already indicates a bit of spaciousness. Becoming bilingual already changes our brain a bit (there is also now a growing literature on the effects of meditation on the brain).

Moments of a Meditator

As a way of speaking about moments or frames of our experience, and to make us a bit bilingual, I have indicated ten moments. I will write:

- [1/1, 1/2, 1/3, 6/4, 6/5, 6/6, 6/7, 6/8, 6/9, 1/10]

The first three moments consist of firings of channel 1—three moments of seeing. Then the next six moments (6/4, 6/5, 6/6, 6/7, 6/8, 6/9) are firings of channel 6—some general analytical cognition or primary or secondary emotion followed by a "return" to channel 1 (1/10).

This analysis is done in order to tone up our capacity to notice *which* channel is firing; such analysis does not engage in the "content" of the experiences, only to become aware of which channel is working, to demonstrate that it is possible to become aware of what channel you are broadcasting on. We have three channel 1 broadcasts (seeing), six subsequent moments of something else (and we have no idea of what the content might be, but we are aware that they were not channel 1, 2, 3, 4, or 5), and then another moment of channel 1 as the tenth.

Beginning Shamatha Experience

The claim of such Abhidharma analysis is that this account of channel firing is a fair profile of how things are occurring for us all the time. Becoming aware of how such channel firings work might be compared to a kind of dawning meditative experience, a kind of beginning shamatha experience.

To give an example used in many Tibetan Buddhist traditions, imagine that your shamatha practice is to stare at a white letter "A." There is an external fixation, a meditation with an object; you are looking at that "A" with your eyes open. Perhaps before you settled into the shamatha, your back was preoccupying you a bit, or, to use Abhidharma language, you were having some intermittent channel 5 firings. Then, maybe some people were making noise (channel 2 firing) so that you could not concentrate. But then finally you hit the target and were able to focus on that "A" (channel 1). A shamatha practitioner learns how to "stay" on the chosen channel broadcast, in this case channel 1, and regards other channels as distractions from which "program" they want to tune in to. In the case diagrammed above, one is able to stay with the chosen object for three successive moments.

Once Again: "Myself" as a Streaming

In this way of analysis, "staying with the object" means staying with it for more than simply a glimpse. The term *streaming* is used not only to name the experiential flow of staying with the chosen object of focus, but also for any segment of this bit of experience.

One can make a distinction between a presmashed and a postsmashed sense of a permanent self. A presmashed individual's discernment is rather dormant, it is not operating at full capacity, and that sense of a permanent self is still mostly intact. A postsmashed individual's discernment, however, is characterized by experiencing the breaking up of that permanence of the self.

Staying without Distraction with One Channel (Undistracted)

In the previous example, there were three moments of staying with the visual object followed by six moments of channel 6, and then, for moment ten, a return of sorts to seeing—that is, direct seeing, channel 1:

- $[1/1, 1/2, 1/3, 6/4, /6/5, 6/6, 6/7, 6/8, 6/9, 1/10]$

The purpose of focus, of shamatha, was achieved in four out of ten moments or frames. That is a 40 percent shamatha practitioner. And the technical term for what was going on in those other six moments is distraction. According to Abhidharma analysis, shamatha practice is learning, at the level of experience, to stay focused on a specific channel. If we are using a visual focus, it is learning how to stay with channel 1. That is to say, it is learning how to extend the number of continuous channel 1 moments with no distracting intermixture of any of the other channels. Here is a diagram of ten moments of channel 1 focus:

- [1/1, 1/2, 1/3, 1/4, 1/5, 1/6, 1/7, 1/8, 1/9, 1/10]

When you note that you are no longer focused on the desired channel, that is called being distracted. The capacity to remain focused is called "mindfulness" (*smriti*), and the capacity to note that you are distracted and then to be able to return to the chosen focus is called "alertness" (*samprajanya*). It involves learning how to become aware that you are distracted. In the parlance of mindfulness instructions this is called "bringing your mind back," or bringing awareness back to the meditative focus.

Recognizing Which Channel Is Firing

The reason why channel 1 is used so often in many Buddhist traditions of mental calmness training is because it is the most powerful and robust of the channels. It is said that it is much easier to note the difference between channel 1 and channel 6 than, for example, channel 5 and channel 6.

The entire schema called dhatu analysis has as its purpose a particular conclusion with respect to having smashed apart this tight self. We want the self to break apart in such a way that we will come to know the difference between channel 6 and any of the other channels. That is to say, we will no longer confuse channels 1–5 with channel 6. We will no longer confuse moments of seeing, hearing, smelling, tasting, or touching with remembering that we saw something or producing that image in our mind's eye. We will be able to know the difference between channel 1, when we are actually looking at something (e.g., the gray rectangle), and a subsequent moment of closing one's eyes and creating that gray rectangle in one's mind. We train ourselves to precisely note that different channels are operating.

For most people—that is, for nonmeditators, those who do not practice shamatha and who do not slow down and take a good look at their minds—if they were to do this analysis of ten moments of what they called seeing, there would be one or two moments of seeing, then moments of thinking about what they saw, then moments of seeing, then moments of thinking about what they saw. So it might be like:

- $[1/1, 1/2, 6/3, 6/4, 6/5, 1/6, 6/7, 1/8, 6/9, 1/10]$

And if you asked them what they were doing, they would say with a completely clean conscience, "I was looking at something," as if for every one of those ten moments it was:

- $[1/1, 1/2, 1/3, 1/4, 1/5, 1/6, 1/7, 1/8, 1/9, 1/10]$

Not only were they experientially lying to us, they were lying to themselves! That "lie" is another way of understanding what Buddhists call the permanent sense of a self.

Vasubandhu suggests that the reason why this entire dhatu analysis was used was to help us note the difference between when we are on channel 6 and when we are on any other channel. This is why—perhaps to your disappointment—there is not too much concern with the content of experience, what is going on *in* channel 6. It is as if only an amateur is concerned with content! The superior practitioner is aware of what the channel is. It is enough to know what frequency one is on.

One Moment of Seeing: Being with the Field

Remember, there are *three* energy packets (dhatus) cooperating together in order for there to be *one* moment of experience. But we do not have access to these three energy packets at the level of experience. At the level of experience, we just have a moment of seeing. For example, if we are looking at the gray rectangle, that is channel 1. The homework was to see if you could note the difference between directly and nonconceptually being with the hue and configuration of a visual field (channel 1) and thinking about it (channel 6). The claim is that, with mindfulness practice, we can have many consecutive moments of experience in a nonconceptual way; we can be tuned in to the sensual given-ness and actual experiential presence of that field of awareness.

There Is No Such Thing as a Gray Rectangle

The point I want to make here, and this goes for all the other channels, is that there is no such thing actually existent out there called gray or rectangle. *Gray* is a word that consists of a series of vowels and consonants in a specific historically constituted language, in this case English. In fact, as a label it is channel 6 and actually refers to a wide variety of different possible hues (so-called gray scale). The same applies for rectangle. They come in different lengths and sizes. In fact, we used these admittedly imprecise words in order to trick us into moving toward an already given visual field in order to have an experience of visual perception. When we say, "look at the gray rectangle," it is just a way of indicating how to move to a certain channel.

Memory

One form of channel 6, a rather important one, is called memory, or mindfulness (smriti). Memory is simply the name of an energy packet, a dharma, a specific functioning characteristic which allows us to stay with an object. Those with a good, robust, and trained memory are able to stay with an object for as long as they want. It is one of the primary energy packets or muscles that we train in shamatha. It is called *mindfulness*.

Mindfulness and memory are the same thing. They refer to the capacity to stay with a focus. Shamatha is sometimes represented in Tibetan Buddhist traditions as a monk chasing his out of control mind, (represented by an elephant). He chases it with two implements: a noose, (representing mindfulness, smirti), and an elephant goad, (representing alertness, samprajanya) This goad of alertness or vigilance is the capacity to note when one has lost track of the mindful focus and is now alerted to bring the mind back to that focus.[111]

Shamatha and Memory

How can you remember afterward that you were having these moments if it would have been only channel 1? There is no reason to remember at all. The instruction in shamatha is: Don't remember that you are looking at something gray. The instruction is simply to be with the object. And when you think, "Oh, what am I doing? Oh, I am focusing on a gray rectangle," that's called a distraction. It is a memory (channel 6) of having been looking at a visual field (channel 1).

Shamatha and Channel Firing: Slowing Down

Now when we slow down and experience things frame by frame, then, to take another example, the moment you were focusing on the pain in your back (channel 5), if you really are with that channel, then the visual world disappears. Visual world means visual for you as a moment of experience. It is a technical term. There is no such thing as visual world apart from visual for me as experience; or—if that is shocking and frightening—whatever way in which the visual world exists right now, apart from an experience for you, is strongly disregarded by these traditions. They are not interested in it and it is considered a distraction.

Remember, this is a description of our experience when we slow down. The idea that there is a visual world out there while we are doing meditation is based entirely on habits of permanence, singularity, and independence. Buddhists called this a wrong view because that view blocks full access to the path which leads one to the goal, the destination, the cessation of suffering and its myriad causes.

We are learning how to translate our ordinary experiences into specialized Abhidharma language. We are becoming bilingual. I would suggest that we take any experience and then ask a question about that experience in terms of Abhidharma language. For example, how would Abhidharmikas model the ordinary experience of hearing an alarm go off while one was doing shamatha concentration on, let's say, the visual field of a white letter "A?" Let's say you are looking at something, and seemingly at the same time you hear an alarm go off. And then you think, "Oh, I have to stop meditating." That habit of saying, "The alarm went off at the same time I was meditating" is not accurate. The experience of "actually-occurring-at-the-same-time" is a distortion. If you slow down enough, you learn that what you thought was a simultaneous experience of looking at an object and hearing the alarm actually consists of different moments: a moment of looking, another moment of looking, then a moment of hearing, then back to a moment of looking, then, perhaps several moments of thinking, and then a moment of thinking, "Oh, that's the alarm. I guess my meditation session is over." There is oscillation, a switching between channels. It's said that if we slow down enough, if we can calm the mind and rest in that state (shamatha), we can become aware of that switching from channel 1 (seeing) to channel 2 (hearing) and then to channel 6 (having the thought that the meditation session is over).

For most people, this snippet of our experiences goes by very fast, and it has a sense of continuity, of verisimilitude. It seems real; we don't really become aware of the rapid channel switching. We have a tendency to get involved in the content of our personal movies, the dramas of our life. We might think, "It's too much effort to slow my mind down; I don't feel like practicing." If we don't learn to slow down, our thoughts and emotions are out of control, and we are more at risk of experiencing the arising of stress, with all its physical and emotional consequences.

8

Exploring Channel Processing

Moments of Seeing: A Channel 1 Experience

Let's look at the channel 1 dhatus:

- [1–7–13] (eye–form–visual perception)

The point here is that for a moment of an experience called seeing, or a frame of experiencing color and shape (channel 1), there has to be an energy packet known as eye, an energy packet known as colors and shapes, and an energy packet as integration. There is a capacity called eye, which is the capacity to process visual information (eye); there is the energy packet known as the visual information itself (hue and shape). The line in the shorthand above linking eye and form (hue and shape) indicates the capacity to see and the visual information have to be working together. And that's not enough; there also has to be the perceptual integration of a well-functioning eye together with the presence of a visual field. All three aspects are necessary for the arising of a moment of seeing. This is an Abhidharma-based way, via dhatu analysis, to represent how an experience of seeing occurs in terms of the contact or functional correlation of all the necessary elements. This is a dynamic model for what we call the broadcasting of a channel 1 experience.

Remember, the extent to which hues and shapes may actually exist outside of a moment of seeing does not seem to be a topic of concern in these Abhidharma contexts. The status of seemingly external objects is talked about elsewhere, but here it is enough to say that when we speak of hues and shapes, sounds, smells, tastes, touches, and other stuff like thoughts, feelings, and so on, we are not concerned with how these may exist independently from our experiences; we are not concerned about the manner in which they may exist when they're not an experience *for us*.

Ten Moments of a Meditator

Picking up from what we said before, imagine a situation in which we're doing a calming meditation practice. We might represent that calming meditation practice as follows: the first moment is channel 1, a moment of seeing. If we're lucky or skilled, maybe we stay with that for one more moment; we're not easily distracted. And there are two contiguous moments; we're staying with the object without an interruption from any other channel. This is said to be the direction we want to go because calming meditation classically defined is the capacity to continue to stay at will on any one channel without an interruption from other channels.

In our example we have two moments of staying with the chosen channel, channel 1, ordinarily called seeing. After two moments of seeing, we have a moment of something I call "other," which is not seeing, hearing, smelling, tasting, or touching (we know by now that according to this tradition there are many different types of "other stuff" that we can process). Here the schema [1/1, 1/2, 1/3, 6/4, 6/5 . . . 6/9, 1/10] represents two moments of seeing, then another moment of seeing, and then for some reason maybe we have the thought: "I'm a good meditator." Then we have another thought: "I have drifted away from the object of meditation." Then we have another thought: "This is not good." And we have another thought: "I don't care, I'm tired." And another thought: "I'm tired because it's too hot." And another thought: "I want to go back to this visual object I was looking at." And then, hopefully, we find ourselves having another moment of simply looking at the object we chose to focus on. This is often how things go in meditation for beginners. This alertness (samprajanya, channel 6) to drifting away from seeing is one of many types of channel 6 processing. It is part of the many possible contents of dhatu 12, "other," non-sense-based factors.

Abhidharma Emphasizes the Channel, Not the Content

In the very flat but precise way of analyzing here in the Abhidharma, what is indicated and is useful is that we're having a moment of seeing, a moment of seeing, and something other, something other, something other, something other, something other, something other. Does that sound familiar? Then we have a moment of seeing again and another moment of staying with the object. We had ten consecutive moments or frames. If we go long enough, we could tell a narrative and at the same time indicate very flatly which channel was activated. From the Abhidharma point of view, what is most essential is not to be fascinated whatsoever by the content, and this is what we do at the level of practice—that is, we try to not be fascinated by the content but rather to simply know when we're seeing, we're seeing, and so on.

What About the Birds?

In the ordinary world, we're used to concentrating on the content of our experiences, right? According to the Buddha, this focus on the drama does not facilitate finding ourselves on a reliable path to liberation. Therefore, it is recommended to cultivate ways of knowing what channel we are on; it is good for our meditation.

As we mentioned earlier, when we are looking at something, what about the sounds that are around us? Our experience doesn't correspond exactly with the way in which it's represented. We know we're in our room, we're focusing on something visually, and we're doing our best. "Ah, but sound of those birds," we might think, but we come back to our object. And then we have thoughts about the birds, and then we come back to our object. So, where are the birds represented in our scheme? It seems we're in a very strange place where there are no sounds whatsoever. What kind of a place would that be? It's hard to imagine. It's an apt question because if we understand the response, we have a precise key about what is and is not represented in this schema and precisely what corresponds to our experience.

All that the schema shows is that there are two moments of being with an object: we are viewing and then being distracted. That distraction may be lovely; it may be frightening; but it's a distraction away from what we decided was our meditation, which was to stay focused on a visual object. But even though we become distracted, we often find that we are able to come back to the chosen object of meditation again.

What about the existence of chirping birds outside my house? In this schema here, there is no moment or indication of hearing at all. This means that, for whatever reason, the sounds coming from birds—including our capacity called ear to process them and our capacity to integrate these sounds into a full experience of hearing—simply didn't occur as an experience for us. It doesn't mean that we don't have an ear. It's not saying that there aren't sounds (in our proximity) that other people may hear at the precise moment that we are in the proximity of those sounds while we are focusing on a visual object. Nor does it mean we have lost our brain capacity to integrate these sounds into an experience. All that is said is that—for whatever reason—there is no contact between the capacity to hear those sounds and integrate them into an experience of hearing. It's not a sound *for us* at this moment.

Now, perhaps this is not a true map of my meditation. Perhaps we had two moments of seeing, and then an actual moment of hearing (channel 2), and then two moments of thinking, "I'm a good meditator" (not noticing that we interspersed this moment of hearing), and then maybe there was even another moment of hearing, so: two moments of seeing, then one moment of hearing, then two moments of thinking, and then, as the sixth moment in this series, another moment of hearing. It would be represented like this:

- $[1/1, 1/2, 2/3, 6/4, 6/5, 2/6 \ldots]$

And these moments come very fast. In three seconds there may be fifty of them. If we're very relaxed, however, then maybe there would not be so many.

It seems that the number of moments that come in a certain objective unit of time is a function of how relaxed we are. It is possible to have the whole thing slow down very much; that's the good news.

Inserting some moments of channel 2 (hearing) into the schema would be a way of honoring how sneaky little moments of bird sound were actually happening *for us*. We have to revise our schema to accord with what actually happened. But it's also possible that the original example of [1/1, 1/2, 1/3, 6/4, 6/5 . . . 6/9, 1/10] is a true picture. We need to represent what actually occurred.

To be precise, the first model shows that even though the birds were out there, the sound of the birds did not arise as an experience for us. It doesn't mean other people didn't hear it. It doesn't mean the birds aren't there. It doesn't mean we lost our ears. But in the first example, there is no presence of the sound of those birds at the level of my experience, whereas in the second one, there is. If we did have the experience of hearing the birds, the second model gives an amended version to be a true picture of what occurred, if it did occur. That is to say, it's entirely possible that after two moments of looking at something, we hear something—that is, channel 2 is firing.

This is how dhatu analysis works. These are the eighteen elements that are very specifically organized and are meant to help us cut through the wrong view, the wrong meditation, the wrong conduct, and the delay of fruition (that is, liberation) that is based on a sloppy way of thinking about things, hearing things, and meditating.

Again, to summarize, if channel 2 is firing in between 1 and 6, it is possible that these firing moments are so short that almost every second during our shamatha meditation (on the level of beginners) would be a firing of the hearing channel of maybe 1/60 of a second. It is so short that it's hardly noticeable that it's a distraction, but it's responsible for this illusion of constant sound being there in your surroundings.

A Stream of Moments

Some may have a concern about posture during meditation. It's likely that while we are in channel 1 and maybe 2 and 6, our awareness of our physical posture (channel 5) might not be present. It's as if our body doesn't exist.

Maybe we think that means that our body is in a slouched or nonconducive-to-meditation posture, which might force further distractions. Maybe, we think, we should not allow ourselves to not be aware of our body. From the viewpoint of the example of dhatu analysis, the concern with what should or should not be the case is not addressed. What is addressed is what *is* the case, for me, in this series of moments. To reiterate, all that is indicated in this example is that there was a moment of seeing, then there was another moment of seeing, and then, in the first example, there were no moments of hearing (even though we know there were chirping birds outside). And then there is a moment of doing something else. There is no romance here, no mystery or melodrama. It's just one darn channel firing after another.

Time and a Moment of Channel Firing

What separates a moment of channel 1 from another moment of channel 1 if there is no time? To say it in the language of the Abhidharma, this would read: channel 1 firing; one full moment; channel 1 firing again; another full moment. You might say a channel continues as a channel until it's interrupted by another channel. And in fact there was some debate within the Abhidharma tradition about this. But it seems they wanted to distinguish the relative level of time; they were interested in *lived* time, not *clock* time. The sense of temporal duration is quite varied from one individual to another and doesn't precisely correspond to clock time.

There are many beautiful stories in Buddhist literature about the experience of time. For example, there is the one about the great yogi who was about to be served a cup of tea and then experienced many amazing events over what seemed experientially to be a long, long time. In this story, the yogi heard a voice, and the person who served him the tea said, "So are you going to drink your tea?" For the one who served the tea, just a moment or so had passed, but in terms of the yogi's experience, there was a great drama that unfolded as if it had gone on for eons. The tea server's "moment" was the yogi's "eon," so time is relative.

Karmic Doors

All behavior is analyzed in the Abhidharma tradition according to the three karmic doors of body, voice, and mind, and they are the expression of a single though powerful dharma, which is called "willing" or "intending" (*chetana*), and also what arises in the wake of that willing, what was willed, the manifest expression of that willing (*cetayitva*). This is a way of talking about karmic behavior, distinguished from unintended responses, those which do not involve intention. Examples of such unintended responses are vocal startle responses and bodily reflex responses. For example, if I am speaking to you, this is called the energy of being vocally intended, and it is said it occurs through the door of the voice. When I move, this is the energy karma via the body.

According to the Abhidharma prior to every speech act, and every intended physical response of ours, there is always present the energy of an intent. To be clear, this technical word—*chetana* in Sanskrit—has received quite varied translations. It does not mean I consciously intended something, and then I decided to express it. Rather it names the force or arc of a prior movement of mind, one that entails the expression (the karmic flow) of speech acts or physical responses. It is classed as one basic factor of experience, one dharma. Vasubandhu dedicates the entire fourth chapter of his *Treasury of Higher Dharma* (*Abhidharmakosha*), which he calls "an investigation into karma" (*karma nirdesha*), to how this one dharma works, both its form as an intending, working through the door of the mind (*chitta*), and also what gets expressed, intended, through the doors of speech and body.

To reiterate, it's said that there is something invisible that always occurs before we express karma. And that which is unseen or unmanifested is on the mind side. It is unmanifest and then it tends toward manifestation through the vocal and physical karmic doors. Every vocal or physical act leaves a karmic trace. That trace goes into a karmic reserve and may serve as the source for another karmic activation later. Every caress and slap leaves an impression. For example, let's say there is a new dog around, and when you reach out to caress it, it steps back. Perhaps that dog reacts this way because it has experienced something other than a caress many times before. It is not about to be hurt, but there is the karmic trace which was left from many past occasions of being

hurt. It remembers and it brings this into the present time as a way of responding. And we are like that dog. We remember. That, more or less, is a full picture
of what we might call karmic behavior according to the *Abhidharmakosha*.

In terms of our experiential model of dhatu analysis, it is enough to know
that talking is a moment of channel 5, and listening is a moment of channel 2,
and so on. Those six channels account for everything that has occurred in the
past, is occurring now, and will occur in the future.

The Experience of Talking

Again, let's slow things down here. What concretely is going on when we say
we are talking? For example, as I'm talking to you, I feel my back a bit (channel 5), I feel my vocal cords (channel 5), I'm looking at you (channel 1), and
I'm having thoughts (channel 6). Within what we usually and sloppily call
"talking" are several different channel firings. We can still honor the way we
actually experience. All of this is not meant to turn us into rigid Abhidharma
machines but rather to enable us to explore and understand with an open
heart and gain the skill of using the sword of precise wisdom discernment so
we can cut through our sloppy habits. It is not meant to make us into robots
but rather to encourage us to dance.

Art and Creativity

According to dhatu analysis, how does creativity work? Painting involves channel 1, which is seeing; channel 5, which is touching; and, of course, thinking and
being open to inspiration, channel 6. In fact, we could give, according to dhatu
analysis, a very flat and unamusing account of, say, Degas in his inspirational
creative process of painting. If we're talking about inspiration, it's simply moments of channel 6 firings. Every thought, experience, and feeling of every great
artist (and also every great criminal) is simply the firings of channel 6.

Tightness in Shamatha Practice?

Our discussion here is not meant to be dragged at all into formal meditation
practice, nor is it meant to change, alter, deviate from, or improve the meditation instructions we've been given. We do our best according to our medita-

tion instruction as we've received it from our teachers. If we are not clear, we are encouraged to not be passive, to seek clarification, and to find a way to not be tight about it. If we find ourselves being tight about it, we need to try to not be tight about being tight about it. It's entirely normal to be tight.

This analysis that we've been engaging in thus far is very good for post-meditative situations. It's not meant to be applied while driving a car or operating power tools; that's point one. Point two is to determine if we can remember what it means to have fun and to see if we can really be spacious in having fun without getting distracted into "should," "ought," or "must." And if we get tight when doing that, we can try to be spacious and relaxed and see what arises.

PART THREE

Mind and Mental Factors

9

Mind

How Do Our "Jumping Frog" Minds Operate?

Now I want to start going into what we have avoided so far, which is the *content* of our experiences. So far, we've looked at how our experience can be represented as one channel firing after another, and we've learned a new way of speaking about and referring to our experience in terms of these channels. More precisely, we've learned to know the difference, at the level of experience, between a moment of seeing (channel 1) and a moment of closing our eyes and creating the image we just saw, which would be a mental experience (channel 6), or, with our eyes open, a moment of remembering that we saw something (channel 6), or remembering that we had created an image in our mind (also channel 6).

The scheme of eighteen dhatus shows us a way to relate to our own experience, to note differences between seeing and remembering what we saw, hearing and remembering what we heard, and so on. The claim is that we can experientially distinguish the difference between the five sense-based channels and a remembrance of what was occurring when those channels were going on, which is channel 6. Why bother to know the difference? It helps loosen up this fixity, this tightness, this so-called self, which is the cause of suffering.

Remember: it is not so obvious, this difference between a moment of seeing and a moment of remembering that we saw. It seems that what we normally call "seeing" is more like a little opera, a drama in which many things—aside from hues and shapes—are going on. It seems that while we are seeing something, there are also sounds, we hear things, and we ponder about the whole opera while it is being enacted. It is all a kind of *melange*.

"What are you looking at?" "I'm looking at *this*."

"What are you thinking about while you're looking at that?" "I'm thinking..."

The Abhidharma says this is exactly the pattern of tightness from which we all suffer. It is a melange of many different factors going on at the same time. We name it our "so-called life." The Buddhists call it "confusion." They say that this swirl, this confusion in which I can be looking at something, hearing something, and thinking about something seemingly at the same time, is not how things are actually occurring. What's more, they say if we learn to experience the difference between a moment of "seeing" and a moment of "remembering" what we saw, this will engender a loosening of the habit of sloppiness and confusion that envelops our so-called life. It will serve to plant the seeds for new, more spacious habits of reflection that will cause our life to be less tight.

One of the best ways to slow down so that we can experience more clearly is to practice shamatha. With practice, we can determine that those things that seem to be happening at the same time are actually not simultaneous but is instead a switching from one channel to another. Meditation practice is the test site, the place and the way to test the points made in this study. The study of dhatu analysis is just the plan of action and, in a sense, a prediction. But without meditation practice, it is just words.

Mapping Dhatus into Dharmas

Let's look again at the variety of different kinds of energy packets—the metaphor we use for the different experiences that are possible according to the *Abhidharmakosha*.

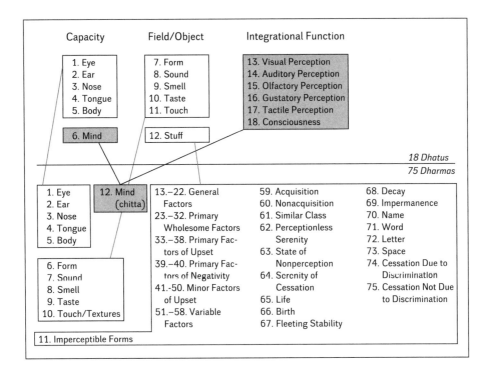

Capacity	Field/Object	Integrational Function		
1. Eye 2. Ear 3. Nose 4. Tongue 5. Body	7. Form 8. Sound 9. Smell 10. Taste 11. Touch	13. Visual Perception 14. Auditory Perception 15. Olfactory Perception 16. Gustatory Perception 17. Tactile Perception 18. Consciousness		
6. Mind	12. Stuff			

18 Dhatus
75 Dharmas

1. Eye 2. Ear 3. Nose 4. Tongue 5. Body	12. Mind (chitta)	13.–22. General Factors 23.–32. Primary Wholesome Factors 33.–38. Primary Fac- tors of Upset 39.–40. Primary Fac- tors of Negativity 41.-50. Minor Factors of Upset 51.–58. Variable Factors	59. Acquisition 60. Nonacquisition 61. Similar Class 62. Perceptionless Serenity 63. State of Nonperception 64. Serenity of Cessation 65. Life 66. Birth 67. Fleeting Stability

6. Form
7. Sound
8. Smell
9. Taste
10. Touch/Textures

68. Decay
69. Impermanence
70. Name
71. Word
72. Letter
73. Space
74. Cessation Due to
   Discrimination
75. Cessation Not Due
   to Discrimination

11. Imperceptible Forms

At this point in the drama of the Abhidharma, we have two sets of actors. We have the *dramatis personae*, the characters known as the eighteen dhatus. And then we bring the group of seventy-five dharmas on stage. So what does this group of seventy-five have to do with the eighteen? We said that all of the seventy-five are hidden under the clothing of the eighteen.

We indicated that the dhatus 1–5 and 7–11 each relate to one energy packet on the list of seventy-five dharmas:

- Factors 1–5 of the seventy-five dharmas correspond to 1–5 of the eighteen dhatus.
- Factors 6–10 of the seventy-five dharmas correspond to 7–11 of the eighteen dhatus.

We also said that the remaining factors are hiding under the costume of dhatu 12. We have now accounted for seventy-five dharmas from the list of seventy-five. We have a somewhat embarrassing situation. A lot has been written about this. How many of these dharmas do we have left? There is one left. But how many of the dhatu players do we have left? There are seven—one capacity (6) and all the integrational functions that have been waiting to be acknowledged, at long last. So, somehow one dharma has to go into seven dhatus—very confusing. We shall see that the one dharma is to be found operating as seven dhatus; its name is "mind" (*chitta*).

Mind (Chitta) Is Varied and It Piles Up

Chitta, or mind, is dharma 12 on the chart of seventy-five. As a Mahayana practitioner, one tries to activate chitta oriented toward enlightenment, and we call that *bodhichitta*. In the *Dhammapada* it says that everything that is important about being human has to do with this mind, chitta. Chitta is the single most important factor for full and complete liberation.

There are many ways we can talk about chitta. Here are two senses. The Indian Buddhist scholar Sthiramati says that chitta can be thought of as quite *varied* (*chitra*)[112] in terms of its expression and also, like a feedback loop, its moments of expression are retained and pile up (*chinoti*).[113] It's not piling up something that is different from its own nature. This defines what it is; it is "a compiler." All of the integrational functions (13–18) are compilers. They lock everything in.

Ways the Mind Piles Up

For living beings, there are three basic ways in which the mind piles up:

1. Things are going well.
2. Things are not going well.
3. Sometimes we are a bit confused, and we cannot precisely say whether things are going well or not.

Going well can mean many things. Normally, we say it's going well if "I" like it. And we say things are not going well if they are not in accord with what "I" want. Our firm basis for deciding what is good and what is not is this position of judging from my viewpoint of "I." But it is not a spacious viewpoint. There is always a holding pattern; there is a tightness.

If we think about it, the sky has no preferences. It simply is, in a spacious and luminous way. When the rays of the sun fully manifest, the rays don't decide, "I should shine more in this direction and not so much in that direction." This habit of judging already means there is a judger. This is a very simple thing to say, but in reality it is very difficult to catch this judger—very, very difficult.

Experiences of Pleasure and Pain

A contemporary meditation master has said that to have a mind means to have experiences of pain and pleasure. That's the primary meaning of mind. All experiences of pain and pleasure occur because of this factor called mind. We can bring this into alignment with the two aspects of mind—it has a variety of ways, but to essentialize, they are twofold—sometimes we experience, judge, and reflect things as going well and are pleasurable, and sometimes we reflect things as not going well and are painful. We have moments of pain and moments of pleasure. Most often we don't reflect on the one who is having those experiences. All the time we get caught up in trying to enjoy, engage in, and increase situations we consider to be pleasurable, and we try to hide from, get away from, or get rid of situations that we consider not pleasurable.

No matter how clever or educated we are, all of our experiences can be divided into these two kinds of patterns: "pleasurable" (meaning it is going our way) and "not so pleasurable" (meaning it is not going our way). When we have an experience that we call pleasurable, and we reflect on it and want to increase it, there is already a holding pattern, a judger, someone who is filtering and deciding. But we don't normally see this. We often, it seems, have to go into retreat to reflect on the question of who is trying to get away from unpleasurable situations. And when we talk to each other, or when we are working in our daily jobs, it's considered a bit off the point if you ask questions about who is the one who is undergoing these experiences. If we persist in asking these questions, we'll probably be fired. We decide that the best policy is "don't ask, don't tell." We are still in the closet. We just go on with our closeted lives as if this were a good thing to do.

The way to proceed is according to a plan. Sometimes there is a plan that says, "Don't do these things." More or less, every plan, every schedule, consists of a way to do something and a way to avoid something, as if the way to proceed is always good and will make us feel good, and the things that we should avoid, because someone judged they're bad, will always make us feel bad. When we see the sign "do not" or "forbidden," someone has decided it is bad. In all the rules and in all the ways of proceeding through life as we do, there is this pattern of deciding and judging.

We might say that all issues of power, politics, and class, and the realms of economics, sociology, and political science are a struggle about definitions of good and bad, definitions of pain and pleasure, and then a struggle about who has the authority to impose their list. We make different groups according to which lists of good and bad we like. This division of good and bad, pleasurable or painful, pervades everything, except maybe the trees and the birds, and of course the sky. We might say that having a mind (chitta) is being caught up in struggling with issues of pleasure and pain, good and bad, with no space to reflect on who is deciding what is good and bad.

Eight Worldly Dharmas

Another contemporary meditation master once shared the following story. He said that he felt that the term *ego*, or *self* (as a translation for understanding of our tightness), is difficult to discover. Precisely, where is this ego? How is this tightness? It then occurred to him that in fact this tightness goes on in eight very distinct ways, ways in which we unsuccessfully try to have situations that flow and are pleasurable, on the one hand, and ways in which we try to avoid situations that are troubling, on the other. This group of eight ways of tightness can be divided into four types of fear of bad stuff that we want to stay away from and four ways in which we hope to increase or be connected with good stuff. If we understand this, it accounts for all the different ways that we are. And realizing this, that master decided for himself that instead of doing a traditional meditation retreat focusing on something like "ego" he would focus on this: from the moment he woke up in the morning until he went to bed at night, he would observe how his mind functioned in these eight possible ways. What are these famous eight ways? How does our pattern of tightness operate?

1. Fear of Pain

From the moment we get up in the morning until we go to bed at night, we fear pain, physical or mental. We make elaborate plans to avoid, or at least delay, any situation that is physically or mentally painful. The first of the eight is fear of pain.

2. Fear of Loss

We also fear and make plans to avoid any loss; we fear losing anything that we regard as ours. We plan to not lose, or we fear that we are going to lose.

3. Fear of Blame

We also fear being criticized by others, being shamed, being told that we did not do a good job or that we didn't do it correctly. We fear this and will avoid being judged in this way if we can. We'll develop a way of being clever or engage in a bit of lying, but maybe for a good reason, so we say, in order to not be the target. We avoid situations of responsibility in this way. This is the third pattern: fear of being blamed.

4. Fear of Bad Reputation

The fourth form of fear is fear of being remembered or talked about with a lack of respect. It is the fear that the gossip about us will not go the way we want the gossip to go. This is the fear of having a bad reputation.

So fear of pain, of loss, of being shamed directly, and fear of a bad reputation are the four ways in which our tightness, our wanting to control, flows with respect to trying to avoid.

5. Hope for Pleasure

We can guess what the other four are. But it is good to remember that from the moment we wake up in the morning until we go to bed at night we are hoping for pleasurable situations, physically and mentally. We make a plan: "These are the pleasurable things that I want to accomplish today, physically and mentally." We hope to increase that, and we don't want to delay it. Hoping for pleasure, the counterpart to fearing pain, takes up a lot of time.

Almost all advertising is a way of trying to make people spend money according to what they imagine will give them pleasure. And, of course, good advertisers know that people need to be educated. They know that people don't really know what they want, so they have to be told and they have to be shown ways in which a particular product—this thing that we can see, hear, smell, taste, touch, think about, or feel—will make them happier if they buy it. That means that advertisers understand very well something about the nature of mind in a relative way. They know that this holding pattern can be educated; it can be influenced. We might say that our education is the training and controlling of this holding pattern.

Sometimes the desire to control the holding pattern doesn't work. The Buddhist teachings talk about turning away from being fascinated by the spectacle of control, which does not correspond to the real situation. They talk about turning the mind away from such engagement, which involves overthrowing the dictatorship of false views that reinforce this tightness. It is said that the way to provoke a revolution at the level of our attitude is to engage in the following four thoughts:

- Think deeply about how rare and precious this human situation is.
- Think deeply about how this precious, rare situation won't last forever.
- Think deeply about how the most important pattern in this precious existence is the way in which our mind goes. And it goes in the two ways of wholesome or unwholesome karma: wishing for happiness to increase (which is wholesome karma and will always bear fruit as ease and well-being) or wishing that happiness would be blocked or decrease (which is unwholesome karma that will always bear fruit as pain and frustration).
- Think deeply about the unsatisfactoriness of samsara. We are told to reflect that the lifestyles that flow from our tight habit patterns, which

are dominated by aggression, acquisition, or ignorance, are really not worth pursuing.

6. Hope for Gain
In addition to spending a lot of time hoping for increased pleasure (the fifth pattern), we try to gain new things that accord with our nature—more things to see, hear, smell, taste, and touch, many new things to think about that we like, many things to feel. This is the sixth.

7. Hope for Praise
The seventh is that we focus our hopes on people praising us. We are very clever at putting ourselves in situations where people will say nice things to us. We want to be right in that place where something nice is happening, and then people will think it had something to do with us. So we plot ways to have praise occur. We all know we will feel good. But actually we will only feel good if it is genuine praise. So we plot all kinds of artificial situations in order to provoke the semblance of genuine and natural praise.

8. Hope for Fame
And the eighth is that we try to manipulate our press. We are always hiring a public relations agent who broadcasts out and leaves pamphlets, brochures, write-ups, and blurbs about how wonderful we are. Have you noticed that when we write a curriculum vitae there is a bit of a selection process? We put the points in there that will attract and fascinate and make people want to praise us and need us. So the eighth is hoping and planning for ways in which history will remember us in a good way.

Worldly Dharmas
These eight factors, these ways of proceeding, are motivations that are called "worldly" because they keep us in samsara. These are ways of avoiding a spiritual revolution.

In fact, everything that is said about ego or self can be rethought as consisting entirely of these eight worldly motivations. On the basis of this insight, one might do a retreat. You make the retreat as you would normally do. Imagine reflecting, in your journal, on moments that you remember that fall into these eight motivations. If you do it with a bit of spaciousness, this is a kind of "shamatha helper." It is not depressing or bad news when you discover this is what you are doing. It explains why you are sometimes exhausted at the end of the day. You set your view with practices in the morning, and then the day begins: time for the eight worldly dharmas, time for "me."

At the end of the day, it's enough to remember this: "What situations did I have today in which I was trying to avoid physical or mental pain? How was I planning for and successful in increasing pleasure?" You can have your eight-worldly-dharmas journal. Don't show it to anyone; just reflect. You don't have to be obsessive about this, trying to catch which of the eight you are in while you are walking around. It is enough to know that this is the hope and fear machine, the dual piston that fires our little motorcar down the little worldly path. It is enough to know that, and then at the end of the day, just reflect. Then rest.

Now who is doing all that? It is mind. Maybe this is an important factor to investigate. We can now investigate in some detail, with a bit of precision, what the Abhidharma traditions have said about the variety of ways in which mind operates.

10

Conditioned and Unconditioned Elements

Our famous list of seventy-five factors is—according to Vasubandhu's *Treasury of Higher Dharma*—considered a full and complete chart of everything that can go on for a living being, and every one of us is inherently born with all seventy-five factors. Within that chart, we can identify two basic patterns called "conditioned elements" and "unconditioned elements."

Conditioned Elements

The chart on page 38 shows conditioned elements that consist of columns I, II, III, and IV. Everything in there is conditioned, meaning subject to cause and effect or, to put it another way, impermanent. And this impermanence is not some vague thing. It means, rather precisely, that there will be a coming into being, a birth (66); there will be a stabilization so that the pattern endures for a while (67); and then there will be a breakup, decay, and dissipation (68). This is true of everything called "conditioned." According to the Buddhist tradition, there is no one who is *creating* these factors; it is simply the nature of these factors to sometimes come together into a kind of coherent vibrational pattern, to stay around for a while, to dissipate, and to break up.

One of the deepest patterns that causes continual suffering and disappoint-ment for human beings is not knowing, in a concrete way, that everything that is conditioned is impermanent. We've been educated in the opposite direc-tion. A revolution of the mind is to turn away from the imprecision and wrong views about how reality is and instead to find a space in which we can directly see how it's actually operating. We have a great number of factors that are con-ditioned; they arise, they stay for a while, and then they go away.

Unconditioned Elements

Fortunately, conditioned factors do not make up the whole picture. In this list of elements (see again the chart on page 38), there are elements that have never come together, nor have they been dissipated. In a sense, they've always been there. There was never a time when they were not. These are called the uncon-ditioned elements.

73. Space or Spaciousness
There was never a time when there was not spaciousness.

74. Cessation Due to Discrimination
This means there's been a breakthrough to a pattern that has always been there. This breakthrough is sometimes likened to what happened to the Buddha sit-ting under the bodhi tree. For the next forty years, from the time of his full and complete enlightenment, all those other factors that were conditioned were extinct or no longer operating. To be awakened means to no longer be subject to the sleep of what is "conditioned."

75. Cessation Not Due to Discrimination
This unconditioned dharma is sometimes correlated with the Buddha's death, his ultimate or final nirvana (*parinirvana*). It's an unconditioned pattern of nirvana in which there is no trace remaining.

Things Can Go Two Ways

The main point here is that at the level of reality experiences operate in two possible ways:

1. They can come into being, stay for a while, and dissipate.
2. There can be a thorough "revolution," a transformation (*paravritti*) such that there are no longer distinctions between arising and falling away. This big revolution is sometimes called "waking up" or "cutting through"; it's nirvana or enlightenment itself.

Learning about the conditioned factors helps in the process of coming into a situation in which this thorough revolution might be possible. We come to focus on the conditioned elements themselves, and we will spend quite some time on column III from the chart of the seventy-five dharmas. We will see that the Abhidharma had very precise knowledge of how the mind works in its variety. It's more or less as it appears on the list. Now we have to see whether we can actually find these factors in our own mind or in our own experience. This is more or less an investigation of channel 6; that is, it refers to situations in which we're not seeing, hearing, smelling, tasting, or touching. Something else is going on.

For those interested in what's going on in channels 1–5, column I of the seventy-five dharmas is sufficient: We have an eye, an ear, a nose, a tongue, and a body (capacities), and they coordinate to have experiences of form, sound, smell, taste, and touch (fields/objects). But somehow this contact between the capacities and the fields is not sufficient. It has to be compiled or organized into something we can concretely experience as seeing or hearing. And so the integrational functions, which are always making contact with the capacities and the fields, are just the various ways in which there operates that pattern of dharma 12 (of seventy-five dharmas), that one dharma called "mind."

This famous mind is very hard to find by itself. It's not even clear what it means. What is mind itself? It seems that we only know mind by how it operates. When it's described in the various ways in which it piles up, it piles up as 13–18 in our dhatu chart.

Column III: Mental Events

Now we are going to investigate not so much mind itself, number 12 of seventy-five, but rather what comes in the wake of the operation of mind. These are primarily the factors in column III of the chart of seventy-five dharmas (see appendix 1). They are sometimes referred to as mental events. We will see that the word *mental*, having to do with mind, is a bit too limited for the full range of what we have here. In fact, column III has forty-six different factors, and it completely corresponds with our dhatu 12. Everything in column III is the information to be processed.

We are talking about the variety of information that we process on channel 6; and the place where that's processed (or the file folder, to use a computer word) is channel 12. Let's examine channel 12 to see what's inside. We're discovering that there's quite a bit inside. We can be very clear that all that is inside, this information that can be processed, does not arise when we're seeing, hearing, smelling, tasting, or touching.

If it seems that we're having a moment of, let's say, 26, "conscience," while we are looking at something, actually, according to this schema, we're having channel 6, "conscience," and then channel 1; we're looking at something, and then maybe going back to channel 6, "conscience."

To make the point again, the eight worldly dharmas, which Dzongsar Khyentse Rinpoche called the living presence of ego or self, is all channel 6—all of it. I make this point over and over again because the Buddhist texts themselves make this point over and over again. Channel 6 and how it works is the most important channel. Being unaware of how mind works at the level of that channel is what keeps us in this round of suffering.

When we study Buddhist literature on the stages of the path, the language of what to pay attention to favors attention to the mind; this is channel 6. We know that even when we are in the so-called formless realm of samsara—the realms of infinite sky, infinite consciousness, nothing at all, and neither perception nor nonperception—this is all channel 6; channels 1 and 5 are not operating there.

Thus, very subtle, spacious forms of meditation, according to the Shravakayana traditions (and some Mahayana traditions), is all channel 6. Distraction, in this case, is defined as being caught up in channels that are not channel 6. It is being caught up with looking at something or hearing something, but then we return to this channel 6.

We've spent quite some time now talking about why this channel 6 is important. Yet we never find it just sitting there, saying, "Hello, I'm your mind." So, let's give a classical definition of what mind is (dharma 12 on the list of seventy-five dharmas) and then we'll move on to the mental events or the things that come in its wake.

Mind: Channel-Specific Awareness

The main source that all the Tibetan traditions refer to in order to define mind is chapter 1, verse 16 of the *Abhidharmakosha*. Here, it says that mind is the name for being able to become selectively aware. It's "selective awareness."[114] I would translate this as "channel-specific awareness."

Remember, here, that the word that is used for mind in its channel-specific functioning is mind (*chitta*), which operates in six different kinds of differentiated awarenesses (vijnana). In the Abhidharma, chitta and vijnana are more or less the same thing. That is to say, if we were to ask where the mind is, it is only in the sixfold integrative and channel-specific places (the column III enumerations).

For now, it's enough to say that mind, or chitta, is the integrative functional aspect that allows us to compile, and to bring such compilations to the level of an experience (vijnana) with respect to seeing (channel 1), hearing (channel 2), smelling (channel 3), tasting (channel 4), touching (channel 5), or anything else, all the emotional and cognitive functions (channel 6). We're going to be focusing on channel 6 and the varieties of so-called mental factors, but the fact that we can have an experience that we can later reflect on, the fact that we can integrate, is mind; it is chitta functioning as vijnana.

Perception

The analysis we've done so far should show that *vijnana* is perhaps poorly translated as "consciousness." We might say mind is alive and well in terms of its perceptive functions. Perceptive means that we're capturing something that's channel specific, a percept.

Some translators call these perceptions "visual perception," "auditory perception," and so on. This "per" means there's a bit of a division or a specificity of channel that is firing, and *vi* in *vijnana* means exactly the same. There's a separation, a tuning in, and a specificity. Vasubandhu states that the *vi* in *vijnana* means "according to the channel."[115] *Jnana* is a general word that means "knowing," an operation that retains information. So vijnana is the retention in a channel-specific way.

Now we know that mind in its variety and ways of piling up does so in six channel-specific ways. Where's the "I" here—that famous guy or gal who's causing all these problems? It's said that it's not given at the level of reality. We just have moments of seeing, hearing, smelling, tasting, touching, and other.

Mind and What Comes in Its Wake

I now want to focus on channel 6, column II, dhatu 12 of the dhatu chart and the processed information associated with it. What is the mind processing by way of information on channel 6? Before Vasubandhu engages in a detailed discussion of all of the factors involved, he says something a bit shocking. He says that this mind and all the stuff that arises as awareness of that "information" (dhatu 12 of 18) happen together. Mind and what comes in its wake happen *together*.

We can analyze these difference aspects, but we should never think that there is something separate called "mind" actually existing apart from "mental events." It's said that mind and mental events[116] actually operate at the same time together in coordination. They are not the same, but they are never discovered as separate. The point here is that the statement by Vasubandhu says "mind" (i.e., knowing, or *chitta*) and "mental events" (the content of what is known, *chaitta*) always arise at the same time.

Factors of Mind

What are these various factors that come together? What's in number 12 of the dhatus? In the chart of seventy-five, we have a group of general functions, a group of good guys, a group of bad guys, even more bad guys, some less bad guys, and then finally those that are neither good nor bad. All these are ways of analyzing all the different aspects of what we can discover in mental reflection. They are always connected with mind in order to be truly there, for that energy packet to be happening, for having an experience.

Column IV

But the Buddha and those who followed in his footsteps noticed something else about reality. They noticed that there seemed to be general laws that regulated consciousness, but those laws were not only true when they were an experience. For example, what is the difference between psychological and logical reality? They noticed just one simple thing for which thousands of pages have been written in the West. And what was observed was the following: they noticed the fact that 2 + 2 = 4 is not only true when we're thinking it. It is not only true when it is an experience for us. This is the vexed problem, the difference between psychological space and logical space. Where is mathematics when I am not thinking it?

A very precise language was developed in the West in the early part of the 1900s to investigate this point. Husserl, in his *Logical Investigations*, criticized the conflation of "truth" as a psychological, present reality and "truth" in the sense of what is logically true, what is not a psychological truth, meaning not dependent on being present for the mind as an experience. This is the difference between "truth of experience," "experiential truth," and "logical truth." Vasubandhu listed factors as "logical truths" in column IV.

Column IV is classified as "not conjoined with mind" (*chitta viprayukta*),[117] meaning the "reality of these factors does not depend on being connected to the mind." Column III has to be connected or conjoined with mind (*chitta samprayukta*)[118] for it to be experientially true. Perception, idea, will, touch, energy, fraudulence, and arrogance all have something rather interesting in common. They're true only when they are an experience for me. They are different from those factors in column IV. Factors in column IV consist of aspects associated with the "truth" of language, logic, and mathematics, as well as other seemingly "abstract" items.

To reiterate, column IV contains factors that are not always present in a moment of consciousness. The technical term for this class of things is *dharmas conditioned but not arising with mind*.[119] It is the difference between psychological or experiential space and logical or mathematical space. This is an attempt to think about what is actually real in domains such as mathematics and language. Think about this: Is the equation $2 + 2 = 4$ only true when I am thinking it? Where does the reality of that "truth" reside, where does the truth of math and logic and language reside? They are not "true" only as the content of an experience. As mentioned above, Husserl's book *Logical Investigations* delves into this, as do others.

Ever-Present and
Object-Determined
Mental Factors

The list of seventy-five dharmas based on the *Abhidharmakosha* by Vasu-bandhu is one way of talking about what makes up all of reality. We gave this list initially in discussions of Abhidharma because this is where one finds the codified definitions. Now, to discuss the mental factors (13–58) from this list in detail, I am going to switch references and touch upon two other books that were written by Tibetans and have modern English translations. Both books are based on and follow the approach of the Abhidharma. These two references are (1) *Gateway to Knowledge* by Jamgon Mipham (1846–1912), a work in which there is a list of all of these factors and their definitions, and (2) *Mind in Buddhist Psychology*, a work by the Tibetan Buddhist scholar Yeshé Gyaltsen (1713–1793) that elucidates the workings of the mind and its mental events. In the back of this translation there is a chart in which the translators correlate some of the factors found in Jamgon Mipham's *Gateway to Knowledge* with what Yeshé Gyaltsen explored.

Both *Mind in Buddhist Psychology* (abbreviated as MBP) and *Gateway to Knowledge* (abbreviated as GK) follow the approach of Vasubandhu, and they both refer to the Abhidharma literature for their technical definitions. As we explore these factors, I will provide the English translation[120] for each factor as found in both GK and MBP (see appendix 2 for a complete list of these factors along with their Sanskrit and Tibetan equivalents).

General Factors

There are ten "general" factors: five ever-present factors and five object-determined factors. All of the general factors have something to do with paying attention or being with an object so that we can report to ourselves that we're having an experience. These are the basic factors involved in cognition. For those who are interested in cognitive science, you might be encouraged to study these ten factors, see what they have to do with experience, and how cognitive science explores the subject matter of these same factors.

These general factors do not have subdivisions at the level of how they actually are but only at the level of how they operate in different ways. As dharmas, they are irreducible to anything else. These factors, these energy packets, are understood to be part of the fundamental building blocks of the universe. They are what actually make up "me" and my "environment." If we develop precision about the actual nature of these energy packets, then we may come to understand how they combine with other energy packets. As suggested before, these factors combine with each other, like atoms combining with other atoms to make molecules and then larger chains of molecules. Whether we are investigating a "plastic bottle" or an experience of, say, "being angry," we can physically or mentally (analytically) tease apart the constituent elements, cutting through to the core of it with the crucial factor of "discernment" (*prajna*). As Vasubandhu says, when one discovers what is irreducible, then, at that level, one discovers what is actually real.

Understanding the scope and definitions of the full list of these factors, one should develop confidence that no aspects of "reality" are being left out. One can learn how our so-called life consists of nothing other than the ways in which these factors (like atoms) combine to make up our phenomenal reality.

EVER-PRESENT FACTORS

	SANSKRIT	GATEWAY TO KNOWLEDGE	MIND IN BUDDHIST PSYCHOLOGY
1.	*vedana*	sensation	feeling-tone
2.	*samjna*	perception	conceptualization
3.	*chetana*	attraction	directionality
4.	*sparsha*	contact	rapport
5.	*manasikara*	attention	demanding

1. Sensation/Feeling-Tone

The first factor, *vedana*, is translated as "sensation" in GK and as "feeling-tone" in MBP. Sensation, a basic energy packet, a dharma, cannot be broken up. It is defined as three different types of experiences (*anubhava*): pleasant (*sukha*), unpleasant (duhkha), and, according to Vasubandhu, neither pleasant nor unpleasant (*asukhaduhka*). Some writers call this last experience "not determined," or they use a term that gets translated as "neutral," as shorthand meaning neither pleasant nor unpleasant. This is not a trivial point, particularly for those who have had some somatic training. Can one actually have a sensation that can truly be called "neutral"? Of course, we do have sensations that are not so easily classified as pleasant or unpleasant. This word *neutral* sounds like a balance. Or it sounds a bit vague. But when one reads the commentaries, they clearly define this third way of sensation as that class of sensations that don't come to us as only pleasant or unpleasant. If we just stick with the words of Vasubandhu, there is pleasant, unpleasant, and neither. There is no "neutral," "undifferentiated," or "indifferent."

It is said that this factor of sensation, within the *Sutta of Mindfulness* (*Satipatthana Sutta*), there is a procedure for reflecting on the nature of sensation. Furthermore, the grouping of conditioned factors into the twelvefold category called "sense bases" is a way of paying attention to how this factor of sensation works. Vasubandhu states that the groupings of factors into five aggregates (skandhas), eighteen elements (dhatus), and twelve sense bases (ayatanas) are studied to counteract a wrong belief regarding the status of an imagined, stable "self" (atman). The twelve sense bases are said to be an antidote for the wrong view that the "self," the sense of "who" I am, is made up of actually existing "material" stuff (this "wrong" view seems to be similar to many Western "materialist" views, such as neural net advocates). Such views do not allow the seemingly "soft" notions of "mind" and "mental events" to enter into their analysis. Materialists believe that all "experience" must be based on brain or brain-related material structures and events, which must, in turn, be based on neurochemistry or perhaps physics.

The point here is that the *Abhidharmakosha* asserts that the twelvefold sense bases are taught in order to be able to cut through the wrong view that the so-called self consists of solid material stuff. The procedure that is used to do this is to discover that "sensations" are more or less always there; they accompany all of our "experiences." In other words, awareness, "mind," and its functioning is always there when there is contact (sparsha) via any of the channels. This is but one example of how the Abhidharma literature refers to certain groupings of this list of factors in order to counteract wrong views (which are regarded as the source of suffering).[121] We can appreciate how exploring this one factor can lead to a deep revaluing of our experience. Such study aids in cutting through the idea that the stuff of experience is material.

2. Perception/Conceptualization

The second factor, *samjna*, has been translated as "perception" and MBP translates this as "conceptualization." [122] The definition of conceptualization is that it is the dharma or factor which can isolate, or pick out, a specific characteristic. It's what allows us to tune in to, in a very fine way, the proper category of what we may focus on. It is the aspect of mental functioning that allows us to pick out a specific characteristic. It is the ability to sort. What we call concepts are the names we give to having been able to make distinctions at the mental level. Both in the Buddhist traditions as well as in the West, there is a lot of deep talk on how we come up with categories and in what ways our categories correspond to reality—that is, how we can sort things into proper categories.

There was a very influential discovery about category formation by University of California at Berkeley professor of psychology Eleanor Rosch. She is also one of the three authors who wrote the book *Embodied Mind*,[123] in which they tried to bring together Buddhist understandings and Western psychological understandings of mind and its functioning. Years before that in 1978, Rosch made a breakthrough. She discovered that in terms of category formation, there is nothing abstract or ideal about "categories" with respect to our experience.[124] For example, there is not an ideal type or category for something called "bird" with respect to which we then learn to identify and associate a particular existent "bird" as being an element or an example of that set called "birds." This discovery seemed to go against prevailing views about category formation.

By working with a tribe in New Guinea, Rosch discovered that there was a "prototypical" existent "bird" and that people classed as "bird" those animals that closely resembled that specific type of "bird." That is to say, the class "birds" meant for that group of people whatever corresponded to a specific kind of bird. Rosch was able to show that what we ourselves might think would be called a "bird" did not always correspond to what they called a bird. They had in mind a prototype, an actual, living experiential example of a bird. The implication regarding category formation based on her work suggests that the "classes" of categories, which are considered general and a bit abstract, are actually never given in experience as such; they are inferentially based on actual prototypes.

This suggests that there is no abstract notion of "bird." "Bird" means anything that looks and acts like that specific prototypical "bird." If a supposed bird deviates too much from the prototype, it will not be referred to as a bird in the language and experience of a given group of people. Prototypical structure of category formation caused a revolution against the notion that categories somehow "exist" out there as abstract things.

This is useful to remember when contemplating Buddhist accounts of what is happening at the level of experience. It seems we have an imprecise way of sorting our experience in terms of categories. Eleanor Rosch (along with Francisco Varela and Evan Thompson) thought deeply about how categories are formed.[125] They concluded that "mind" and cognition in the Buddhist tradition refers to embodied experiences of knowing, the different ways in which we experience. "Mind" is, in that sense, always an embodied knowing.

The factor called "idea" or "conceptualization" is also one of the five aggregates (skandhas). Idea or conceptualization is defined as the capacity to grab or isolate certain recurring factors. In English, the term *concept* means "grabbing on to something." The same sense is found in Latin and in German: both the Latin *conceptus* and the German *Begriff* (which comes from *be-greiffen*) convey a sense of grabbing on or selecting. The Buddhist view, we might say, is that for most people there is a conflation or a confusion between our concepts and reality.

Our capacity to show that our mind is able to make distinctions that correspond to reality depends a great deal on this factor called "conceptualization." If there's a defect in our ability to pick out a specific characteristic, it is very difficult to have a precise experience in our lives. We can read about this at some length, but it's enough to know that it's the name for being able to pick out, or grasp, a distinguishing feature, a specific characteristic.

3. Attraction/Directionality

The third factor, *chetana*, is translated variously as "attraction" or "directionality or, as previously discussed, as "will" or "volition." It is the factor that is a full explanation—when we understand its dynamics—of karma. As discussed before, there is no dharma, no factor called karma. There is the dharma called "directionality (of mind)," as it is rendered in MBP. One of the ways mind works is to bend or to move toward its objects.

Yeshé Gyaltsen quotes an Abhidharma text by Asanga, stating, "This particular movement of mind is an activity that propels the mind forward. It has as its function making the mind settle on what is either positive or negative or in between. It's a mental event or a factor that arouses and urges awareness toward its object."[126]

The *Abhidharmakosha*, in the very beginning of chapter 4, the chapter on karma, says that karma consists of that factor called "directionality" and what follows in its wake (what was directed, *chetavitya*).[127] We previously discussed this when we explored the Abhidharma understanding of how karma works. As previously discussed, it is the moving and having been moved. Everything that has been moved as karma can be classed as either a bodily or a vocal act.

So, this movement, or directionality, or intentionality, is a moving-forward of our awareness, and it's a very important factor. Understanding this one dharma allows us to fully understand karma. Once again, we are reminded that the details and dynamics of that one factor are given a full treatment in chapter four of the *Abhidharmakosha* (*karma nirdesha*).

This factor can also be understood in the sense of "attraction," as it is translated in GK. This translation captures the aspect of the movement of mind, which is attracted toward different ways of being. Of course there is quite a difference in English between "attraction," "will," "volition," or "directionality," so maybe it's helpful to know that all these different words are attempts to capture some aspect of what is meant by that one factor chetana.

4. Contact/Rapport

The fourth factor, *sparsha*, is translated as "contact" and "rapport." This is part of the twelvefold chain of dependent co-arising. Contact means something coming together. While the term *contact* is used in GK, *rapport* is the translation found in MBP. Rapport means that something is working together in a good way. Whether you say contact or rapport, both mean that there is the coming together, the meeting, or the working together of three aspects.

You'll be happy to know that these three aspects are columns I, II, III. Already our dhatu analysis helps us a bit. It's the coming together of column I, the sensory capacity or faculty (indriya), together with column II, the sensory field (alambana), and also column III, the perception, consciousness, or integrative capacity (vijnana). When there is rapport or contact, it supports the arising of a full experience. If there's any damage or defect in the rapport, there will not be an experience.

5. Attention/Demanding

The fifth factor, *manasikara*, is sometimes translated as "attention." What does attention mean? It's a process regarding how the mind works: it fixates on an object of concern.

Can we just stay with these objects? MBP, says that this is a factor in which there is a continuity, a being able to hold the mind on its object or its reference point.

What is the difference between a directedness (*chetana*) and attention (*manasikara*)? Both are movements, but what is the difference? The answer given is that directionality is a general movement of the mind, bringing the mind toward its object. We move toward an object: we do not have a specific object in focus yet, but we're just moving toward it. Attention, however, is having the mind fixed on a particular object. Here we have given a sense of the meaning of these five basic factors. Even though they are very important factors involved in our experience, to date there is no uniformity of agreement on how to translate these factors.

OBJECT-DETERMINED FACTORS

	SANSKRIT	GATEWAY TO KNOWLEDGE	MIND IN BUDDHIST PSYCHOLOGY
1.	*chanda*	intention	interest
2.	*adhimoksha*	interest	intensified interest
3.	*smriti*	recollection	inspection
4.	*samadhi*	concentration	intense concentration
5.	*prajna*	discrimination	appreciative discrimination

1. Intention/Interest

The first object-determined factor, *chanda*, is translated as "intention" in GK and "interest" in MBP. Interest is the desire to endow a thing with this or that particular attribute. It's an awareness that gets a bit more involved in the object. It has the function of laying a foundation for actually developing a sense of enthusiasm regarding that object of focus. It seems that if we're not a bit involved with a subject, it's a bit hard to develop enthusiasm regarding it, right? This factor is translated in GK as "intention" in the sense of trying to possess a desired object. It supports the application of exertion.

2. Interest/Intensified Interest

Factor two, *adhimoksha* or *adhimukti*, is translated in GK as "interest." Remember that MBP translated *chanda* as "interest," and they translate this factor here, adhimoksha, as "intensified interest," being able to stay focused on the object. We get interested or involved in something, which is "chanda," and that serves as a basis for developing enthusiasm. And adhimoksha is an intensification of that interest.

These are not random lists; in many cases they are developmental processes. For example, here, there is a sense of how we first get involved in, and then can stay with, any object of awareness. It is the way of the Abhidharma to have lists that have an order and a purpose. What we're seeing here is how we develop the capacity to stay with any object or focus whatsoever. If there's a defect in any of these, if some of these factors are not fully present, then the chosen object of our awareness will not be vivid or clear.

The definition of this intensified interest, according to MBP, is to be able to stick with the thing that has been determined. Its function is so that you cannot be taken away from it. You're not so easily distracted. We might say then that the relationship between chanda and adhimoksha is this: we get a bit involved in something, and this serves as a basis for developing an enthusiastic interest, but unless we can intensify this being involved, it's easy to get distracted.

3. Recollection/Inspection

There are many translations for factor three, *smriti*. It is most commonly translated as "mindfulness" (the Pali for this term is *sati*, as in *satipatthana*). This key factor has been translated in GK as "recollection" and in MBP as "inspection." It names the capacity to stay with an object of focus, so that one does not become distracted. Whatever the focus of the mind is, it doesn't slip away. It doesn't forget or go away from whatever it focuses on; it can stay with that object of awareness.

Remember that this factor of mindfulness is one of the two major factors which are cultivated in shamatha meditation. We previously spoke of a monk chasing an elephant (his out-of-control mind) with a noose (a symbol for being mindful). In time that monk will tether that elephant, thereby taming him, which means he will have calmed his own mind. The Buddha often used this analogy of anchoring the mind with the tether of inspection, or mindfulness.

The function of inspection here is that we won't be so easily distracted. A good calm-abiding meditator can stay with whatever "channel" they have chosen to focus on. They won't just have one moment of seeing (channel 1) and then lots of moments of being absorbed by other channels. They can stay with the chosen object, the chosen channel, moment after moment; they will not be distracted. The name for that capacity to stay with an object is inspection, or more commonly "mindfulness." This is the primary way in which this factor is known. Buddhist practitioners are trying to be sufficiently calm to be able to mindfully stay focused on the object they choose, without being distracted.

But this factor of inspection also has another meaning, one that seems rather different from the technical definition of mindfulness as it is usually understood. This other sense of mindfulness is what is termed "memory." We say that someone has a "good memory" or has a "poor memory." What does that mean? This same factor of inspection accounts for both the capacity to bring into present experience something that occurred in the past (memory) and the ability to stay with it (mindfulness). A person who has a bad memory cannot so easily select and bring into present experience something that has previously occurred.

The Buddhists, as "psychologists," made the following claim, which is amenable to verification: The difference between having a good or bad memory is determined by having good or bad mindfulness. That is to say, an indication for one's memory is whether or not one can mindfully stay with a chosen object without getting distracted. You can see how these two come together.

Perhaps one of the reasons why we are distracted, why our mindfulness and memory are not so good, is because we choose to forget all the unwholesome actions that we have committed in the past. In fact, in Tibetan Buddhist Vajrayana traditions, there's a very powerful way of bringing to the surface and then banishing to "another place" all the past accumulations of unwholesome karmic activity. It's known as the practice of Vajrasattva. The practice of bringing to the surface and then acknowledging such unwholesome past actions is said to cleanse and purify our mental continuum.[128]

Now we can see that "inspection," "recollection," "mindfulness," or "memory" are different ways of talking about the same function, which is the capacity to stay with whatever is chosen as an object of focus.

4. Concentration/Intense Concentration

We come to factor four, *samadhi*, which is rendered by GK as "concentration" and by MBP as "intense concentration." It's defined as being able to have the mind singly fixed. This refers to the well-known notion of "one-pointedness" in Buddhist texts; it is a single-minded concentration. If we can do this, its function is to support correct or "right" cognition. According to Buddhist traditions, if we want to see things "as they are," we have to go into deep and precise focusing, deep and precise concentration. It doesn't mean thinking hard about something. It means, rather, bringing the entire working of the mind, laser-like, to a very precise capacity to focus. This is what allows a full and correct awareness to emerge.

A common translation for this is "meditation." Meditation here doesn't mean some vague sense of being calm or spacious; it means being able to bring the mind to a very precise focus so that we can see what is going on *as it goes on*. You can see that, in a way, all of these factors are moving to an ever more focused and precise focusing. We can learn to apply that to any object whatsoever, any object that we may want to focus on.

5. Discrimination/Appreciative Discrimination

Now we come to the fifth object-determined factor, *prajna*, which I have translated here as "discernment," but is also translated in GK as "discrimination" and in MBP as "appreciative discrimination." It's the ability to precisely note and firmly establish what is going on with these various factors. This factor has as its definition the capacity to know factors,[129] and its function is to cut through any sense of confusion or doubt regarding the nature of the factors.

12

Wholesome Mental Factors

Now we come to a consideration of Abhidharma categories regarding so-called wholesome and unwholesome factors of existence. So far, we've explored, in the same order of discussion found in works by Vasubandhu and other Abhidharma-inspired texts, general and object-specific factors of experience. But, of course, we do things with our minds other than simply being aware of objects; we get involved in them, in ways that make things go well and in ways that make things go poorly. Now we move on to a discussion of styles of attention and distraction, ways of getting involved in focusing the mind. We will first look at the eleven "wholesome" or "good news" factors before examining the "unwholesome" or "bad news" factors.

Remember that all of these factors have one thing in common: They are all the basic building blocks of the universe; they are the factors of existence; they are the energy packets; and they constitute "us" and our "world." As such, one would expect to find a listing and description of not only basic cognition and processes of attention but also listings and descriptions of "wholesome" and "unwholesome" factors. As we've said before, karma seems to go in two different ways; things are either going well or they're not. If we cultivate the factors called good or wholesome, it will result in situations of ease, spaciousness, and relaxation. Eventually, a good thought bears as its fruit (some time in the future) an experience of well-being; a bad thought, an unwholesome thought, will bear as its fruit an upsetting or painful experience.

"Wholesomeness" is defined in the Buddhist traditions as that which truly moves us away from tendencies toward suffering. That's the concise way it's defined. Wholesome means truly moving along on the path to cessation of suffering. Wholesome means that which, when cultivated, moves us out of a narrow way of being and suffering and along the path toward full and complete enlightenment. That's the sole criterion of judging, and only secondarily does it have something to do with social norms and standards.

WHOLESOME FACTORS

	SANSKRIT	GATEWAY TO KNOWLEDGE	MIND IN BUDDHIST PSYCHOLOGY
1.	*shraddha*	faith	confidence/trust
2.	*hri*	conscience	self-respect
3.	*apatrapa*	shame	decorum
4.	*alobha*	nonattachment	nonattachment
5.	*advesha*	nonaggression	nonhatred
6.	*amoha*	nondelusion	nondeludedness
7.	*virya*	diligence	diligence
8.	*prasrabdhi*	pliancy	alertness
9.	*apramada*	conscientiousness	concern
10.	*upeksha*	equanimity	equanimity
11.	*avihimsa*	nonviolence	nonviolence

After a consideration of these wholesome factors, we will explore the "un-wholesome" factors—first the primary ones and then the secondary ones. At that point we will come to see that "unwholesomeness" is anything that blocks, suppresses, or mystifies our movement along the path to the cessation of suf-fering. And when I say "mystify," I mean being conditioned by something that does not correspond to reality; it's blocking wholesomeness. This is why "wrong view" is an unwholesome factor. Anything that increases our habits of suffering is unwholesome (the words *good* and *bad* are a bit heavy, and evil certainly does not apply in these Buddhist contexts). The key point, throughout these explorations, is how we are with our "mind," our habits of attention, and our awareness. In the *Dhammapada*, there is a phrase that is worthy of continued reflection in this regard: "We are what we think, having become what we thought."[130] So, let's now go through these wholesome factors, one by one.

1. Faith/Confidence/Trust

The first wholesome factor, *shraddha*, is translated as "confidence," "trust," or "faith."[131] The *Abhidharmakosha* talks of having a mental certainty, a "clarity" and "surety."[132] It is not "faith" so much as being clear about three things: the Buddha, the Dharma, and the Sangha. If we have mental clarity about what Buddha, Dharma, and Sangha means, this factor called "confidence" is present. It has nothing to do with believing or having "faith" in the sense of blind allegiance or superstition. Such a sense would, in fact, seem to go against basic Buddhist understandings of "wholesomeness." This is perhaps a rather important point. If people ask you, "Oh, so you're a Buddhist; what do you believe in?" what would you say? I would probably reply that I try not to "believe" anything or take it "on faith." Another way to put this is that such "faith" can be understood as not having correct view.

There are two other topics that are elaborated with respect to this term "confidence." One is being mentally clear about the four noble truths. When we are mentally clear about suffering, its cause, its end, and the path to that, there is confidence present. The other concerns karma. When we understand, when we're mentally clear, about karma, its causes, and its results, there is confidence present. For those who don't have a religious or spiritual bent, they can leave aside talk of the Buddha, Dharma, and Sangha. Maybe they can even leave aside talk of the four noble truths. But surely they might be encouraged to think deeply on the relationship between their intentions and their subsequent experiences. As they begin to see that there is a very close connection between these two, something might begin to occur. And that "something" is also called "confidence."

In the Tibetan Buddhist tradition, *The Words of My Perfect Teacher* by Patrul Rinpoche says that when one goes for refuge, this *going* means that one is learning what corresponds with a true refuge. Refuge is a metaphor here. It means "a shelter." Refuge refers to a true and real shelter that we can go to and that will protect us or bring us to a state of being completely beyond the wind and the rain of changing circumstances that cause upset and confusion.

Patrul Rinpoche also says that one of the indications that one has learned how to go for refuge is that increasingly this factor of confidence and trust is present in us. If we are not so confident or trusting, from this point of view, among other things, perhaps there is a defect in our understanding of how to go for refuge.

2. Conscience/Self-Respect

The second wholesome factor, *hri*, is translated as "self-respect" or "having a conscience." The great fourteenth-century Tibetan Dzogchen master Longchenpa developed a rather interesting approach to talking about these factors. He said, in summary, that most people have no idea about karma, about causes and effects. To discover how this works is already a great revelation. And to discover that there are two ways in which karma operates is even more precise. That is to say, there are unwholesome and there are wholesome ways of proceeding. We already said that wholesome means it will be of benefit and we will feel good later. Unwholesome means the opposite. He said this factor of self-respect can be glossed as "me" or "face" and "hot," which together makes a "hot face,"[133] thus referring to "embarrassment." That means that we have the capacity to know whether or not our life is in accord with wholesomeness or unwholesomeness. I know the difference, and I'm working with that difference.

If we're disturbed, if we're traumatized, we will be scattered, we will be chaotic, and then even the ten factors of general functioning will be disturbed. We won't know how these good and wholesome factors work. We'll have the opposite going on, so it's a little bit difficult. But sometimes we say, "Ah, this is wholesome; I should cultivate that. This is unwholesome; I should leave it alone." Sometimes we have a little bit of space to note that something we are about to get involved in is unwholesome and shouldn't be practiced. It doesn't correspond to what is most basic from the viewpoint of a spacious heart. Having not engaged in that action, even though provoked to do so, indicates the presence of self-respect, a conscience. Those who have a very shaky sense of self-respect have not been able to cultivate or stabilize this factor.

3. Shame/Decorum

The third factor, *apatrapa*, is sometimes rendered as "shame" or "decorum." These days the English word *shame* does not have a good connotation. It sounds a bit abusive, as if we're blaming someone, right? What does this factor connote? It is, in a way, similar to "self-respect," and the two are often mentioned together. Whereas "self-respect" has as its reference seeing that some behavior does not correspond with our "true" nature and then not engaging in that behavior, leading to a growing sense of "self-respect," "decorum" has to do with recognizing that a possible behavior with respect to a group affiliation (like being in a sangha or an intentional community) might be going against the norms of that group. "Decorum" is related to other groups of people or perhaps a sangha situation, where we are agreeing to a set of rules and procedures that are wholesome. We voluntarily entered into this agreement and we do our best. From time to time we may note that we are being provoked to engage in an unwholesome action with respect to that group, meaning we are about to go against the collective norms. We are not going against a set of coercive, imposed laws but rather against the norms of an intentional community that is trying to work to bring about a greater situation of well-being.

With that difference, both "self-respect" and "decorum" are similar. We're provoked, but there's a bit of space to know the difference between what is wholesome and unwholesome. When we know something is unwholesome and we do not engage in it, there is a feeling that one has, in a wholesome way, maintained a sense of self-respect and decorum. Whether it's with respect to a group or with respect to oneself, they both have to do with being on the brink of being provoked to engage in an unwholesome action and not succumbing to performing the action. We don't do it and we feel good. Longchenpa reminds us that having the knowledge that karma works in two ways, either in a wholesome or unwholesome way, allows us to begin to work with what to do when we are tempted to engage in something unwholesome.

Perhaps it is useful to recall a phrase in the Pali version of the Vinaya that describes how one trains to avoid unwholesomeness. In spite of many translations which say "Thou shalt not steal, kill," and so on, here, the precise language is different. The phrase "do not" or "thou shalt not" is not used. Rather, the term *training* (Pali *sikam*) is employed. One undergoes "training" in abstention from unwholesome actions. To this word is added the phrase *step-by-step* (Pali *padam*); thus, we train in stages (Pali *sikam padam*) to avoid unwholesomeness.

According to the Sri Lankan Theravadin monk Bhante Seelawimala, the word *padam* in this phrase has two meanings: One such meaning of *stage* is according to what your stage is in the practice of living according to the codes of conduct in the vinaya, that is, according to whether you are a beginner (a novice monk or nun) or a more seasoned ordained follower of the Buddha, a fully ordained monk or nun. The other sense of stage is according to your status in life—that is, whether you are a layman or laywoman, a novice monk or nun, or a fully ordained monk or nun. One's training depends on one's status in those senses. The last part of the phrase is *samadiami*. Here "samadiami" (I go) carries the sense of "I am voluntarily going or following this step-by-step training." This means I am going into it voluntarily. I am gradually training myself in, for example, abstention from such and such. This is quite different from the directive "thou shalt not," right? So, according to these understandings, we are encouraged to train our ethical muscles gradually; according to our status and lifestyle, we learn to honor these codes of training in good conduct. The training programs are different depending upon one's status in life, whether one is ordained (as a monk or nun) or is a nonordained householder. And even within those divisions of ordination, there are differences: the training of a novice monk or nun is somewhat different from a fully ordained one, according to the number of vows they have taken.

I think we might refer to both "self-respect" and also "decorum" as the Buddhist equivalent of what in the West are called "healthy boundaries." How might a Buddhist practitioner engage in healthy boundaries? The response might be that one is learning to work with provocations to engage in unwholesome activities. And when we don't, that is wholesome.

The key to this, again based on Longchenpa, is that only when these wholesome factors are alive and present in us can they help to stabilize the factor of confidence. In other words, it's very difficult to have confidence if we don't have the habit of self-respect and decorum, if we do not respect ourselves. Longchenpa says when decorum and self-respect are present, they support the emergence of confidence. This suggests that if there's a defect in our confidence, we should perhaps look at these factors of self-respect and decorum. Maybe our way of working with what we imagine to be wholesome and unwholesome, for example the adoption of the moral phrases such as "thou shalt not," may feel a bit coercive and externally imposed and not corresponding to our nature.

Longchenpa goes on to say that if we have self-respect and decorum, and we're really experiencing this confidence, then we're in a good situation to benefit from the presence of a spiritual friend or teacher. Many problems regarding the ability of working well with a spiritual friend or teacher could be traced to an interruption or a lack of stability in terms of our own self-respect, our own decorum, and our own confidence.

4. Nonattachment

Now we move on to the fourth factor, *alobha,* is translated as "nonattachment." It is the first of three factors—which include nonattachment, nonaggression, and nondelusion—that are wholesome factors that seem to have as their definition the absence of unwholesomeness. This is something to think about. That is, the absence of these factors, not having attachment, aggression, or delusion, is said to be positive.

We can remember what *positive* means in this context and that it is translated in different ways: wholesome, good, or positive. As we said, these are factors that help to move us along the path in the direction of going beyond all suffering and sources of suffering. It does not at all mean these are factors that make us *feel good*. Feeling good is not the basis for deciding what is positive, nor is feeling bad a basis for declaring something is "unwholesome." Though we mentioned this before, it probably bears repeating: both "wholesome" and "unwholesome" are defined, in Buddhist contexts, in terms of the goal of Buddhism, or, we might say more precisely, in terms of the goal of a spiritual being, which is to come to a certain settled presence of spacious awareness that is beyond all upset, forever. It is to become liberated from suffering and its sources. For now, it is enough to know that these factors called "positive" move us in that direction. If we don't have confidence or trust that this is so, that lack of confidence or trust itself may upset us, which we will talk about shortly.

Now to the factor called "nonattachment." What is it? Nonattachment is the state in which one is not attached to anything that occurs in this life and all the things involved with it. In fact, many Tibetan Buddhist teachers have said that the primary difference between an ordinary being and one who really has a spiritual calling—one who may be, as is said in Buddhist texts, "on the path"—may be linked to this factor of nonattachment.

It is said that ordinary beings do everything as if only this life matters, a way of being that is oftentimes supported by the wrong view that there is *only* this life. Being not attached means one has discovered a way of being in which one is not so obsessed or involved with the various things that arise in this life.

We might take solace from what Trungpa Rinpoche once asked: What might it look like on the ground concretely to not be so attached to this life? To this, he suggested that it's not that we are indifferent or unaware. It's not that at all. It's that we find a way to go through life that's a bit more workable. If we talk about driving a car, at some point when we are learning to drive a car, we have to learn how to turn corners. In the beginning, of course, when we are just learning to drive, we pray that all the roads will be straight. But at some point there comes a special teaching, that sometimes even if you don't want to drive on a curvy road, those curves are there. And if you want to go on that road, you must find a way, even though it doesn't correspond to our nature or our beliefs about the way things should be. Maybe turning ourselves in our car, in a somewhat coordinated way, with the curvature of the road of life, as it actually presents itself, is not such a bad thing.

In the beginning, we might be shocked when a turn in the road comes. This turn in the road is sometimes called a problem or a situation that has to be dealt with. When we say that, we are already a bit upset. Why does there have to be such a situation? My idea of the road is that it should be straight, and I had a plan that was a straight plan. I had not planned to go on a road that had turns. If we are a more seasoned driver, we know, of course, that many roads have turns. We may insist and demand a full and complete map of precisely where and when every turn will come. (This analogy is almost obsolete now with the advent of GPS. But the analogy still holds, especially when that GPS suddenly fails, right?) That map better correspond to what the actual landscape is. But if you talk to somebody who's been around for a while, they will say, "We will do our best, but there is no guarantee."

Attachment to how we imagine events "should" occur makes us a bit shaky. In fact, what we might call "this life" consists only of "events." Nonattachment is learning how not to be so attached to what occurs in this life. It's a very deep thing. One more thing to mention about nonattachment is this: now that we know how pervasive its importance is, is it operating and present only when there are moments of not being so obsessed or attached? Not being attached is the positive actual presence of something that is real. The Abhidharma texts go on to ask, what is its function? What's so positive about it? (When we say function, I want to be very clear what we mean here. This is an energy packet. This is an actual, vivid, living presence of something that's real. It is not a mental thing according to these traditions.) It says something rather nice and startling. It says that the function of nonattachment is that, when it is present, it serves as a basis for us not being so easily caught up in unwholesome activity of any sort whatsoever. This is not a small thing.

5. Nonaggression/Nonhatred

Now we come to the fifth factor, *advesha*, translated as "nonaggression" or "nonhatred." Nonhatred is the absence of the intention to harm living beings. It is also the absence to engage in arguing or quarreling in situations that we find frustrating. Nonhatred is also the absence of engaging in causing suffering for those whom we regard as the cause of our frustration. Thus, nonhatred is the absence of inflicting suffering on those who cause frustration in us. This is something positive. And it is said that it functions when it is present to serve as a basis for not getting caught up in what might call "bad" karma, something that will be bad for us in the future. It goes on to say that this nonhatred or nonaggression is the awareness that, in some situations, we have no intention whatsoever to pay it back, to inflict it upon others. And this is considered a good thing. It is good for us and good for others.

6. Nondelusion/Nondeludedness

The sixth factor, *amoha*, is translated as "nondelusion" or "nondeludedness." It's kind of a catchall term. Nondelusion is said to be active when there's a thorough understanding that comes from having received spiritual instructions, having thought about them deeply, and then coming to an understanding of their import. When there is a thorough comprehension of the instructions we have received, this is called being nondeluded, and again, like the other two, it serves as a basis for not becoming involved in unwholesomeness.

One studies so as to become clear about the subject matter, to be clear about the goal, or the target. But study is never enough. When you do engage in "target practice," it doesn't mean simply identifying the target. There is something more involved. In archery it is not the point to simply locate the target; something called a bow and an arrow are also involved, right? Having studied what a target is, that's the study part. Then, you are actually encouraged to bend the bow, aim the arrow, and with a very relaxed, calm mind and body, using the eye of discriminating awareness, finally to release the arrow. Then we "practice" actually hitting that target. When we give these definitions here, all we're doing is listing them and how they function. We can then see whether or not we want to pursue an actual experience of these factors. But we may be surprised. Have you ever noticed that when you read what the ingredients are in something you thought you might want to eat that list often doesn't correspond to your experience of eating it? And then for some silly reason we get upset; it's rather a strange reaction. It's as if there should not have been a "curve in the road."

Beginners are easily upset when there's a curve in the road. Intermediate practitioners know there's going to be a curve, and they probably try to get a more precise map of where the curves will come. They might even no longer think about where that road is going to end up. But they still obsess about those curves; they want to get the *essential teaching* on where and when those curves will be coming up in their journey. Intermediate folks obsess about getting teachings about those curves, those possible pitfalls. They might feel that, armed with such a map, they're not going to be so surprised when they hit a curve. But quite often they don't negotiate the curve with much of a sense of panache, of confident joy. They're rather uptight. Have you noticed?

Advanced, or "seasoned," Dharma practitioners do not obsess so much. They've learned the habit of knowing that when the curve will come is not certain, nor is it even reliably predictable. They may have had many years of being fascinated by secret teachings on the true nature of those curves, and they sometimes remember that relaxation and acceptance is a key; they discover that because the teachings never completely correspond to (nor can they be used to absolutely guarantee) how things will be. When they hit the curve, they're not so anxious, they're not so attached, and it shows in how they take the curves.

As an extreme, of course, we've read about and even watched on television those who engage in "extreme sports." Those race-car drivers, who are experts at negotiating curves at extremely high speeds, serve as an inspiration to all of us. But we shouldn't think that our body and car is the same as their body and car. Hence the warning: "Don't try this at home, professionals only." Ngor Tartsé Khen Rinpoche, the former abbot of the Sakya Ngor Monastery, had a very interesting translation for the word *yogis*.[134] He called them professionals. Maybe we don't have to be so uptight about those curves in the road.

7. Diligence

Next comes the seventh factor, *virya*, translated as "diligence." The so-called general factors of "interest" serve as the basis for the arising of diligence. A professional has lots of diligence.

What is diligence? It is an attitude which moves in such a way that it is always active, devoted, not shaken or thrown off, not easily turned back, and not defeated. It's said that when this factor of diligence or energy is there, it brings to realization everything that is in accord with what is spiritually positive.

We should say "spiritual diligence" here because we might think, "Well, some great criminals have lots of diligence; they are devoted and active in not turning away from their activities, even though they might be regarded by others (or sometimes even themselves) as unwholesome." In this context, however, one understands that diligence is being continually focused on what is positive, what is wholesome. Vasubandhu reminds us that diligence is an antidote against spiritual laziness, and it's the presence of that energy that moves us toward what is spiritually positive.

Let us think a bit about this. If the presence of this factor called "spiritual diligence" is defined as focused or helping spiritually positive factors, then we have a very precise key to thinking about our own level of "energy," which here means the flow of our intentions, our desires to engage in different activities. It is said that the presence of spiritually positive energy helps us with our true energy, our authentic spiritual core. This kind of energy is said to correspond to our basic nature or actual state; it is not the energy of addiction or aggression. When we've learned to cultivate positive factors, at some point we will discover that we have more energy. It's like a snowball effect. The more we learn to cultivate what is positive, the more energy we have.

The opposite is also true, which is to say, having unstable or shaky energy is often a sign that we have not cultivated and brought forth in our life spiritually positive factors. This is a very important term, and if we think, "How is it possible that all those bodhisattvas, all those teachers seem to be so energetic? I don't have that energy," we have a key to how and why they might have access to such energy. Perhaps they are cultivating positive wholesome actions. Perhaps they are cultivating nonattachment, nonaggression, and nondelusion. It's as if to say the cultivation of not being attached, aggressive, or deluded, just that, helps with our energy.

8. Pliancy/Alertness

The eighth factor, *prasrabdhi*, is translated as "pliancy" or "alertness." There are two forms of it: pliancy with respect to the body and pliancy with respect to the mind. When this factor of pliancy of body and mind is present, it functions to shift us away from feelings of being sluggish, of having no energy.

We have sluggishness in our body and in our mind. Maybe this factor of pliancy is why "bodywork" is so popular. For people whose energy is low and stuck, or even for people who are a bit depressed (not clinically depressed), bodywork is a way of shifting energy or, in the language of the Abhidharma, of cultivating pliancy. It's said that when one is relaxed and pliant in the body, one may feel like a piece of cotton floating in the air. When we have stabilized that feeling—this lightness, this buoyancy—what we call "the body" can be directed toward any positive action whatsoever; it won't be blocked. This is a very positive factor. This is pliancy with respect to the body.

There is also pliancy with respect to the mind. Mental pliancy means that we are sufficiently relaxed with our powers of concentrating. This removes mental sluggishness. When we don't have mental sluggishness, it's said that the mind can move toward any object of concentration whatsoever, and it will operate smoothly. The great Tibetan Buddhist savant Tsongkhapa and many others have said that concentration is the "king" that rules the mind. When he is seated, he is immovable like Mount Meru. If this king travels, he can go wherever there is positivity, and in moving like this he brings about great happiness. The form of the great happiness that he brings consists of pliability of body and pliability of mind. This is a way of not being conditioned or trapped by sluggishness. When one learns to integrate this feeling, it's said that it spreads, increases, and becomes pleasurable. It becomes very intense and a means of doing away with any obscuration whatsoever. It's an important factor.

9. Conscientiousness/Concern

The ninth factor, *apramada*, is translated as "concern," "conscientiousness," or being "careful." The Buddhist master Thinley Norbu Rinpoche would quite often remind his students to not be careless but to be careful. It is a very special kind of awareness.

This factor works together with nonattachment, nonaggression, nondelusion, and diligence. When those factors are present, it makes it easier to be conscientious. Conscientiousness here means that which protects the mind against engaging in activity that cannot truly satisfy or be of benefit. It doesn't mean being very concerned about this and that. It's a way of protecting and guarding against going in a direction that will just cause trouble in the future. It protects against that which is not reliable.

One large class of things that are not reliable is all the various factors of upset (which we will explore at length in the next section on "unwholesome" factors, both primary and secondary factors). It's said that conscientiousness protects against getting involved in or falling prey to upset, as if to say, whenever we are upset, it is a result of having been careless. It's said that if we learn how to go through life with great care, it becomes a very helpful way of cultivating what is truly excellent, and Buddhists seem to feel this is true for both this world and the world beyond. It helps one to cultivate the inherently wholesome qualities, all the positive values associated with the enlightened, awakened state of being. And it is also considered to be of benefit in cultivating what is truly positive in this worldly state of affairs. If we learn to proceed with care and not too much attachment, aggression, or delusion, and if we apply a bit of energy and pliancy, we will soon be able to taste, concretely at the level of experience, what is truly excellent and truly beneficial. All of these factors work together.

10. Equanimity

The tenth factor, *upeksha*, is translated as "equanimity." Equanimity is said to be the opposite of emotional instability. It is calm and spontaneous presence of awareness. Equanimity functions to protect from the arising of emotional instability. Equanimity is the name given to when our awareness is abiding in a state of nonattachment, nonhatred, nondeludedness, and perseverance. It means that we can then take our awareness and fully concentrate on any object whatsoever. It is related to having present all the means and techniques associated with the practice of calm abiding. For it's said that when one has fully mastered all the nine phases of calm abiding, one is no longer at risk of or subject to being overexcited or depressed, the two primary forms of distraction in such practice. So, as the text says, when there is equanimity, the mind is there, spontaneously as it is.

11. Nonviolence

The last factor here, *avihimsa*, is translated as "nonviolence" and is related to loving-kindness. It's related to a form of not hating, and its function is not to become malicious. It is also related to patience and acceptance because maliciousness has the energy of impatience within it. It's said that nonviolence is patient in a particular way. It is patient acceptance that tends toward and expresses itself with the thought or sentiment: "How wonderful it would be if those who suffer could be released from their suffering." This is the technical definition of nonviolence. It has as a defining characteristic an attitude in which one cannot find even the slightest hint of wishing to inflict or repay suffering with suffering.

What These Wholesome Factors Have in Common

Next, there's a section that talks about what all of these wholesome factors have in common and that clarifies in what way they are wholesome or positive. And there's a very long section that encourages us to cultivate these factors and that thoroughly shows how each of these factors is truly positive and how they will help us to negotiate all those curves in the road without being so upset. When these factors are not so stable, or when we think they're not that important, this lack of positive factors being present is unwholesome, meaning we are at risk for being upset (if not now, then in the future).

Unwholesome factors of upset are very important to identify. As a matter of fact, one way of talking about the path to going beyond suffering is simply to be rid of upset, and to stabilize those realizations beyond upset.

Getting rid of upset clears a space for the arising of realization, and these two aspects of the path are very closely linked.

Wholesome Sense of "I"

There is a healthy, cool sense of "I" that actually helps us walk the path; that is self-respect, decorum, feeling good, and loving-kindness. Everybody seems to need it. And everybody has access to this sense of wholesomeness. Everybody can increase it. But, of course, there is also a bad, or "unwholesome" sense of "I." What I mean by "bad" here is that it blocks the path. We think things are going to stay the way they are. Or we think that things should stay the same. And such concern is driven by hope and fear; it is driven by what we characterized previously as eight worldly dharmas.

13

Unwholesome Mental Factors

Now we will look the primary factors of upset and their relation to the secondary factors of upset. First, however, it's important to say something about the use of the term *upset*. Sometimes people refer to these factors simply as varieties of "emotional" upset. But, for instance, it's not clear that "belief" (number 6 in the list of primary factors) is an "emotional" upset. I use this word *upset* for the Sanskrit word *klesha* because it indicates something is a bit out of balance. Also, it avoids this problematic term *emotion* or *emotional*. We might say that there are both "mental" and "emotional" aspects of upset.

There are six primary factors of upset and a list of twenty secondary factors of upset. What is the relationship between the primary and secondary factors? The primary factors are rather like parents, whereas the secondary factors are like their children; they "come from" or are rooted in those primary factors.

Anger and Its Secondary Factors

Let's give an example. Factor number 2, anger, of the primary factors has as its "children," its progeny, secondary factors numbered (1) fury or indignation, (2) resentment, (4) spite, and (10) malice.

We might say that these children are experientially accessible, living factors of upset. The primary factors, then, are more like tendencies or basic orientations. For instance, when the factor of anger is being expressed actually and concretely in our lives, this energy of aggression tends toward rather different and specific forms. One of them is number 1, fury or indignation. Can we relate to that in our lives? It is present when we might feel: "How dare you! How could you! Things were so perfect, and then you (or someone) spoiled it!" That is the energy of "indignation"; it is very precise; it is related to and rooted in "anger" as the "parent." In that moment, when we have to deal with this out-of-control child of upset called "indignation," we forget who the parents are. If we are very clever, we might want to call the parents and say, "You need to control your child." This is an example to help us understand the relation between the primary and secondary factors. Secondary here means "the child of." And every child had parents who "gave birth" to them.

Another child of arrogance or anger is "resentment." The great German philosopher Friedrich Nietzsche wrote about the importance of resentment. Even within technical Western philosophical literature this factor of resentment, coming from repression, is a wide and pervasively observed phenomenon. Sometimes we feel resentment, and we are just waiting for something to confirm our being justified in that resentment. Then it comes out, and we express it. Often there is a time lag; this factor of waiting is largely unconscious. There has been a repression. There have been previous acts of unkindness and aggression that have pushed down the energy. It is just waiting, as if under pressure. And then the slightest little thing can set us off. Both indignation—how dare someone!—and a sense of resentment are concrete expressions of the energy called anger.

Number 4, "spite," in the list of secondary factors, is also associated with that "parent" anger. Spite means we are enjoying inflicting pain on others. Spite or malice is intending to make someone feel bad.

Anger, the parent, expresses itself through its children; it flows sometimes in the form of wanting to harm, sometimes in the form of taking pleasure, and sometimes in the form of outrage. We begin to see the children of that angry parent. We will need to go into some of the details of these really interesting factors. They may even seem to be more interesting than the wholesome factors; maybe this is because it is a bit easier to identify them in our everyday life. One of the things we might discover is that what we call our energy of spaciousness, our basic sanity, is hidden or obscured by our habits of upset. The biggest "habit" of upset, which doesn't even seem to be an emotion, is the primary factor number 6, belief. We have a lot of opinions, a lot of beliefs. We think this actually corresponds to the way things are.

Attachment and Its Secondary Factors

We gave the example of anger, and I will now give another example. The very first primary factor on this list is "attachment." Attachment is a rather broad thing. We do not go around saying, "I am attached. I wish I was not attached." We have rather concrete experiences, and it is interesting to see which "children" of this parent upset are actually running around—that is to say, which ones of my actual experiences of upset belong to the family of attachment. The main work here is to see who these children are because they correspond rather closely to what we would call "having" an upset. It seems that there are at least twenty ways in which we can be upset, twenty basic energy packets of upset. This list seems to cover a great deal of what I experience in my life; it goes a long way in helping me identify the many forms of upset which are common occurrences. It allows me to expand my vocabulary. I do not just say, "I am miserable" or "I am upset." I have twenty different ways to sing that song.

For instance, with respect to the primary upset called "attachment," it might be helpful to know who the children are. Let's think concretely in terms of energy. The energy of attachment, and being fascinated or involved in attachment, flows in many different ways. There are nine different "children" associated with the parent "attachment." These nine secondary factors of upset are:

- Being stingy, or having avarice or parsimony (6)
- Being pretentious or deceitful (7)
- Being dishonest or hypocritical (8)
- Being a bit self-infatuated or inflated (9)

- Having a lack of conscience or being shameless (11)
- Having a lack of propriety (12)
- Being lethargic or gloomy (13)
- Being a bit overexcited or ebullient (14)
- Being a bit desultory or distractible or just being distracted (20)

How Emotional Upset Occurs

These lists of primary and secondary factors of upset provide a rich source for what one might call an "experiential phenomenology of upset"—that is, a study of the phenomena of how emotional upset occurs, both in its overt expression (twenty secondary factors) and also in the predispositions that set us up toward such expression, the prior conditioning (the six primary factors). For example, how is it that when this primary factor called attachment is rather active, any of its the children may come out and play?

In the contexts we are now exploring, the term *emotion*, or *emotional upset*, corresponds more precisely to the list of secondary unwholesome factors, the so-called children whose parents are the primary factors of upset.

Furthermore, if we look at the six factors listed as primary—attachment, anger, arrogance, ignorance, doubt, and belief—three of them (ignorance, doubt, and belief) might not seem like upsets to us. Whether primary or secondary, however, all of them have in common the potential movement of a disturbing energy. We may not be disturbed by ignorance or doubt, and certainly my beliefs do not disturb me, right? But belief here means you believe "This is me." This is the energy that works in the background and impedes and upsets our ability to walk on the path to full and complete liberation. This is what these Buddhist texts suggest.

Another, more contemporary way to think about these primary and secondary factors is that they indicate there is "a disturbance in the force." It's as if there is some kind of Star Wars going on. The Buddhist version of this war, however, would be to suggest that sometimes there is no disturbance in the force. And that is the good news. The positive factors we talked about previously help the disturbance in the force to settle down and make possible a clearing, a way in which we can actually see how to proceed. We might say, then, that the big difference between the positive factors and the factors of upset has to do with this "force" (our basic sanity, our buddha nature). Even though we might not presently feel upset, there is still a stirring, an imbalance, and a lingering energy of potential upset, right? It may be repressed; it may be from the past, but it is there. We will give a very brief definition of the six primary factors before launching into the fun part—those twenty secondary factors.

PRIMARY FACTORS OF UPSET

	SANSKRIT	GATEWAY TO KNOWLEDGE	MIND IN BUDDHIST PSYCHOLOGY
1.	*raga*	attachment	cupidity-attachment
2.	*pratigha*	anger	anger
3.	*mana*	arrogance	arrogance
4.	*avidya*	ignorance	lack of awareness
5.	*vichikitsa*	doubt	indecision
6.	*drishti*	belief	opinionatedness

1. Attachment

The first of the six primary factors of upset, *raga*, is translated as "attachment." It is the energy that makes us run after anything in the three levels of samsara. The first level is the desire realm. Each of the six life forms (the hell beings, the hungry ghosts, animals, humans, titans or quarreling beings, and the so-called divine ones) is part of the desire realm because they each have a primary factor of upset that motivates them. Hell beings are primarily motivated by anger, pretas or hungry ghosts are primarily motivated by being stingy or avaricious, and animals are primarily motivated by being ignorant or rather clueless, having dangerous confusion. The so-called human realm is dominated by a fickle and changeable fascination. (By the way, this is why advertising works so well with humans; we are always wanting something "new" or "better.") The so-called titans, the quarreling ones (would-be gods), are dominated by jealousy, and the so-called gods are primarily motivated by pride or arrogance.

Whenever any of these factors of upset is primary, we are "in" that realm of desire. If we are dominated by anger, everything is hellish, and our experience for that period of time is called being a hell being. It is as if to say who we are is what we are thinking, and how we think is where we are. The Abhidharma gives us a clue, which helps break down a solid idea of self that is separate from the world. Who we are, where we are, and what we are doing are all the same thing, asked in different ways. You can even make a practice out of this: Who we are is where we are. Who we are is what we are doing. Where are we? What are we doing? There is no escape. It is a rather sly game. It is not the way we think. We think, "I am this way and I just happen to be doing that." But according to this scheme, if we are angry, we are hell beings. If we are arrogant, we are so-called gods, etc. These six realms are not at all some mythological locations that exist apart from exactly the precision of our own mental processes. Attachment is running after things dominated by these primary factors of upset. And that is called the desire realm.

The second level of samsara involves running after the realm of form, which means meditative experiences, and the third level of samsara involves running after experiences of the formless realm, which means extremely subtle meditative experiences. All these three types of experience constitute samsara, whether focused on "desire," "form," or "formless" modes. And all such experiences are temporary; they won't last. This, then, is the range of that primary factor called attachment. We are attached to and run after or are driven by charged situations and meditative experiences, and that accounts for our whole life.

2. Anger

Factor number 2 is anger. Anger here means, as we explored previously, to have a vindictive attitude toward sentient beings we do not like, toward frustration, and toward whatever might cause our frustration. We do not like frustration. We want to reject and push away frustration altogether. Insofar as other people may be the source of frustration, we want to push them away too. We have a very low capacity for accepting or being present with frustration. The function of anger (now that we know something about how it is defined) is that it serves as a basis for our finding fault with almost anything that occurs in our life, and it blocks us from having any concrete experiences of happiness.

3. Arrogance

The third factor, *pratigha*, is translated as "arrogance." Arrogance is defined as the quality of having a mind that's a bit inflated. This factor serves as a basis for the arising of disrespect. We think we know what is going on, so we disrespect and we don't pay attention to what does not correspond to what we think is going on. That is a sense of arrogance. We do not necessarily go around saying "I am arrogant." We say, "I know," meaning "I know better." We disregard what does not correspond to what we say we know. It also serves as a basis for frustration when what is actually going on does not correspond to my inflated sense of what should be going on. This primary factor has a full treatment in the Buddhist literature. The MBP lists seven kinds of arrogance: (1) arrogance, (2) excessive arrogance, (3) taking pride in having excessive arrogance, (4) arrogance which has the habit of reflecting "me," (5) the arrogance of showing off, (6) the arrogance of dismissing or of thinking small or demeaning things, and finally (7) the arrogance that is completely perverted, the arrogance that completely turns away from what is actually true.

4. Ignorance

The fourth factor, *avidya*, is translated as "ignorance" or "lack of awareness." This is the most pervasive of all factors of upset. Ignorance is the most basic root cause of all suffering.

5. Doubt

The fifth factor, *vichikitsa*, is translated as "doubt" or "indecision." This is the opposite of confidence or trust. If we are not confident, we have doubts. It's as simple as that. If there's doubt or indecision, it means there is no confidence.

A confident state means a state from which decisive action can occur. If we are not clear about how to proceed, we are indecisive.[135] We have doubts about what is "true." The truth may be like this or like that; we are not exactly sure. Our mind is not really clear.

As you may remember, being mentally clear was the term used to talk about confidence. The presence of doubt or indecisiveness functions in such a way that it blocks or prevents us from becoming involved with positive things. It is defined with respect to what is positive. We may have doubts about how to overcome being controlled by upsetting factors, and it may seem that we do not know how to do that. The more we doubt, the more indecisive we are; the more we lack confidence and understanding, the less likely and less capable we are of getting out. The text goes on to ask: How is it that we are blocked from going in the positive direction? Well, we do not understand the truth of suffering, its cause, its end, and the way to end it. (This means we might be confused about the "truth" of the four noble truths.) We do not understand the relationship between our actions and our subsequent experiences. This blocks everything positive in our lives. In particular, it blocks having a true vision and understanding of what is actually the case, the true nature of things. Whenever we see and understand something that is true, indecision is banished, and there is confidence present. One should be interested in how to get rid of all the different opinions that we have that we are not clear about. Opinions and beliefs are like the playthings of those who are indecisive. The more indecisive we are, the more playthings called beliefs we have. The more we believe, the less we know. It is as simple as that.

6. Belief/Opinionatedness

The last factor, *drishti*, is translated as "belief" or "opinionatedness." There are five ways to discuss this factor:

1. We have lots of opinions regarding what is perishable, what will break down. That means that we have lots of opinions, fictions, and things we accept or claim to be the case about a self or things that belong to a self. We do not understand that this "self" is itself a belief. In fact,

there is a multiplicity of factors that work together to create the illusion of a self, which will break down.

2. There is opinionatedness regarding extremes. We really think, extremely, *this* is the way it is or *that* is the way it is. And these extremes also lead to the third point.

3. There are opinions regarding ideologies. This is a nice translation for what in Tibetan is called "a cherished view." Our view is very precious to us, and we cling to it. We have lots of opinions about cherished views.

4. There are opinions regarding ethical conduct and certain things that *ought* to be done. People are very tight about what should be done. The tighter we are, the less we know.

5. There are opinions that are simply wrong, meaning we have beliefs that don't correspond to reality.

SECONDARY FACTORS OF UPSET

	SANSKRIT	GATEWAY TO KNOWLEDGE	MIND IN BUDDHIST PSYCHOLOGY
1.	*krodha*	fury	indignation
2.	*upanaha*	resentment	resentment
3.	*mraksha*	concealment	slyness-concealment
4.	*pradasa*	spite	spite
5.	*irshya*	envy	jealousy
6.	*matsarya*	stinginess	avarice
7.	*maya*	pretense	deceit
8.	*shathya*	hypocrisy	dishonesty
9.	*mada*	self-infatuation	mental inflation
10.	*vihimsa*	hostility	malice
11.	*ahrikya*	lack of conscience	shamelessness
12.	*anapatrapa*	shamelessness	lack of propriety
13.	*styana*	lethargy	gloominess
14.	*auddhatya*	excitement	ebullience

	SANSKRIT	GATEWAY TO KNOWLEDGE	MIND IN BUDDHIST PSYCHOLOGY
15.	*ashraddhya*	lack of faith	lack of trust
16.	*kausidya*	laziness	laziness
17.	*pramada*	heedlessness	unconcern
18.	*musitasmritita*	forgetfulness	forgetfulness
19.	*viksepa*	nonalertness	inattentiveness
20.	*asamprajanya*	distraction	desultoriness

1. Indignation/Fury

The first secondary factor listed in the chart is indignation or fury. Now we are getting closer to the surface of what is easy to experience. Now we are dealing with the "children" who sometimes run amok. Perhaps some of us have never had an experience of some of these factors. To those people we have to say: "Good for you, but stay tuned." There is a famous example of a yogi who was practicing "patience" in a cave for many years. Someone came along and asked him, "What are you doing?" The yogi replied, "I am practicing patience." "Oh, really? Can you tell me about that practice?" At that point, the yogi became angry and lost his "patience."

Indignation is said to be a vindictive intention associated with the primary factor of upset called anger. Let's imagine that we have a chance to hurt someone because they did something that outraged us, and now that chance to get back at them is close at hand. We were not even thinking about it, and then suddenly this really irritating person comes along, and we think, "Now I have my chance to exact revenge." That sentiment is associated with indignation. Indignation sparks the thought that says, "Now I'll get them. Now I can hurt them." The texts say very clearly that even just that quick thought coming into our mind is the basis upon which, for example, a knife might be picked up and someone is killed. It's the moment right before picking up that knife. In order for that physical act to occur, there is this factor of fury or indignation. It is a factor that causes a lot of harm.

2. Resentment

Resentment is the energy of not letting go of an obsession connected with anger. We are obsessed, we are angry, and we are not letting go, and this works together as resentment. When resentment is present, we cannot endure anything. We just cannot bear it. We cannot let go of continuously feeling this way. It puts us in a position of what we call being "trigger happy." We are just waiting to pull the trigger. We just cannot wait to retaliate, measure for measure.

3. Concealment

The third secondary factor is concealment, or being sly or sneaky. It is a very special state in which we cannot resolve something. We are not quite sure what is up or how to be. It is associated with being dull and stubborn. Even when we are urged to do something positive, we are not sure it corresponds to our nature. We do not just directly and in an unconcealed way go toward what is positive. Being concealed causes us not to be able to make a clean break from what's not positive, as if we conceal our own best energy with this habit. We're unresolved; we can't decide. Quite often the teacher will say, "drop it; cut it." He or she says this because if we can, we can be relieved. Concealment also functions to cover up our unwholesome tendencies. We are hiding, and we do it with an attitude of stubbornness. When a spiritual friend, meaning one who would walk with us on the path out of suffering, would desire to help us, we stubbornly refuse, or we resist. Then our small problem becomes larger and larger, until this indecision becomes a lifestyle and makes it very difficult to just drop it or cut through anything at all. As a result, we have the continuing state of being stubborn, sly, concealing, and dull.

4. Spite

Spite is a vindictive attitude preceded by a feeling of being indignant and a feeling of resentment. When we feel indignant, when we think, "How dare they!" and then feel resentment, thinking, "I don't like that, that, and that," we have an energy of wanting to get back at those who have wronged us. It's very much connected with anger. This serves as a basis for letting loose harsh and strong words with our mouth. On the one hand, it increases unwholesomeness; and on the other hand, no matter how harsh we are on others, it bounces back on us and we don't feel happy. We have no intention of making a clean break with this whole thing. We are still part of the problem. Many Buddhist texts warn about reviling or criticizing with harsh words or engaging in ridiculing others. It is a very prevalent factor.

5. Jealousy/Envy

Then we come to jealousy, or envy. The first thing that is said about jealousy is that it is a highly disturbed state of mind, as if it is a bit more dangerous or powerful than some other secondary factors of upset. Vasubandhu also indicates that jealousy is strongly associated with hatred and aversion. It takes as its point of generation not being able to hear about the well-being or excellence of other people. We hear about the good qualities of another and we hear this little voice: "What about me? When do I get the medal? When do I get the loving smile?" It says this is caused by being overly attached to gain and honor. (You will remember the famous list of eight worldly motivations.)

Its result, its function, is that it makes us really unhappy. It blocks happiness. We know the antidotes to jealousy: rejoicing in the good deeds and the merit of others is one of them. Another antidote to jealousy is the capacity to cut through to the root of the idea that there are others out there who are more special and more important than I am. Once again that famous "I" appears: "I am less important. I have a problem with other people's success." We think there is an "I" and then later there is a problem. But, from these perspectives, the "I" is already the problem. And so it goes, round and round, the circle of samsara fueled by this rigid fixation on "I."

6. Stinginess/Avarice

Stinginess or avarice is defined as being overly concerned with and being overly attached to physical things in this life because somehow we think there is a relationship between physical things and our honor. We think that being well thought of has something to do with things that we have or things that are associated with us. This factor is connected to passion or lust, the desire to have those things. How does this avarice function? It is continuously feeding on itself; we become continuously obsessed by material things. We're attached to the body and to what the body may accumulate. We have no thought for what might happen once this wonderful body is gone.

7. Deceit/Pretense

Deceit or pretense is our capacity to display what is not real. In a slightly different context, Jean-Paul Sartre once said that one of the characteristics of being human is having the capacity to learn how to lie. This is interesting because it means there is some basis for distinguishing what is true and what is not true. Deceit and lying are unwholesome. But at the basis of the unwholesome display is our knowledge of the difference between what is real and what is not real. Deceit involves our capacity to make others feel that what we are displaying is real. This is associated with both passion and lust but also with bewilderment. We may enjoy doing this. We may enjoy deceiving others. We see the effect it has on other people. That is the passion. But the bewilderment is the fact that we don't understand that this does not do us any good.

This factor of deceit, this act of displaying what is not real and enjoying it while being unclear that it isn't doing us any good, is also very closely attached to beliefs about wealth and honor. When we cultivate this, it results in a whole lifestyle based on deceit. Because these lifestyles do not correspond at all to walking out of suffering, they are referred to as perverse or wrong lifestyles. Here is a list of the "perverse" lifestyles that follow from deceit:

1. There is the lifestyle that consists of hypocrisy. Everyone who cultivates this lifestyle knows that one is a hypocrite with other people. We can find this in business. You say, "He is a hypocrite. You can't believe what he said." But the other person says the same about you. Still, you have meetings and you make business deals. But it doesn't make you very happy.

2. Another lifestyle is based entirely on flattery. The flatterers get together, and they have their flattery meetings. You talk smoothly; you only say agreeable things. But you want something from it.

3. Then there are people who are overly praising. They go over the top all the time. The text says: first you start with flattery and then you heap praise upon praise. You praise people's possessions because you want them.[136]

4. Another lifestyle of deceit involves those who seek wealth by means of wealth. This refers to those who brag about what they have by saying, "This great person blessed me; he gave me these things." You are using the wealth of words to attract wealth and attention to yourself.

8. Hypocrisy/Dishonesty

Closely related to deceit, the eighth factor is dishonesty. One desires wealth and honor and, based on this desire, confuses what is unwholesome with what is wholesome. This dishonesty works in tandem with deceit. The function of dishonesty is to conceal your shortcomings because you don't want your honor to decline. You try to keep your mistakes a secret, but when people find out, you become a bit meek and a bit more prudent. These two together, deceit and dishonesty, keep us from seeking the good advice of those who could lead us in a positive direction. This is a specific form of unpleasantness or unhappiness called not meeting spiritual friends. One of the things that blocks us from meeting spiritual friends or teachers is being dominated by a deceitful and dishonest heart. It is not a small thing.

9. Self-Infatuation/Mental Inflation

Next, we have the factor of self-infatuation, or mental inflation. We all know this feeling, I think. It's called the joy or rapture of thinking about our health, youth, good looks, and our abundance of pleasure. It causes us to be unconcerned or careless with respect to other aspects of life.

10. Hostility/Malice

Now we come to the tenth factor, which is translated as malice, or as hostility. Malice is associated with anger It is associated with anger, number 2 of the primary factors. It is defined as lacking loving-kindness, compassion, and openheartedness. It's defined by the lack of something positive. When we were examining the wholesome factors, we saw that some of them were defined as the lack of something negative. This lack does not mean that nothing is there; it's as if to say there is a space created that's not filled up. This lack means there is a space. When there is a lack of negativity with some of the positive elements, this lack of negativity is itself positive. There's a space for something to come in. In this case, the same principle is involved but from the opposite perspective. Malice names the energy where there is no loving-kindness, no compassion, and no openheartedness.

It's said that this lack of loving-kindness, compassion, and openheartedness functions in a specific way. How does it flow? We treat others abusively. That is the definition and that is its function. For those of us interested in psychology, if you ask the question, "Why is that person treating that other person abusively?" the answer here would be, in part, that temporarily there is no loving-kindness, compassion, or openheartedness in that individual. This is something rather profound. And, in fact, we are not exempt because there is both subtle and gross abuse. There's abuse in the outward, overt expressions, through our words and deeds, but there can also be abuse through our thoughts.

This is one of the reasons why those in the Buddhist tradition put a lot of emphasis on cultivating loving-kindness, compassion, and openheartedness. It is not enough simply to rest in a state of what one calls "emptiness." In the traditions that I know, the view and practices of cutting through and emptiness are always mixed with or alternated with practices of loving-kindness, compassion, and openheartedness.

To say a little bit more about this factor of malice, it is the desire to treat others abusively, and involves the energy of not having kind feelings toward other beings. This is a very deep thing. It is not the mere absence of shouting or hitting someone, for instance. When we open to others, when we relate to others, are we doing so out of a sense of obligation or coercion—as if to say, they're there, so we have to involve them? As we are speaking, as we are moving, if we look a bit inside ourselves, do we have a kind feeling in our heart toward others or not? We know very well, from being a child up until now, what a kind feeling is. Everyone, and not only human beings, knows what kindness is when they experience it. You can tell with a cat or a dog. If they feel that you are a kind person, they will come toward you. There is that nonconceptual, direct, energetic link; there is the experience of being sympathetic. In that respect, all living beings are the same—we open to others when we sense there is kindness. That's just the way it is. When we're kind toward ourselves, we open to ourselves and we're more tolerant. If we're unkind to ourselves, we shut down to ourselves. If we don't feel kindness, if we feel the opposite, if someone else is not being kind, then something in us shuts down.

But we still need to function, so there arises a bit of a division between our thoughts and our speech and actions. This lack of loving-kindness is a good definition for samsara. Samsara would be totally transformed if all beings were cultivating loving-kindness continuously. This factor of malice, then, delves into what happens when that loving-kindness is not occurring. So abuse, in the inner sense of that term, means temporarily not having kindness present.

The text not only speaks of the lack of loving-kindness but goes on a bit further to speak of the lack of compassion and openheartedness. It says that a lack of loving-kindness is our inclination to treat others abusively, a lack of pity or compassion is our inclination to induce others to treat others abusively, and a lack of openheartedness or a lack of affection is to take enjoyment from hearing or seeing others acting in such an abusive way.

11. Lack of Conscience/Shamelessness

The next two factors may cause a bit of confusion due to the translations. Sometimes "shamelessness" occurs as a translation for both of them. These negative or upsetting factors correlate very precisely with the wholesome factors 2 and 3 discussed previously. Again, we see that when we lack conscience, or we lack self-respect, when we lack this wholesome factor, there is a negative

factor present. That negative factor is called the lack of conscience; the termi-
nology I prefer is the "lack of self-respect." Similarly, when we lack decorum,
there is the factor 12 of upset, shamelessness, or lack of propriety. (We spent
some time talking about the importance of these two wholesome factors and
how they help us explain to psychologists a "Buddhist" understanding of a
healthy sense of self.)

The text says that shamelessness, to use this term, or lack of conscience involves not restraining oneself and indulging in one's perverted ways of being as
if they were the true way to be. This means, as we mentioned when we spoke
about the opposite of this, as a positive wholesome factor, that there's no interest and possibly no knowledge of wholesome versus unwholesome whatsoever. As you might remember, this factor of self-respect only makes sense if one
truly can experience the difference between wholesome and unwholesome. It's
very important not to confuse "wholesome" with "feels good" and "unwholesome" with "feels bad."

A contemporary Buddhist teacher once cautioned, "Beware of the logic of
feels good," the logic that says, "if it feels good, it is good," and "if it feels bad,
it must be bad." If one does not know the difference between wholesome and
unwholesome, the result is that we are always confirming our own perverted
or distorted way of being and regarding it as the basis for everything. On the
basis of being able to distinguish wholesome from unwholesome, when we're
provoked to engage in an action that we know is unwholesome, sometimes
there is enough space and we don't engage in it. The name of the experience
that might follow is self-respect. It's not a matter of resisting or suppressing our
engaging in unwholesomeness. It's not so easy to resist or repress.

One unwholesome lifestyle is called alcoholism. The recovery program
called Alcoholics Anonymous (AA) is a peer group; that is to say, there's no
therapist, and everyone is on the same level. The main book, the reference
point for those in AA, states someplace at the beginning (something that is
not agreed to by allopathic medicine) that addiction is a spiritual disease. The
reason I bring this up here is because in the context of resisting or fighting alcoholism in AA, they say that when we find ourselves not engaging in the unwholesome action (in this case, drinking), it's a blessing. We didn't decide. The
theory is that this humility of realizing that one's life is a bit unmanageable,

that it can't be controlled, relaxes and removes a bit of the shame which says, "I am guilty, I am weak, I should be able to overcome this." So, in a way, we might say Buddhism is a program of recovery. In AA it's called a twelve-step program; in Buddhism it's the eightfold path.

So, just on this point, there's something similar between recovery from addiction on the one hand and Buddhism on the other. Sometimes we find that there's enough spaciousness and relaxation, so that when we are provoked to engage in something unwholesome, we don't. Then how do we feel? "Aah." We feel relieved. The name for that feeling is self-respect. It's not thinking, "I have self-respect, and every self-respecting citizen of the realm will vote for me." This is the marketing of self-respect. It's different from what we're talking about here. If someone is taking their inability to distinguish wholesome from unwholesome as the norm and does as they please we say, "That person is shameless." We use that word for others, but usually it means, "I do not approve of their behavior."

Let's go deeper here. This negativity is involved in greed, hate, and delusion and acts as a catalyst for all forms of upset. There's a strong involvement of *attitude*.[137] When this factor of lack of self-respect is present, there is a strong attitude at work; we don't want to change the way we are, and we don't want to think of our attitude as narrow. We don't think that we have shortcomings, and we think we're the standard of measurement for what is okay. We take our ideology as the norm. It says the opposite of this is self-respect. This is a factor that is furthered with respect to greed, hate, and delusion. When our attitude changes a bit, we change our habits called greed, hate, and delusion.

This is a big change. It's as if our attitude is a very deep rudder on a boat going across the ocean of samsara, and on that journey, we discover it is possible to change the rudder. That rudder change might be likened to an attitude changer. As we change the angle of the rudder the difficulty of working with deep patterns of addictive self-infatuation begin to change. And our journey in that boat becomes less arduous. If you're in a boat in the turbulent ocean and you want to see something different, change the angle of that rudder.

12. Shamelessness/Lack of Propriety

The next factor, shamelessness or lack of propriety, means going against the wholesome norms that have been established with respect to behavior toward others. (Remember our discussion of the wholesome factor called propriety, or "decorum.") We do not live alone; we live in society, in community. We're encouraged to think about what is wholesome and unwholesome with respect to collective activity or with respect to others. The lack of propriety is to say, "I don't care what others do"; it's to be closed off to others being a source of wholesomeness. We judge others by whether or not they vote the same way we do. We never think their point of view is worthy of reflecting on. An antidote to this is to consider under what conditions others might be worthy of respect. (It's the opposite of being a bother.)

Both lack of self-respect and lack of propriety work to reinforce all the different kinds of emotional upset. If we do not want to refrain from unwholesomeness, then there is no way to protect ourselves from its effects. We have to *want* to refrain.

When we desire or wish for something to be permanent, unique, or isolated, that becomes a source of suffering. But when we wish for all living beings to be beyond suffering, this is the best wish in the world. On this point, many texts say that this is the best wish, because it's the longest-lasting wish one could ever have. This wish is great in terms of how long it will last, and it is magnificent in terms of its range of application because it concerns all sentient beings. The word *all* here means "infinite." It means that whenever we think we are finished, we are not; there is always one more being to help. So, in fact, one's job is never done. According to the Mahayana, the alleviation of suffering and the cultivation of an altruistic intent to work continuously to bring that about *never ends*.

If we do not want to refrain from unwholesomeness, we cannot protect ourselves from its effects. You will remember the technical definition of wholesome and unwholesome: unwholesomeness will always blossom as suffering. Fortunately, the opposite is also true. The fruit of the seed of wholesomeness will eventually bear the fruit of well-being. Both lack of self-respect and lack of propriety are involved in every unhealthy attitude.

13. Lethargy

This leads to the next factor, "lethargy." Actually, lethargy and excitement (factor 14) are a pair. If you have done some training in calm-abiding practice, you will know that these are the primary unwholesome factors that one is working with. Some of the more exotic factors of upset, like hypocrisy, resentment, and envy, have been somewhat cooled out when we are doing calm-abiding practice. But there are these two unwholesome factors that come out on stage and do their dance more or less continuously during our meditation session, and these are the factors of lethargy and excitement.

When we take calm-abiding instructions (shamatha)—and here we are only speaking of shamatha with an object since it is easier to pay attention with an object to start with—we use the term *distraction*. One is encouraged to note when there is distraction. But what does this distraction consist of? It is said that distraction occurs when our energy has withdrawn from the target of focus. The culprit, the thief, the one who steals away our mindfulness, is actually made up of these two factors of upset. That factor of lethargy has to do with becoming drowsy, whereas excitement is operative when we become agitated, or overenthusiastic. Think of them, maybe, as the "Bonnie and Clyde" thieves who rob us of calm abiding.

Isn't it rather a miracle, that we can ever become aware that we have drifted away from our target of focus? We go, "Ah," and then we bring ourselves back. That moment of saying "Ah" and bringing ourselves back is "alertness," a factor we have previously discussed. It is likened to the elephant goad in the previous example of the monk chasing the wild elephant of his mind. Alertness leads the wild elephant of our awareness back onto the path. So, both factors lethargy and "excitedness" are the factors which cause our distraction away from our meditative focus. When we are working with these factors, in the beginning we do not see them at all; we are just chasing the elephant. We cannot control it. Finally, with the noose of mindfulness, a positive factor that we talked about before, we can tame the mind and be calm a bit.

What does lethargy mean? It is a way in which the mind is not functioning properly. This is associated with a feeling of bewilderment, being very unclear, or being murky. This murkiness, this woolly-headedness, aids every form of upset. It is like mold growing on top of the upset. This heaviness, or sluggishness, is also analyzed in terms of the body and the mind, so if you can shift the energy, it is possible to restore your alertness.

14. Excitement

There is also the factor of being excited, or manic. Together, factors 13 and 14 are the "manic-depressive" states not only associated with cultivating calm abiding but actually and subtly underlying most states of so-called awareness. Discovering that this is true is part of the practice of shamatha. It is not at all the case that a good meditator never has these energy patterns. A good meditator is one who is learning how to note when they arise and how to bring oneself back.

This factor of excitement is a restlessness of mind. This factor is linked to desire or passion and gets involved in things that are judged to be fun or enjoyable. Its function is that it obstructs or blocks calm. Additionally, overexcitedness means running after or craving, particularly for things that we think will be pleasurable. According to the text, not every time we go toward something which we think is interesting is a case of this manic-ness; it occurs only when there is an overabundance of attachment.

When we are able to stay with an object of focus, it means that the dynamics of manic-depression are not operating. In fact, this is a good definition of mindfulness. It is being able to stay with the object of focus. The longer we can stay with the object of focus, the stronger our shamatha practice.

When our mind is not with the object of focus, then mindfulness is not present. So where, then, is the mind? It is doing something else. We may have an experience of blankness, of being a bit spaced-out. One of the things good meditation teachers try to caution against is trying to force this meditation with an object. When we force it and we're not so relaxed, we split off; we become a bit hypnotized, and we dissociate.

This is why in many Buddhist traditions it is said to be very good to do many short meditation sessions. One wants to keep one's attitude fresh. If, from the very beginning, you are doing thirty minutes or an hour, what in fact are you probably doing? We may develop a sense of lethargy or discouragement or being split off, and then we are not enjoying the session; we are not sharp and fresh. This way of practicing helps us to be fresh and also to be able to note when we have become distracted (due to excitement or gloominess) so that we can bring our mind back into focus.

To use an analogy, the two muscle groups that we are exercising when we do shamatha are (1) seeing, experiencing just the mindful flow of being with the object, so-called being mindful (smriti), and then (2) being able to note or be aware when we are no longer with the object, not being so caught up in the drama of Bonnie and Clyde and all of their adventures. We note: "Uh, Bonnie and Clyde again," and just bring our mind back, so-called alertness (samprajanya). This is a way of working through and no longer being hypnotized by excitement and gloominess.

15. Lack of Faith/Lack of Trust

The fifteenth factor is lack of trust, or lack of faith. This is the absence of the factor of trust or confidence. Patrul Rinpoche talks about different styles of not having trust in the teacher. In *The Words of My Perfect Teacher*, he mentions that some want to hunt the teacher because we believe the teacher has something that we want to get, as if the teacher were a musk ox, and we want to get that musk and extract the perfume. We want to soak ourselves in that smell. But that smell is the stench of inauthentic spirituality. You can find that being advertised everywhere all the time. That is a form of lack of trust. We are confirming our own convictions. We might say one of the hallmarks of lack of trust is that we always bring our agendas with us. We have a list of all the things we want to get from the teacher and the teachings.

Lack of trust occurs wherever trust is blocked. It is not a mere absence of trust. We do not have a deep conviction or trust in the teachings and so, consequently, we have no trust and we have no desire for wholesomeness, for what is positive. We may have tremendous desire and conviction in things that are unwholesome. We might not even know the difference between wholesome and unwholesome. This lack of trust is very closely related to lack of self-respect. Here, it says that the function of lack of trust is that it becomes a basis for spiritual laziness. One of the root causes for not doing Dharma practice is a lack of self-respect and also a lack of trust.

The Mahayana as a path emphasizes the discovery that the greatest and best desire of all and the greatest possible source of happiness is working to bring happiness to others. This involves activating an altruistic intention (bodhichitta).

When we suffer lack of trust, it fosters the blockage of the positive flow of energy. It causes spiritual laziness. It seems that we have lots of energy for all kinds of ordinary things, but lack of trust is when we do not know how to cultivate a deep conviction regarding the relationship between cause and effect in our own life.

For those on the path, this also means not being clear about why the Buddha, Dharma, and Sangha are jewels, precious things. We have no trust in the rarity and preciousness of the actuality of what the word *Buddha*, the word *Dharma*, and the word *Sangha* point to. We do not know. We do not care. So we get a little bit lazy, and finally, we have no faith, no confidence whatsoever. We have not developed the confidence of longing for full and complete liberation, the best kind of desire in the whole world.

16. Laziness

Laziness, here, factor 16, is defined as not having the energy of engagement with what is positive. It is spiritual lethargy and is associated with being bewildered, being spaced-out, and being deluded. The form that this spaced-out deludedness takes is being habituated to being drowsy. We want to resist just cutting through something. One form of spiritual laziness is to obsess about our current situation. We can be extremely energetic about it. But here, we are exploring *spiritual* laziness. We just want to lie down and wallow in our current problems. We do not want to get up from them. If somebody suggests to us, "Cut through it, get on with your life, do something different, and go for it," this laziness changes to one of the other factors of upset.

In all this immersion in our problems, we have totally forgotten that there is a way out. Whenever we are obsessing like that, where is the Buddha, Dharma, and Sangha in that obsession? We do not have a refuge then, temporarily. I think spiritual lethargy or spiritual laziness is a much better translation than simply being lazy because this can be a highly energized state, a self-indulgent state. It means we just do not have the energy for making a difference in our lives. If someone comes along and suggests, "Here is something you can do," we will resist this. We may fall asleep and continue to sleep our whole lives.

17. Heedlessness/Unconcern

We come to the factor of being careless or heedless or not having concern. We might also say we are spiritually sloppy. It's like when you make crème brûlée and it tastes really good, until you realize that you are covered all over with it. It is fine as long as it does not prevent you from breathing. The idea that we could get out of samsara at all is rather shocking and somewhat disturbing. This factor of being careless refers to the habit of not being sensitive to and not paying attention to what is spiritually wholesome. That habit makes us vulnerable to becoming fascinated by things that can never fully satisfy us.

This so-called carelessness, this heedlessness, means not being sensitive to what is wholesome and having no sense of the need for protection or sobriety with respect to being attacked by the energy of greed, hate, or delusion.

18. Forgetfulness

Forgetfulness is a defense against becoming sensitive to what is positive and wholesome. In fact, forgetfulness is the opposite of mindfulness.

We do not stay with an object. We do not stay with an energy pattern. We say it is not important, maybe, or we have no way of distinguishing between what is healthy and unhealthy. Forgetfulness here does not just mean, "I forgot that bit." It is a flash of awareness during which the mind is not clear, so that it cannot hold to what is positive.

Forgetfulness is what makes distraction possible. Distraction, then, is any situation in which we do not have present the desire for and the fact of the possibility of full and complete liberation for all living beings. According to Mahayana traditions, if there is even the slightest moment in which that desire is not present, we are spiritually distracted.

19. Nonalertness/Inattentiveness

The second to the last factor is not being alert or not being attentive with respect to the actions of our body and our speech and also the intentions that precede them in our mind. We might say that we are not being attentive to the three karmic doors of body, speech, and mind. With that habit, we can lose our status of being a sensitive, open, and attuned human being. That is what inattention can lead to.

20. Distraction/Desultoriness

In the very last factor, we are really distracted; we are wavering a lot. We are a bit out of control. This refers to being scatterbrained; we are a bit all over the place on a regular basis. Especially these days, we might even think this is normal and natural. We have become an omnivore of distraction. We are always "eating" according to aggression, greed, or bewilderment. We are swayed by our emotions. We are really scattered. This is monkey mind. We are scattered with respect to things we see, hear, smell, taste, and touch. We are distracted by things that appear externally. We are distracted by all of our thoughts and emotions. We are distracted from, or pay no attention to, the fine points of our experience. We are fascinatedly distracted by all kinds of activities that are not wholesome, and we are distracted with our great schemes that rationalize why this distraction is appropriate.

VARIABLE FACTORS

	SANSKRIT	GATEWAY TO KNOWLEDGE	MIND IN BUDDHIST PSYCHOLOGY
1.	*middha*	sleep	drowsiness
2.	*kaukritya*	regret	worry
3.	*vitarka*	conception	selectiveness
4.	*vichara*	discernment	discursiveness

1. Sleep/Drowsiness

We now come to four factors called "variable." Variable factors means that they operate in various ways. First in the list is sleep or drowsiness. When we make drowsiness our basic state of being, then that is how we relate to everything. We are drowsy with respect to most everything: what is positive, what is negative, what is appropriate, and what is not appropriate. This drowsiness basically means that time is slipping away. We are losing our ability to make a positive change in our lives. We become rather helpless and stuck in our habitual drowsiness. We are inwardly involved with our own drama, and we have a sense of heaviness in our body, maybe weariness, maybe laziness. It is good to remember that the time for sleep is at night!

2. Regret/Worry

The next factor is regret or worry. This is defined as being obsessed with what is unwholesome or wholesome, what is appropriate or inappropriate, what is intentional or not intentional. Its function is to obstruct the mind from being calm. It has as its habit becoming addicted to what is not pleasing. Such regret and worry is addiction to that which is not pleasing.

3. Conception/Selectiveness

The next factor is conception or selectiveness. It is said to be a very coarse mental operation. These are not necessarily negative, though I am presenting a negative sense of them. We can have conception and selectiveness regarding what is wholesome too. This factor, as all the variable factors, can have both positive and negative consequences. This factor can be the basis for either happiness or unhappiness. In that sense it is variable.

4. Discernment/Discursiveness

It is said that discernment involves tuning in to what is there. Comparing selectives with discernment is likened to the activity of a potter: the first one, selectiveness, is likened to firmly grasping on to a pot—one has selectively locked on to a situation—then discernment involves tuning in to some of the aspects of that pot one is holding—like that situation that you have grabbed on to.

Benefits of Abhidharma Study

It is good to remind ourselves why studying the Abhidharma is beneficial. I want to step back a bit and say something about the context. Among all the Buddha's great teachings, where does this fit? We have already said this, but it is good to remind ourself of the way of organizing the Buddha's teachings according to three turnings.[138]

In the first turning, the Buddha spoke about the four noble truths, and he also gave advice on proper conduct; these are the sutras and the vinaya. The sutras are a collection of all the different occasions on which the Buddha addressed different kinds of people in quite varied situations. He taught to each group of people according to their capacity, but there is a thread running throughout. This idea of a thread or a tight fitting together, a sewing together in a way that makes sense, is what the word *sutra* itself means. "Discourse" is not a good translation for sutra. The Sanskrit word *sutra* and the Latin word *suture*—a kind of tightening up or fitting together for a positive reason—have the same root. A sutra is not rambling, gossip, or amusement; it is really to the point.

There are those who came and tried to codify the essential points in the Buddha's teachings, this thread in the sutras, and they noticed that the Buddha on more than one occasion spoke about various grouping of factors of experience: he spoke of the five skandhas, the twelve ayatanas, and the eighteen dhatus.

According to historical studies the Abhidharma literature came from notes (*matrikas*)[139] that were put at the end of the sutra collections; they were probably memory devices. These matrikas were ways of recording essential distinctions that were mentioned by the Buddha, ways of recalling the various numerical lists he spoke about.

It is said that in time there were those who developed a fascination and an interest in making a study of those notes, and so began the elaboration on his teachings found in the sutras. They wanted to know what the five, the twelve, and the eighteen categories meant, what they referred to. And they regarded such inquiry as the "higher" Dharma, that this was the way to get to what the Buddha actually meant. These notes were appended at the end of some of the sutras when those were written down. We don't have access to how the Abhidharma might have existed when it was transmitted orally. But in time it became a separate collection, a "basket" (*pitaka*), which contained the essential teachings of the Buddha. The Abhidharma became one of the three collections of the Buddha's teachings; the other two consisted of his talks (sutras), and guidance on ethical conduct (vinaya).

It is said that different temperaments attract one to different collections of the Buddha's teaching. Those who were on the greed or lust side were encouraged to study the vinaya, such study being an antidote to lust; Those who were prone to aggression or anger were encouraged to study the sutras. And those who were dominated by bewilderment and confusion were encouraged to study the Abhidharma.

The texts go on to say that the style of the sutra teachings is metaphor and simile. It's narrative; it's a story. But the style of the Abhidharma is analytical and involves making distinctions and definitions.

Dharmas: The Basic Building Blocks

Now that we have completed the Abhidharma teaching, I would like to remind you what the purpose of this kind of in-depth analysis is. We can remember that all these different factors—positive, negative, and general—according to the first-turning teachings of the Buddha are the primary energy packets. This is what's real.

With prajna, the energy packet that can focus itself in a precise, swordlike way (like a collider beam), we can smash what we thought was ultimate and basic. We thought all of our problems, all of our meditative experiences, and all of our insights were solid and unchanging. But when this collider beam known as wisdom mind is focused on these fuzzy, murky ensembles, sometimes, momentarily, they burst apart and leave a little bit of a trace, just like when subatomic particles burst apart. In that space, in the wake of the application of wisdom mind, sometimes we can see and discern directly the way things are. (Then, of course, these factors come together again and it's a bit murky. Again we can smash apart these murky ensembles.) The best way to smash is to develop the habit of calm, mindful, and relaxed presence. If we're tight in body or tight in mind, it will be extremely difficult to experience what may occur in the spaciousness.

At any rate, whether we are aware or not, all of these factors are combining and recombining with each other all the time. Unconsciously or consciously, they are streaming, they are flowing, they are working when we're meditating, when we're not meditating, when we're sitting, walking, sleeping, and laughing. There's no situation in which these basic factors are not present. All of them together, as they get together—this is reality. It allows us, with a degree of precision that is not so easily seen in some other Buddhist teachings, to tune in to the variety of all the different factors that make up our thoughts, our emotions, our experiences.

In the very beginning we used the analogy of these factors being like an atomic chart. This is thought to be a completely comprehensive and precise list, one that describes each of these atoms, their qualities, and the various rules for how they combine with each other.

This is kind of how we go through life, right? We have a rather sloppy, imprecise, bewildered, or arrogant way of relating to our experiences. We have a habit of actually making prostrations to this arrogance and bewilderment on a regular basis. We do so with the utterance "I," and sometimes, to vary it, "mine" or "you," "yours" or "not yours," and sometimes "not mine." This is the way most of us proceed through our lives, and at the end of our life we're a little exhausted. We have huge demeritorious piles of arrogance and bewilderment, with a completely clear conscience.

The good news is that the Abhidharma says we can break that habit; we can cut it. We can tune in and have as a target exactly this habit of arrogance and bewilderment. When we do tune in, there's a smashing; there's a bit of calm and clearing. In that calm clarity we may glimpse a bit how things actually are. One of the proofs that we have actually glimpsed this is a slight disinclination to continue to prostrate to this arrogant, bewildered heap. It becomes a little bit more difficult to say so quickly and with a clear conscience: "my," "my problem."

The Abhidharma is an invitation to smash, to break down, to cut through, and to completely destroy and overcome every tendency toward extremes of arrogance, greed, and bewilderment. Remember that what allows us to do this is a special kind of wisdom energy. (prajna). Prajna is a dharma, a basic energy packet, that has as its function the capacity to know, through analysis, the specific differences of all the other dharmas, and how they combine into conglomerations which make up the totality of our selves, our world, our experiences, both actual and possible. You can go quite far with this prajna; you can perfect it.

Elements (Dhatus)

As we've seen, one of the schemes of smashing through is the eighteen dhatus. We went through the analytic explanation, but we will remember that in practice, when we're doing "dhatu analysis," we are simply and precisely aware of which channel we're broadcasting on. Simply cultivating the habit of knowing what channel we're broadcasting on is a very powerful way of smashing through the arrogant bewilderment that makes the noise "I." The purpose of doing this analysis is so that we can know what channel we're on, or more precisely, that this "I," when smashed, is simply a hexamodal complex.

If we smash what we call an "I," we have six channels. All living beings have six channels. This practice of dhatu analysis alone is extremely powerful and, unlike some other extreme yogic practices, won't send you to the chiropractor. It's not too hard. We spend quite a bit of time recounting the stories of what kind of smashing occurred on channel 6, studying the various energy packets that are involved in channel 6. Now we have an inventory of all the different programs that have ever been broadcast on channel 6, anywhere, anytime.

We may want a story; we may want them to combine with each other. We have these stories all the time. But all those stories are made up of nothing but these elements: the general ones, the wholesome ones, the unwholesome ones. You can weave any story you want.

Sense Bases (Ayatanas)

There is also another way of combining or making sense of our experience. Just for a sense of completeness here, this is the group of twelve ayatanas. We already explored this in the context of "sensation" (vedana) and saw how all of our experiences can be seen to involve a sensation, a response of some sort, either pleasant, unpleasant, or neither. The model consists of two groups of six—six called internal and six called external. It says that these internal sense bases are the doors through which experience enters. *Aya* means "arrives or emerges or is born" and *tana* means that which "furthers or extends or goes or spreads." What is arriving and then spreading is called "sensation," which is differentiated in six ways. Remember that sensation is one of the factors of experience. We know that sensation is either pleasant, unpleasant, or neither one nor the other. We might say that the ayatanas are things that further the arising of sensations. The internal ones are the doorways through which sensations arrive, and the external ones are those which have contact with sense fields, six in number (the six channels). Each time there's contact, the internal and external sense bases are coordinated; there's a resonance or there's a vibration. It is at that point that there arises a sensation. Sensation, here, is not a physical thing. Remember that the ayatanas were taught in order to counteract the wrong belief that the so-called self is made up of physical stuff.

When one is analyzing or experiencing in the way of ayatanas, one is training oneself to pay attention to how our channels fire. (We can still think of channels as the arising and spreading of a sensation.) One is encouraged to pay attention to the arising and spreading of different sensations as they occur. If one is practicing the ayatana way of viewing, one is focusing one's mind on the arising of sensation. When I look at something, channel 1, I don't focus on what I'm seeing (that would be dhatu analysis) but rather on the sensation which is arising due to the activation or firing of that channel. You are paying attention to the arising of sensations. The object of attention is the sensation. We hear something; that's channel 2. What is the associated sensation which is arising? For those who are rather in their heads a lot, who are preoccupied with mental stuff and cut off from just feeling and tuning in to sensations, they will find this kind of analysis a bit of a challenge. They're not so much in their bodies, so this might be taken as an invitation to explore the rumor that we do indeed have a body, that our cognitions are embodied. Body means there's a sensation. That means a living being is there.

The claim is that there is always a vibration, a sensation, and that you see that this is so if you can relax a bit and focus on detecting and noting the arising of sensations. When we do so, we'll note, so says these texts we are exploring, that there arises one of three sensations: pleasant, unpleasant, or neither. Breaking things apart this way, we can see how, indeed, this might be a very powerful way of cutting through a fascination with inert forms, let alone objects, let alone simply knowing what channel you are on. This is one way of working with the sense bases.

One shouldn't mix dhatu analysis and ayatana analysis; they are different in approach. Dhatu analysis is knowing what channel you're on. Ayatana analysis is being aware of the arising and spreading of differentiated sensations. They are differentiated with respect to what channel is firing, but we are not concerned about which channel we are on. We are just noting the sensation: is it pleasant, unpleasant, or neither?

The Five Aggregates (Skandhas)

Now we come to a consideration of the grouping of the five aggregates (skandhas).

Form

The skandha or the grouping called "form" consists of ten obvious factors, ten "dharmas," plus one "form-like" but intangible factor that is not manifest (*avijn-*

apti). This latter factor names the tangible force or form of taking a vow. The ten main factors are the five capacities to see, hear, smell, taste, and touch—that is, the "senses" (indriyas), factors 1–5—and also what is being perceived or processed, the information or objects consisting of colors and shapes, sounds, smells, tastes, and touch (what we labeled as factors 7–11). When one analyzes according to the aggregates, one does not at all pay attention to each single channel. Rather, we just group channels 1–5 together and say it's not mind; it's the aggregate of "form." Of the five skandhas, only one of them classifies the five sense fields according to the capacity to process and also the objective fields, the domains that are processed. The form aggregate does not involve those dhatu factors 12 or 13 through 18. Those are grouped separately, as we shall see. Because the teaching of the skandhas is said to be for those who think the self is "mind"—that "mind" is one thing—there is a breakdown of "mind" into four separate aggregates. Skandha teachings classify "mind" into four. In its classification, it is the opposite of the emphasis in the dhatu schema, which has only one channel concerning "mind." Only seven dhatus out of eighteen are concerned with "mind" (numbers 12 and 13 through 18). The point in doing skandha analysis is to be able to discern the difference between form stuff and four different kinds of mind stuff.

Sensation

Sensation consists of one entire aggregate, which is only one dharma. You may wonder: How can one dharma be an "aggregate" or a group? Vasubandhu informs us that this is classed as an aggregate since it can refer to every possible sensation from the past, present, and future. And it is also the aggregation of all possible sensations of "pleasant," "unpleasant," or "neither." It is the multiplicity of recurring sensations as one whole group.

Conception

There is also the skandha of being able to sort or isolate, to have a concept. Every situation of the past, present, or future has that skandha of conception. We previously discussed this as part of the list of "ever-present" factors, and it was defined as ever-present factor 2, "conceptualization," *samjna*. And its definition is the capacity to isolate or to grab on to specific features. As an aggregate, it names all such occurrences in the past, present, and future.

Karmic Formation

This is the grouping which aggregates the most number of dharmas, of factors of conditioned existence (*samskrita skandha*) It includes all of the seventy-two factors of conditioned existence, except those four aggregates grouped as the "form aggregate," "sensation aggregate," "conceptualization aggregate," and "mind, or consciousness aggregate." And it includes all those factors as they occur in the past, present, or future.

Consciousness/Mind

The last of the five aggregates groups together that one dharma called "mind" (chitta). It should be understood as aggregating the six different forms of "consciousness" or "perception" (vijnana), dhatu numbers 13 through 18. It is said that of the five skandhas it is this last one, consciousness, that "transmigrates." It is the vijnana skandha that goes on and on from one life situation to another. It is not the forms, nor is it the sensations, the conceptualizations, or even karmic formations that transmigrate. Only our "habits of awareness" continue on after our so-called death. These habits of awareness and perception, the fifth aggregation, continue on into different possible forms. That is why so much focus is placed on "attention" and "awareness" near the time of death; that is why it is said that "mind" is king, mind is sovereign.

Conclusion

In conclusion, I hope that the details and approaches we've explored at great length will engender an interest in the further study of Abhidharma literature and contribute to an emerging sense of what might now be properly called a "Buddhist psychology of awakening." I am keenly aware that many topics discussed in Vasubandhu's *Treasury of Higher Dharma* (*Abhidharmakoshashabhasya*) were not explored at all. I've tried to keep the discussion to what I've regarded as most salient for a contemporary audience of hopefully avid learners. May it be of benefit to many.

My foremost wish is that the somewhat detailed explorations in this little book will attract the attention of those who are inspired by the words of the Buddha to really make a difference in their lives. To that end, I have tried to give a suggestive, and perhaps innovative way of reflecting on these noble traditions in a way that might be of interest to contemporary readers. But the Buddha cautions us to make the teachings real for ourselves, not to fake it, not to pretend with an outward show but instead to develop a habit of honesty with ourselves.

As we do our best to study and practice, there will be many problems, of course. But let us not be so bewildered and arrogant as to be conditioned by these problems as they arise. Pretty soon we won't be here. Each year we will see who is no longer alive, and you know in time each of us will walk that path. These teachings are not just for now but are also for the future. And so by way of completion, I would give myself the advice that I also share with you. How should we be? The advice is simply to do our best and try to relax.

Appendix 1

The Seventy-Five Dharmas

The Seventy-Five Dharmas according to the
Abhidharmakosha by Vasubandhu

Conditioned Elements (saṃskṛta-dharma)

COLUMN I: FORMS (*RUPANI*) GENERAL FUNCTIONS

	SANSKRIT	TIBETAN	GATEWAY TO KNOWLEDGE	MIND IN BUDDHIST PSYCHOLOGY
sense capacities/faculties				
1.	*cakṣus*	*mig*	eye	eye
2.	*śrotra*	*rna*	ear	ear
3.	*ghrāṇa*	*sna*	nose	nose
4.	*jihva*	*lce*	tongue	tongue
5.	*kāya*	*lus*	body	body

	SANSKRIT	TIBETAN	GATEWAY TO KNOWLEDGE	MIND IN BUDDHIST PSYCHOLOGY
sense fields/objects				
6.	rūpa	gzugs	form	form
7.	śabda	sgra	sound	sound
8.	gandha	dri	smell	smell
9.	rasa	ro	taste	taste
10.	spraṣṭavya	reg bya	texture	touch
imperceptible forms				
11.	avijñapti	rnam par rig ma yin pa	imperceptible forms	

COLUMN II: MIND (*CITTA*)

	SANSKRIT	TIBETAN	GATEWAY TO KNOWLEDGE	MIND IN BUDDHIST PSYCHOLOGY
12.	citta	sems	mind	mind

COLUMN III: CONCOMITANT MENTAL FACTORS (*CITTA-SAMPRAYUKTA-SAMSKARA*)

GENERAL FACTORS

	SANSKRIT	TIBETAN	GATEWAY TO KNOWLEDGE	MIND IN BUDDHIST PSYCHOLOGY
13.	vedanā	tshor ba	sensation	feeling-tone
14.	saṃjñā	'du shes	perception	conceptualization
15.	cetanā	sems pa	attraction	directionality
16.	sparśa	reg pa	contact	rapport
17.	chanda	'dun pa	intention	interest
18.	prajñā	shes rab	discrimination	appreciative discrimination
19.	smṛti	dran pa	recollection	inspection
20.	manasikāra	yid la byed pa	attention	demanding

	SANSKRIT	TIBETAN	GATEWAY TO KNOWLEDGE	MIND IN BUDDHIST PSYCHOLOGY
21.	*adhimokṣa*	*mos pa*	interest	intensified interest
22.	*samādhi*	*ting nge 'dzin*	concentration	concentration

PRIMARY WHOLESOME MENTAL FACTORS

	SANSKRIT	TIBETAN	GATEWAY TO KNOWLEDGE	MIND IN BUDDHIST PSYCHOLOGY
23.	*śraddhā*	*dad pa*	faith	confidence/trust
24.	*vīrya*	*brtson 'grus*	diligence	diligence
25.	*upekṣā*	*btang snyoms*	equanimity	equanimity
26.	*hrī*	*ngo tsha*	conscience	self-respect
27.	*apatrapā*	*khrel yod pa*	shame	decorum
28.	*alobha*	*ma chags pa*	nonattachment	nonattachment
29.	*adveṣa*	*zhe sdang med pa*	nonaggression	nonhatred
30.	*avihiṃsa*	*rnam par mi 'tshe ba*	nonviolence	nonviolence
31.	*praśrabdhi*	*shin tu sbyangs pa*	pliancy	alertness
32.	*apramāda*	*bag yod*	conscientiousness	concern

PRIMARY FACTORS OF UPSET

	SANSKRIT	TIBETAN	GATEWAY TO KNOWLEDGE	MIND IN BUDDHIST PSYCHOLOGY
33.	*moha*	*gti mug*	delusion	deludedness
34.	*pramāda*	*bag med*	heedlessness	unconcern
35.	*kausīdya*	*le lo*	laziness	laziness
36.	*aśrāddhya*	*ma dad pa*	lack of faith	lack of trust
37.	*styāna*	*rmugs*	lethargy	gloominess
38.	*auddhatya*	*rgod pa*	excitement	ebullience

	SANSKRIT	TIBETAN	GATEWAY TO KNOWLEDGE	MIND IN BUDDHIST PSYCHOLOGY

PRIMARY FACTORS OF NEGATIVITY

	SANSKRIT	TIBETAN	GATEWAY TO KNOWLEDGE	MIND IN BUDDHIST PSYCHOLOGY
39.	āhrīkya	ngo tsha med pa	lack of conscience	shamelessness
40.	anapatrāpya	khrel med pa	shamelessness	lack of propriety

MINOR FACTORS OF UPSET

	SANSKRIT	TIBETAN	GATEWAY TO KNOWLEDGE	MIND IN BUDDHIST PSYCHOLOGY
41.	krodha	khro ba	fury	indignation
42.	mrakṣa	'chab pa	concealment	slyness-concealment
43.	mātsarya	ser sna	stinginess	avarice
44.	īrṣyā	phrag dog	envy	jealousy
45.	pradāśa	'tshig pa	spite	spite
46.	vihiṃsā	rnam par 'tshe ba	hostility	malice
47.	upanāha	khon du 'dzin pa	resentment	resentment
48.	māyā	sgyu	pretense	deceit
49.	śāṭhya	gyo	hypocrisy	dishonesty
50.	mada	rgyags pa	self-infatuation	mental inflation

VARIABLE FACTORS

	SANSKRIT	TIBETAN	GATEWAY TO KNOWLEDGE	MIND IN BUDDHIST PSYCHOLOGY
51.	kaukṛtya	'gyod	regret	worry
52.	middha	gnyid	sleep	drowsiness
53.	vitarka	rtog pa	conception	selectiveness
54.	vicāra	dpyod pa	discernment	discursiveness
55.	rāga	'dod chags	attachment	cupidity-attachment
56.	pratigha	khong khro	anger	anger

| 57. | *māna* | *nga rgyal* | arrogance | arrogance |
| 58. | *vicikitsā* | *the tshoms* | doubt | indecision |

COLUMN IV: INTERPRETIVE SCHEMATA/ ELEMENTS NEITHER SUBSTANTIAL FORMS NOR MENTAL FUNCTIONS (*CITTA-VIPRAYUKTA-SAMSKARA*)

	SANSKRIT	TIBETAN	GATEWAY TO KNOWLEDGE	ALTERNATIVE TRANSLATION
59.	*prāpti*	*thob*	acquisition	acquisition
60.	*aprāpti*	*ma thob*	dispossession	nonacquisition
61.	*sabhāgatā*	*ris mthun pa*	similar class	communionship
62.	*asaṃjñika*	*'du shes med pa*	perceptionless serenity	fruition of thoughtless heaven
63.	*asaṃjñika-samāpatti*	*'du shes med pa'i snyoms 'jug*	state of nonperception	thoughtless ecstasy
64.	*nirodha-samāpatti*	*'gog pa snyoms 'jug*	serenity of cessation	annihilation trance
65.	*jīvita*	*srog pa*	life	life
66.	*jāti*	*skye ba*	birth	birth
67.	*sthiti*	*gnas pa*	subsistence	stability
68.	*jarā*	*rga ba*	aging	decay
69.	*aniyata*	*mi rtag*	impermanence	impermanence
70.	*nāmakāya*	*ming tshogs*	names	name
71.	*padakāya*	*tshig tshogs*	words	sentence
72.	*vyañjanakāya*	*yi ge*	letters	letter

Unconditioned Elements (asamskṛta-dharma)

	SANSKRIT	TIBETAN	GATEWAY TO KNOWLEDGE	ALTERNATIVE TRANSLATION
73.	ākāśa	nam mkha'	space	space
74.	pratisaṃkhyānirodha	so sor btags 'gog	cessation due to discrimination	extinction through intellectual power
75.	apratisaṃkhyānirodha	so sor btags min 'gog	cessation not due to discrimination	extinction due to lack of a productive cause

Appendix 2

The Fifty-One Mental Factors

The Fifty-One Mental States according to
Gateway to Knowledge and Mind in Buddhist Psychology

EVER-PRESENT FACTORS (*SARVATRAGA*)

	SANSKRIT	TIBETAN	GATEWAY TO KNOWLEDGE	MIND IN BUDDHIST PSYCHOLOGY
1.	*vedanā*	*tshor ba*	sensation	feeling-tone
2.	*saṃjñā*	*'du shes*	perception	conceptualization
3.	*cetanā*	*sems pa*	attraction	directionality
4.	*sparśa*	*reg pa*	contact	rapport
5.	*manasikāra*	*yid la byed pa*	attention	demanding

OBJECT-DETERMINED FACTORS (*VIṢAYANIYATA*)

	SANSKRIT	TIBETAN	GATEWAY TO KNOWLEDGE	MIND IN BUDDHIST PSYCHOLOGY
1.	*chanda*	*'dun pa*	intention	interest
2.	*adhimokṣa*	*mos pa*	interest	intensified interest
3.	*smṛti*	*dran pa*	recollection	inspection
4.	*samādhi*	*ting nge 'dzin*	concentration	concentration
5.	*prajñā*	*shes rab*	discrimination	appreciative discrimination

WHOLESOME FACTORS (*KUŚALA*)

	SANSKRIT	TIBETAN	GATEWAY TO KNOWLEDGE	MIND IN BUDDHIST PSYCHOLOGY
1.	*śraddhā*	*dad pa*	faith	confidence/trust
2.	*hrī*	*ngo tsha*	conscience	self-respect
3.	*apatrapā*	*khrel yod pa*	shame	decorum
4.	*alobha*	*ma chags pa*	nonattachment	nonattachment
5.	*adveṣa*	*zhe sdang med pa*	nonaggression	nonhatred
6.	*amoha*	*gti mug med pa*	nondelusion	nondeludedness
7.	*vīrya*	*brtson 'grus*	diligence	diligence
8.	*praśrabdhi*	*shin tu sbyangs pa*	pliancy	alertness
9.	*apramāda*	*bag yod*	conscientiousness	concern
10.	*upekṣā*	*btang snyoms*	equanimity	equanimity
11.	*avihiṃsa*	*rnam par mi 'tshe ba*	nonviolence	nonviolence

PRIMARY FACTORS OF UPSET (*MULAKLEŚA*)

	SANSKRIT	TIBETAN	GATEWAY TO KNOWLEDGE	MIND IN BUDDHIST PSYCHOLOGY
1.	*rāga*	*'dod chags*	attachment	cupidity-attachment
2.	*pratigha*	*khong khro*	anger	anger
3.	*māna*	*nga rgyal*	arrogance	arrogance
4.	*avidyā*	*ma rig pa*	ignorance	lack of awareness
5.	*vicikitsā*	*the tshoms*	doubt	indecision
6.	*dṛṣṭi*	*lta ba*	belief	opinionatedness

SECONDARY FACTORS OF UPSET (*UPAKLEŚA*)

	SANSKRIT	TIBETAN	GATEWAY TO KNOWLEDGE	MIND IN BUDDHIST PSYCHOLOGY
1.	*krodha*	*khro ba*	fury	indignation
2.	*upanāha*	*khon du 'dzin pa*	resentment	resentment
3.	*mrakṣa*	*'chab pa*	concealment	slyness-concealment
4.	*pradāśa*	*'tshig pa*	spite	spite
5.	*īrṣyā*	*phrag dog*	envy	jealousy
6.	*mātsarya*	*ser sna*	stinginess	avarice
7.	*māyā*	*sgyu*	pretense	deceit
8.	*śāṭhya*	*gyo*	hypocrisy	dishonesty
9.	*mada*	*rgyags pa*	self-infatuation	mental inflation
10.	*vihiṃsā*	*rnam par 'tshe ba*	hostility	malice
11.	*āhrīkya*	*ngo tsha med pa*	lack of conscience	shamelessness
12.	*anapatrapā*	*khrel med pa*	shamelessness	lack of propriety

	SANSKRIT	TIBETAN	GATEWAY TO KNOWLEDGE	MIND IN BUDDHIST PSYCHOLOGY
13.	*styāna*	*rmugs pa*	lethargy	gloominess
14.	*auddhatya*	*rgod pa*	excitement	ebullience
15.	*aśrāddhya*	*ma dad pa*	lack of faith	lack of trust
16.	*kausīdya*	*le lo*	laziness	laziness
17.	*pramāda*	*bag med*	heedlessness	unconcern
18.	*muṣitasmṛti*	*brjed ngas pa*	forgetfulness	forgetfulness
19.	*vikṣepa*	*shes pa bzhin ma yin*	nonalertness	inattentiveness
20.	*asaṃprajanya*	*rnam pa gyengs ba*	distraction	desultoriness

VARIABLE FACTORS

	SANSKRIT	TIBETAN	GATEWAY TO KNOWLEDGE	MIND IN BUDDHIST PSYCHOLOGY
1.	*middha*	*gnyid*	sleep	drowsiness
2.	*kaukṛtya*	*'gyod*	regret	worry
3.	*vitarka*	*rtog pa*	conception	selectiveness
4.	*vicāra*	*dpyod pa*	discernment	discursiveness

Appendix 3

The First Karika of the
Abhidharmakosha
and the Commentary

Abhidharmakosha-karikas

As we have said, the *Abhidharmakosha* consists of two parts. The first part is written in verse form for memorization, as an aid to remember. These are the *Abhidharmakosha-karikas*. *Karikas* means short verses for memorization. It was a custom in India, when studying Buddhism, to memorize these karikas. The great masters of these traditions took great care in composing these karikas in a way that all the essential terms were there. They have the form of an analytical outline or a table of contents, and they are made in such a clever way that they might be easy to memorize.

In the living tradition of the study of the Abhidharma, one memorizes the karikas and then uses them as the basis for going in depth into particular points. As an aid for going into depth, in addition, Vasubandhu wrote a commentary, the *Abhidharmakoshabhashya*, in which he expanded upon the points just briefly mentioned in the more than four hundred karikas. For the living tradition of Tibetan Buddhism, the Abhidharma in the Shravakayana sense consists primarily of those two works written by Vasubandhu, who lived from the fourth to the fifth century. We should know that the *Abhidharma-kosha* was not just a local hit in Gandhara (present-day Kashmir) but was read and studied by many.

The *Abhidharmakoshabhashya* is divided into eight principal chapters, with a ninth chapter as an appendix. In the eight main chapters, Vasubandhu surveys all the ways in which these seventy-five dharmas work together. He first composed it in Sanskrit, and it was later translated into Tibetan during the great time of translations of Buddhism from India to Tibet, sometime after the founding of the first great state-sponsored Buddhist monastery known as Samyé in the eighth century.

Invocation from the *Abhidharmakosha*

I would like to invoke here the beginning of the *Abhidharmakosha*, as a way of creating *auspiciousness* with this noble tradition.

Vasubandhu begins, according to the Tibetan translation, as follows:

Om. Homage to the Buddha.
He has, in an absolute manner, destroyed all blindness;
He has drawn out the world from the mire of transmigration:
I render homage to Him, to this teacher of truth, before composing the
    treatise called the *Abhidharmakośa*[140]

Vasubandhu continues:

Desiring to compose a treatise, with the intention of making known the greatness of his master, the author undertakes to render him homage and to first present his qualities.

"He" refers to the Buddha, the Blessed One.

"He has destroyed all blindness," that is to say, by him or through him blindness with respect to all things is destroyed.

"Blindness" is ignorance, for ignorance hinders the seeing of things as they truly are.

By this, the Buddha, the Blessed One, is sufficiently designated, for he alone, through the possession of the antidote to ignorance, has definitively destroyed all ignorance with respect to all knowable things, so that it cannot rearise.

But the Pratyekabuddhas and the Śrāvakas have also destroyed all blindness, for they are freed from all ignorance defiled by the defilements.

But they do not know the qualities proper to the Buddha, objects very distant in space or time, nor the infinite complex of things; therefore, they have not destroyed blindness in an absolute manner, for the ignorance freed from the defilements is active in them.

Having thus praised the Blessed One from the point of view of qualities useful to himself, the author praises him from the point of view of qualities useful to others: "He has drawn out the world from the mire of transmigration." Transmigration is a mire, because the world is bound up in it, and because it is difficult to traverse. The Blessed One, having pity on the world that finds itself drowned without recourse in this mire, has pulled it out, as much as possible, by extending to each one the hands of the teaching of the Good Law.

"I render homage," by prostrating myself even to my head "to this teacher of truth."

Notes

Introduction

1. There are several translations of the *Visuddhimaga* into English. See, for instance, Bhikkhu Nyanamoli (2011).

2. Patrul Rinpoche, *The Words of My Perfect Teacher* (Boston: Shambhala Publications, 1998), 369.

3. Note that in the Tibetan translation they do not say *shyiwa (zhi ba) or shyiwar shok* (*zhi bar shog*), which would mean "be calm." They say *shyinè* (*zhi gnas*), calm abiding.

4. This exchange from the *Ayacana Sutta*, translated by Bhikku Thanissaro, can be found on the Access to Insight website: www.accesstoinsight.org/tipitaka/sn/sn06/sn06.001 .than.html.

5. See, for instance, the *Dhammacakkappavattana Sutta*.

6. If you think linguistics is not important, I would remind you of the words of the maha-siddha Kanha, who once said that the path is blocked by vowels and consonants.

7. I always remember a story in the life of the Buddha. He had one karmically very gifted disciple who, upon sighting one slightly graying hair, completely understood that the nature of all conditioned phenomena was impermanent and thereupon instantly became an *arhat*.

8. A condensed and profound text on the relationship between right view and right thought is the *Wheel of Analytic Meditation* (*Chegom Khorloma*) by Lama Mipham.

9. Patrul Rinpoche, *The Words of My Perfect Teacher*, trans. Padmakara Translation Group (San Francisco: HarperCollins, 1998), 102. With respect to the ten negative actions to be avoided, three of these ten are physical acts: taking life, taking what is not given, and sexual misconduct. Four are verbal acts: lying, sowing discord, harsh words, and worth-

less chatter. And three are mental acts: covetousness, wishing harm on others, and wrong views.

Chapter 1. What Is the Abhidharma?

10. *Satipaṭṭhāna Sutta.*
11. *Smṛtyupasthāna Sūtra.*
12. *Abhidharmakośa.*
13. For an English translation, see Leo M. Pruden, *Abhidharmakośabhāṣyam* (Berkeley: Asian Humanities Press, 1991).
14. *Abhidharmakośabhāṣya.*
15. Skt. *kośa.*
16. Skt. *kārikā.*
17. Skt. *prajñā*; Tib. *shes rab.*
18. Skt. *dharmanam pravicaya.*
19. Asanga, *Abhidharmasamuccaya: The Compendium of the Higher Teaching (Philosophy)*, trans. Walpola Rahula and Sara Boin-Webb (Fremont, CA: Jain Publishing, 2015).
20. Patrul Rinpoche, *The Words of My Perfect Teacher*, 15.
21. Butön Rinchen Drup, *Butön's History of Buddhism in India and Its Spread to Tibet: A Treasury of Priceless Scripture*, trans. Lisa Stein and Ngawang Zangpo (Ithaca, NY: Snow Lion Publications, 2013).
22. *Vyākhyāyukti.*
23. Skt. *jñeya*; Tib. *shes bya.*
24. Skt. *mārga*; Tib. *lam.*
25. Skt. *nirvāṇa*; Tib. *mya ngan las 'das pa.*
26. Skt. *mano viṣaya*; Tib. *yid kyi yul.*
27. Skt. *dharma āyatana.*
28. Skt. *puṇya*; Tib. *bsod nams.*
29. Skt. *āyus*; Tib. *tshe.*
30. Skt. *buddhavācana*; Tib. *sangs rgyas kyi gsung rab.*
31. Skt. *bhavanā*; Tib. *sgom pa.*
32. Skt. *niścaya*; Tib. *nges pa.*
33. Skt. *nīti*; Tib. *chos lugs.*
34. Skt. *dhṛ.*
35. Skt. *saddharma*; Tib. *dam pa'i chos.*
36. This is a *tatpuruṣa* Sanskrit compound of the *shashthīsamāsa* type (Skt. *sato=sambuddhasya dharma iti saddharma*).
37. This is a *karma-dhāraya* Sanskrit compound.
38. Skt. *satah satpuruṣasya caritavyo dharma iti saddharma.*
39. Skt. *āgamadharma*; Tib. *lung gi chos.*
40. Skt. *ādhigama-dharma/ādhidharma*; Tib. *rtogs kyi chos.*
41. Skt. *eka rasa*; Tib. *ro gcig. Ro* means "flavor" or "taste," and *chik* in the sense of *gcig pu* means "unique, special."

42. Tib. *rten 'brel.*
43. Skt. *vimokṣa*; Tib. *rnam grol.*
44. Tib. *dge ba'i rtsa.*
45. Skt. *prajñāpāramitā.*
46. Skt. *dharmanam pravicaya*; Tib. *chos rnams la rab tu rnam par byed pa.*
47. Skt. *śruta*; Tib. *thos.*
48. Skt. *cintā*; Tib. *bsam.*
49. Skt. *bhavānā*; Tib. *sgom.*
50. *Saṃdhinirmocana Sūtra.*
51. Skt. *abhimukhya*; Tib. *mngon du gyur.*
52. Skt. *abhīkṣṇam*; Tib. *yang.*
53. Skt. *abhibhū*; Tib. *zil gnon.*
54. Skt. *abhisamaya*; Tib. *rtogs pa.*

Chapter 2. Everything Is Dharmas

55. Skt. *Vibhājavādin.*
56. Skt. *sarvaṃ dharmam.*
57. Vasubandhu, *Abhidharmakośabhāṣyam*, vol. 1, 56.
58. Being reborn into samsara.
59. Vasubandhu, *Abhidharmakośabhāṣyam*, vol. 1, 57.
60. Ibid., 57
61. Ibid., 57
62. Skt. *abhimukha.*
63. Vasubandhu, *Abhidharmakośabhāṣyam*, vol. 1, 57.
64. Skt. *prāpti.*
65. Skt. *aprāpti.*
66. Skt. *jāti.*

Chapter 3. Exploring the Nature of Self and Reality

67. Skt. *asaṃskṛta.*
68. Skt. *ahētuka.*
69. Skt. *ātman.*
70. Skt. *brahman.*
71. Skt. *catuṣkoṭi.*
72. Obsessional fixity is permanent (Skt. *nitya*), singular (Skt. *eka*), and independent (Skt. *sva-indriya*).
73. Skt. *tṛṣṇā.*
74. *Suhṛllekha.* For an English translation of a Tibetan commentary to Nagarjuna's text, see Mipham Rinpoche, *Golden Zephyr*, trans. Leslie S. Kawamura (Berkeley: Dharma Publishing, 1998).
75. Skt. *ātmagraha*; Tib. *bdag tu 'dzin pa.*
76. Skt. *anātman.*

77. Skt. *pudgala.*
78. Skt. *skandha.*
79. Skt. *āyatana.*
80. Skt. *dhatu.*
81. *Arhat = ari* (enemy) + *hantā* (to kill).
82. Tib. *gang la gang 'dul.*
83. Pali. *Puggala paññatti.* See B. C. Law, trans., *A Designation of Human Types* (Lancaster, UK: Pali Text Society, 1992).
84. A greed type (Skt. *rāga*), a hate type, (Skt. *dveṣa*), or an ignorance type (Skt. *moha*).
85. There's a wonderful book by Carl Jung on the history of thinking deeply about this issue of personality in the West. See Carl Jung, *Psychological Types: The Collected Works of Carl Jung, Vol. 6* (Princeton, NJ: Princeton University Press, 1976).
86. Skt. *avidyā.*
87. Skt. *bodhī.*
88. Skt. *preta.*
89. Skt. *tathatā*; Tib. *de bzhin nyid.*
90. Skt. *Tathāgata.*
91. Skt. *tathāgatagarbhā.*
92. Skt. *Uttaratantra Śāstra*; Tib. *Rgyud bla ma.*

Chapter 4. Six Channels of Perception

93. Skt. *pudgalanairātmya.*
94. Vasubandhu, *Abhidharmakośabhāṣyam*, vol. 1, chapter 2, verses 14 and following.
95. Skt. *saṃtāna*; Tib. *rgyun.*
96. Skt. *durgati*, lit. "the gone bad realms."
97. Skt. *dhyāna*; Pali *jhana*; Tib. *bsam gtan.* This is often translated as absorption or meditative trance.

Chapter 5. Dhatus and Channel Processing

98. Vasubandhu, *Abhidharmakośabhāṣyam*, vol. 1, chapter 1, verses 20 c–d, 81.
99. Skt. *abhimukhya*; Tib. *mngon du gyur.*
100. This is sometimes translated as "organ."
101. Skt. *sparśa.*
102. Skt. *ālambana*; Tib. *dmigs pa.*
103. Skt. *vijñāna*; Tib. *rnam shes.*

Chapter 6. Tuning In to Experience

104. Skt. *sa ālambana*; Tib. *dmigs bcas.*
105. Skt. *nir ālambana*; Tib. *dmigs med.*
106. Skt. *viṣaya*; Tib. *yul.*
107. The Buddha, who was called the Māhāvibhājavādin, the Great Analyzer, could discern

all the subtle differences of our everyday experience so as to be able to enter into compassionate communication with those who experience imprecisely. He did this in order to encourage people to slow down and to take delight in paying attention with a mind and heart that is not so tight. By doing this they would then know that their problems are not solid and fixed, and they could find a way to make life slightly more workable.

108. Skt. *grāhya*; Tib. *gzung*.
109. Skt. *grāhaka*; Tib. *'dzin*.

Chapter 7. Moments for a Meditator

110. One of the differences between the Shravakayana, Mahayana, and Vajrayana is how long it takes to blast through the pattern called self. According to the Mahayana traditions, it only takes seven lifetimes to cut through the pattern. In the Vajrayana tradition, they say it can occur "in this body and in this lifetime."
111. For a full discussion of nine stages of mindfulness, see: Geshe Gedun Lodro, *Walking Through Walls: A Presentation of Tibetan Meditation*, trans. and ed. by Jeffrey Hopkins (Ithaca, NY: Snow Lion Publications, 1992), 163–98. And for a visual presentation of a monk chasing his elephant mind around nine turns in the road, see the online diagram at https://terebess.hu/english/oxherd27.html.

Chapter 9. Mind

112. Skt. *citrā*.
113. Skt. *cinoti*.

Chapter 10. Conditioned and Unconditioned Elements

114. Tib. *so sor rnam rig*.
115. That Sanskrit prefix *vi* as a specificity comes up over and over again in translations into Tibetan as *rnam* and *rnam pa*.
116. Tib. *sems, sems 'byung*.
117. Skt. *cittaviprayukta*.
118. Skt. *cittasamprayukta*.
119. Skt. *cittaviprayukta saṃskāra dharma*.

Chapter 11. Ever-Present and Object-Determined Mental Factors

120. Here is a note on translation and cognitive clarity. One can ask, how is our sense of clarity sometimes an obstacle? If one were to read Carlos Castaneda, one would know that there were two primary obstacles to becoming a warrior. The first was fear. We can identify with that very easily. The second one was clarity. How can clarity be an obstacle? Clarity means we become accustomed to thinking we understand and that this is sufficient. So we hear the same word in all kinds of translations, not realizing or not caring that it is translating different words because no one is controlling translation. There

is no *Académie française* for translation of Buddhist texts. It is a free and rather chaotic business. We may see a translation of a word, and when it comes up in other lists, we naturally think it is the same thing. This causes a lot of confusion. This is the state of Buddhist studies. When you have a great teaching by a lama, if it has to be translated for you, you are more or less at the mercy of the translator. We so want to grasp the meaning, and then later, thinking we understood, we find that this clarity had been an obstacle because it was a false clarity.

I'll give one humorous example. This was told to me by Erik Pema Kunsang, who was translating for His Holiness Dilgo Khyentse Rinpoche. Many different people would come to see Dilgo Khyentse Rinpoche at Shechen Monastery in Kathmandu, Nepal. On one occasion a man came and asked for an essential teaching. This man seemed to know a bit of Tibetan, so Erik was not needed at all; he just sat there. And Khyentse Rinpoche gave this man an essential teaching and the man immediately was totally happy and went away satisfied. Now, as it happens, the Kathmandu Valley is a very small place, so sooner or later you hear about everything. And it got back to Erik that this man was saying that he had received a very special high teaching from Khyentse Rinpoche, directly. And he was sharing what he had learned: "Life is a flower." Erik told Khyentse Rinpoche and they both had a really good laugh. In fact, what this fellow had heard Khyentse Rinpoche say was: *Tsé metok* ("Life is a flower"), but Khyentse Rinpoche had actually said: *Tsé mitak* ("Life is impermanent"). So this is a concrete example. We ourselves might laugh at this story, but we ourselves are at risk for thinking that what we "hear" about the Buddhadharma confirms the way we feel. Our so-called "hearing," however, might be defective, obscured by the obstacle of thinking we have clarity. So in honor of that incident in Kathmandu, we might henceforth call this the delusion of clarity called "Life Is a Flower."

121. From a slightly different Abhidharma tradition, the Burmese Buddhist teacher S. N. Goenka has also written about meditation on sensation. See William Hart, *The Art of Living: Vipassana Meditation as Taught by S. N. Goenka* (New York: HarperCollins, 1987).

122. I tend to prefer to use the word "perception" for vijnana (often also translated as consciousness).

123. See Francisco Varela, Evan Thompson and Eleanor Rosch, *The Embodied Mind* (Cambridge, MA: MIT Press, 1991).

124. Eleanor Rosch and B. Lloyd, eds., *Cognition and Categorization* (Hillsdale, NJ: Lawrence Erlbaum Associates, 1978).

125. See Rosch, 1991.

126. See Yeshé Gyaltsen. *Mind in Buddhist Psychology*, p. 25.

127. Skt. *cetayitva*; Tib. *bsams pa*.

128. A Tibetan Buddhist teacher once said that when he was confronted with the task of memorizing many pages of Tibetan text, he found that when he did Vajrasattva practice, his capacity to remember, his capacity to memorize, increased.

129. Skt. *dharmanam pravicaya*; Tib. *chos rnams la rab tu 'byed pa*.

Chapter 12. Wholesome Mental Factors

130. P. Lal, trans., *Dhammapada* (New York: Noonday, 1967).
131. I think that the word "faith" is not a very felicitous translation, but many do translate this term *shraddha* that way.
132. Tib. *sems dang ba*.
133. Tib. *ngo tsha*.
134. Skt. *yogi*; Tib. *rnal 'byor pa*.

Chapter 13. Unwholesome Mental Factors

135. The Tibetan term for doubt or indecision is sometimes given as *som nyi*, meaning to be of two minds about what is true. We note here that the English words *doubt* and *double* are related.
136. This is a complete teaching on the world of finance, right? It is a world in which evaluation of other people is based entirely on what they do or might possess.
137. The word here for attitude in Tibetan is *blo*. This is a very important word; it occurs in *blo ldog*, the attitude that changes or reverses our upsetting habitual attitudes.

Chapter 14. Benefits of Abhidharma Study

138. In Tibetan, these are (1) *ka dangpo* (*bka' dang po*), the first coming-forth of the speech of the Buddha, (2) the *ka barma* (*bka' bar ma*), the middle one, and (3) the *ka tama* (*bka' mtha' ma*), the last one.
139. Skt. *mātṛkā*.

Appendix 3. The First Karika of the *Abhidharmakosha* and the Commentary

140. Vasubandhu, *Abhidharmakośabhāṣyam*, 55–56.

Bibliography

General References

Asanga. *Abhidharmasamuccaya: The Compendium of the Higher Teaching (Philosophy)*. Translated by Walpola Rahula and Sara Boin-Webb. Berkeley: Asian Humanities Press, 2001.

Bhikkhu Nyanamoli, trans. *The Path of Purification, Visuddhimagga*. Kandy, Sri Lanka: Buddhist Publication Society, 2011.

Butön Rinchen Drup. *Butön's History of Buddhism in India and Its Spread to Tibet: A Treasury of Priceless Scripture*. Translated by Lisa Stein and Ngawang Zangpo. Ithaca, NY: Snow Lion, 2013.

Chim Jampaiyang, *Ornament of Abhidharma: A Commentary on Vasubandhu's Abhidharmakosa*. Translated by Ian James Coghlan (Library of Tibetan Classics). Boston: Wisdom Publications, 2019.

Govinda, Anagarika. *The Psychological Attitude of Early Buddhist Philosophy*. Allahabad, India 1937; reprint New Delhi: Motilal Banarsidass Publishers, 1992.

Guenther, Herbert V. *Philosophy and Psychology in the Abhidharma*. Delhi: Motilal Banarsidass Publishers, 1974.

Hart, William. *The Art of Living: Vipassana Meditation as Taught by S. N. Goenka*. New York: HarperCollins, 1987.

Husserl, Edmund. *On the Phenomenology of the Consciousness of Internal Time (1893–1917)*. Translated by John Barnett Brough. Dordrecht, Neth.: Kluwer, 1990.

Jung, Carl. *Psychological Types: The Collected Works of Carl Jung, Vol. 6*. Princeton, NJ: Princeton University Press, 1976.

Lal, P., trans. *Dhammapada*. New York: Noonday, 1967.

Law, B. C., trans. *A Designation of Human Types*. Lancaster: Pali Text Society, 1992.

Lodro, Geshe Gedun. *Walking Through Walls: A Presentation of Tibetan Meditation.* Translated and edited by Jeffrey Hopkins. Ithaca, NY: Snow Lion, 1992.

Minkowski, Eugène. *Lived Time: Phenomenological and Psychopathological Studies.* Translated by Nancy Metzel. Evanston, IL: Northwestern University Press, 1970.

Mipham Rinpoche. *Gateway to Knowledge, Vol. 1.* Translated by Erik Pema Kunsang. Hong Kong: Rangjung Yeshé Publications, 1997.

———. *Golden Zephyr.* Translated by Leslie S. Kawamura. Berkeley: Dharma Publishing, 1998.

Patrul Rinpoche. *The Words of My Perfect Teacher.* Translated by the Padmakara Translation Group. San Francisco: HarperCollins, 1994.

Rosch, Eleanor, and Barbara L. Lloyd, eds. *Cognition and Categorization.* Hillsdale, NJ: Lawrence Erlbaum Associates, 1978.

Thanissaro Bhikku, trans. *Ayacana Sutta: The Request.* Translated from the Pali by Thanissaro Bhikkhu, 1997, 2013, "Ayacana Sutta: The Request" (SN 6.1), translated from the Pali by Thanissaro Bhikkhu. *Access to Insight* (BCBS Edition), November 30, 2013, www.accessto insight.org/tipitaka/sn/sn06/sn06.001.than.html.

Varela, Francisco J., Evan Thompson, and Eleanor Rosch. *The Embodied Mind: Cognitive Science and Human Experience.* Cambridge, MA: MIT Press, 1991.

Vasubandhu. *Abhidharmakośabhāṣyam.* Translated into French by Louis de la Vallée Poussin, English translation by Leo M. Pruden. India: Asian Humanities Press, volume 1, 1991.

Yeshé Gyaltsen. *Mind in Buddhist Psychology.* Translated by Herbert V. Guenther and Leslie S. Kawamura. Berkeley: Dharma Publishing, 1975.

Specialized References on the History and Development of Abhidharma

Bareau, Andre. *Les Sectes Bouddhiques du Petit Véhicule.* Paris: École Française d'Extrême-Orient, 1955.

Buswell, Robert E. Jr. "The Proliferation of 'cittsviprayukatasamskara-s' in the Vaibhasika School." *Journal of Indian Philosophy* 25, no. 5 (October 1997): 451–66.

Funahashi, Issai. "Abhidhamma" and "Abhidharma." *Encyclopedia of Buddhism,* vol. 1, edited by Gunapala Piyasena Malalaksekera, 37–90. Colombo, Ceylon: Ministry of Cultural Affairs, 1984.

Gold, Jonathan C. *Paving the Great Way: Vasubandhu's Unifying Buddhist Philosophy.* New York: Columbia University Press, 2015.

———. "Vasubandhu." In *Stanford Encyclopedia of Philosophy.* Stanford University, April 22, 2011. Substantive revision April 27, 2015. https://plato.stanford.edu/entries/vasubandhu/#Bib.

Hirakawa, Akira et al. *Index to the Abhidharmakośabhāṣya.* Tōkyō: Daizō Shuppan, 1973–78.

Kragh, Ulrich T. "The Extant Abhidharma Literature." *The Indian International Journal of Buddhist Studies* 3, no. 3 (2002) 123–68.

Potter, Karl H., ed. *Abhidharma Buddhism to 150 A.D.* Vol. 7 of *Encyclopedia of Indian Philosophies,* with Robert E. Buswell Jr., Padmanabh S. Jaini, and Noble Ross Reat. Delhi: Motilal Banarsidass, 1996.

Rigpawiki.org. "Treasury of Abhidharma." Last modified September 6, 2018. www.rigpawiki.org/index.php?title=Treasury_of_Abhidharma.

Index

45–59
60–71